IMAGES
*of America*

# WEBB CITY

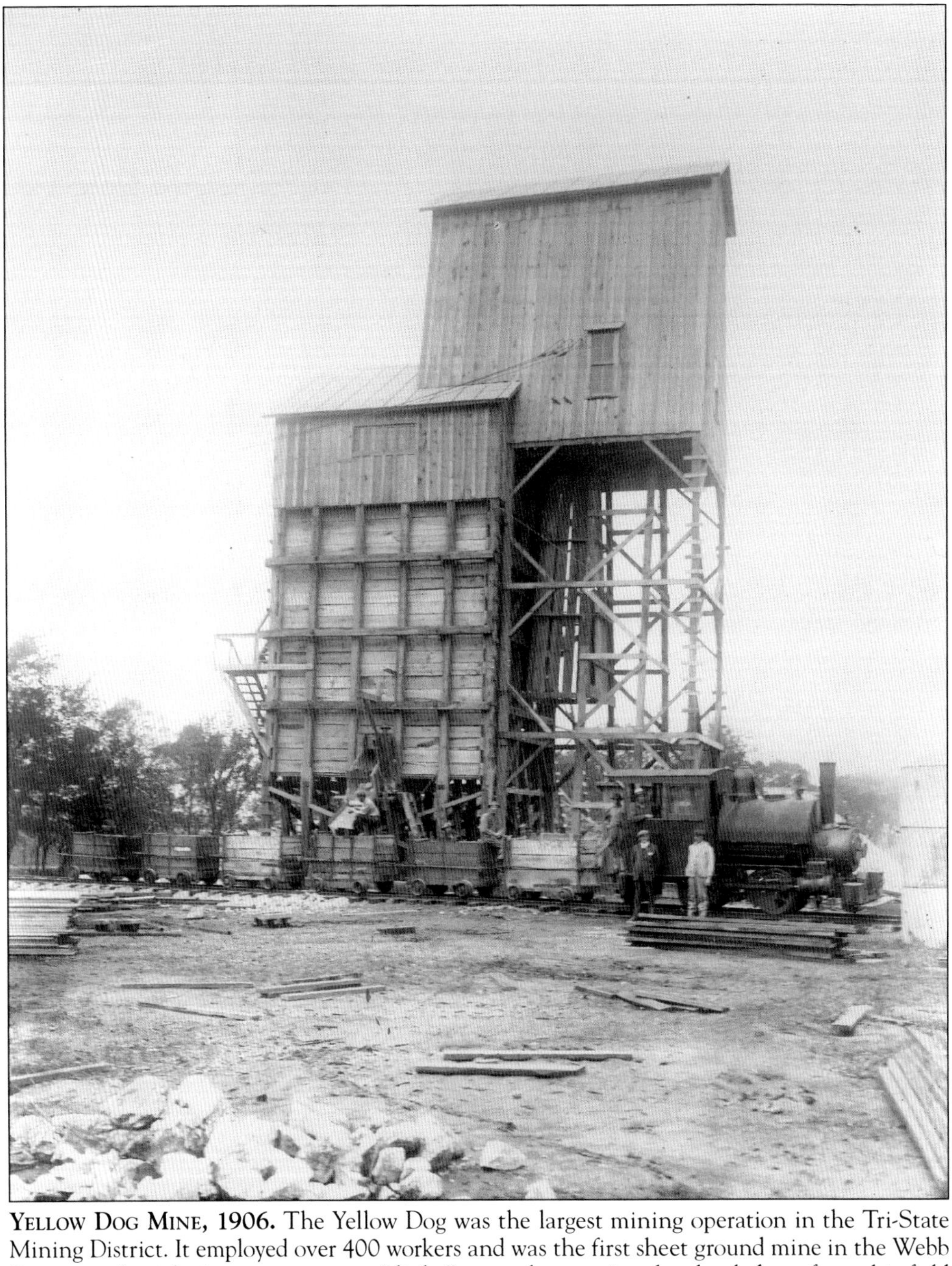

**YELLOW DOG MINE, 1906.** The Yellow Dog was the largest mining operation in the Tri-State Mining District. It employed over 400 workers and was the first sheet ground mine in the Webb City area. At right is a narrow-gauge "dinky" steam locomotive that hauled ore from this field shaft. (Courtesy of Missouri Digital Archive.)

*ON THE COVER:* **DRILLING CONTEST, OCTOBER 4, 1914.** Sam Long and Weed Smith from Webb City held the contest record, drilling 30.75 inches in 15 minutes in 1913. The contest was sponsored by Hercules Powder Company. Pictured here a year later at the contest are, from left to right, H. Haines, Weed Smith, and Edward Haines from the Beulah S. Mine in Webb City. (Courtesy of Missouri Digital Archive.)

IMAGES of America

# WEBB CITY

Priscilla Purcell Brown

ARCADIA PUBLISHING

ISBN 978-1-4671-1357-1

Published by Arcadia Publishing
Charleston, South Carolina

Printed in the United States of America

Library of Congress Control Number: 2014948583

For all general information, please contact Arcadia Publishing:
Telephone 843-853-2070
Fax 843-853-0044
E-mail sales@arcadiapublishing.com
For customer service and orders:
Toll-Free 1-888-313-2665

Visit us on the Internet at www.arcadiapublishing.com

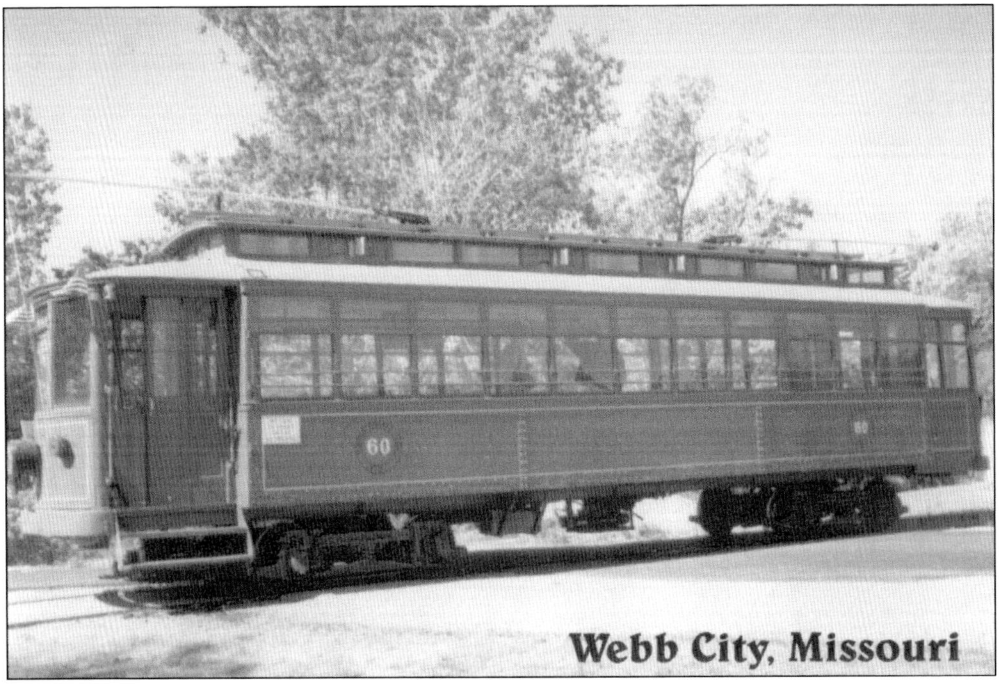


**Southwest Missouri Electric Railway Company.** The streetcar seen in this postcard travels only a short distant today. It runs on tracks around King Jack Park in Webb City. (Courtesy of Bradbury Bishop Deli and Route 66 Diner.)

# Contents

# ACKNOWLEDGMENTS

The photographs found in this book were assembled by the cooperative efforts of my family and friends. I would like to thank Robert King and George Twigger for their encouragement and help to see that the content is accurate. Dixie Dorlene Riley, Sherry Purcell, Jim Bunch, William H. King Jr., Mickey Bulger, Allen Twigger, Joseph P. Wittich Jr., and the Martin family shared photographs from their personal collections. I want to thank Larry Wood for his support. Thank you to Webb City Public Works, Steve Weldon at Jasper County Recorders Center, Webb City Police Department, Bradbury Bishop Deli and Route 66 Diner, Missouri Digital Archive, Webb City Route 66 Visitors Center, and Cooper's 66 Eatery. I would also like to thank my daughters Jamie, Angel, and Amber, and their husbands, Erik, Mike, and Jake. And, last but not least, I thank my grandchildren Courtney, Kyra, Ashlynn, and Asher.

Unless otherwise noted, all images are courtesy of the author's collection.

# INTRODUCTION

At the foothills of the Ozark Mountains, just before one reaches the great prairies of the Midwest, sits Webb City. The beautiful old mansions and the tall trees that form canopies over the city's streets hint to long-ago eras. To look at the city today, one would never know that at one time it was part of the greatest lead- and zinc-mining district in the world.

It was agriculture, not mining, that brought the first pioneers to Webb City. The main attractions were an abundance of freshwater and some of the richest land in the world. Settlers found abundant land for farming, horticulture, and raising stock. It was a good place to build homes and rear families. John Cornwall Webb moved his family in 1856 from Tennessee to southwest Missouri. On the first day of June 1859, he purchased 240 acres at the General Land Office in Springfield, Missouri. He farmed this land until 1873, when he found lead lying on top of the ground while plowing his cornfield. After two years of mining, Webb became discouraged and leased his land to W.A. Daugherty and G.P. Ashcroft. This decision would become very profitable for him. In September 1875, Webb platted the township of Webb City, also called Webbville, on part of his land. He donated property for schools and churches and built the Webb City Bank and the first hotel. Webb's journey from farmer to wealthy mine owner may be a unique story to the world, but it was common to southwest Missouri during the mining boom.

In 1876, the Center Creek Mining Company began operations on Webb's land. Soon, the area was flooded with an influx of miners. For the most part, they made their homes in rowdy Joplin, where there were gambling halls, saloons, and brothels. The mine owners made their homes in more prosperous Webb City. Soon, the city needed a means of transportation, not only for getting the miners to and from their jobs at the mines, but to reach recreation, entertainment, and shopping. In 1889, Alfred Harrison Rogers launched a horse-drawn streetcar. Within four years, it became the Southwest Missouri Electric Railway Company.

At first, it was thought that only lead had any value; zinc was discarded as waste and called "black jack." When zinc increased in value from $3 a ton to $87 a ton in 1907, the rush was on. The nickname "Zinc City" was posted on signs at both the east and west ends of town. Another nickname for Webb City is "Flag City" because of the large number of irises growing around town. "Flag" is an old-time name for the flower.

Like everything in life, there were both good and bad aspects of the mining boom. Miners from the Tri-State Mining District became plagued with silicosis, an occupationally acquired lung disease caused from dust that often led to tuberculosis. The residents of Jasper County stepped up and passed a bond issue for the construction of a hospital. Women and children were also being affected from the dust brought out of the mines that attached to the men's clothing. James A. Daugherty donated land, and in 1918 Elmhurst Tuberculosis Hospital opened.

Webb City's mining boom was at its peak while World War I was raging in Europe. With the end of the war in 1918, falling ore prices, and the discovery of a richer ore in Oklahoma, Webb City turned its attention to manufacturing. Factories soon became large employers of women in the area, producing shoes, clothing, and cigars. Bricks, caskets, gaskets, scales, and sheet-metal products were manufactured in Webb City. With manufacturing companies came office jobs for both men and women. Many products were shipped by train, but truck-driving jobs became more available as America's highways improved. As automobiles became more affordable and dependable, more individual households owned a car. Streetcars were used less, and by 1939 Southwest Missouri Electric Railway ended all routes. This was the end of an era for streetcars and mining.

It was now on to the next big thing in Webb City's history. That next big thing happened in 1926. Webb City took its place in American pop culture as Route 66 wound its way through the city. After World War II, people were traveling the popular highway as they never had before. Webb City, like other communities, saw businesses spring up to accommodate the travelers. Today, "The Mother Road" attracts people from all over the world.

Another attraction to Webb City is its high school's proud football legacy. Its teams have led the school too many championships. Records of winning teams first begin in 1907. During the Depression, in order to boost employment, the Works Progress Administration (WPA) was established. WPA workers built Hatten Athletic Field on land donated to the city by Amos Hatten and Harry Easley. Today, it is the site of Webb City High School.

Mining devastated the land, leaving tailing piles and ruins for miles surrounding Webb City. Now, 100 years later, the Environmental Protection Agency has projects that attempt to clean up the toxic waste. The community is divided over how this is benefiting the city. Some people feel that by removing all ruins, a part of Webb City's mining history is being destroyed.

Webb City is a beautiful place to live. It has survived because of its ability to reinvent itself, from mining to manufacturing. Regrettably, the city limits are locked in from the north by Oronogo, in the south by Joplin, to the east by Carterville, and to the west by Airport Drive. This gives the city no place to grow.

# One

# Zinc City

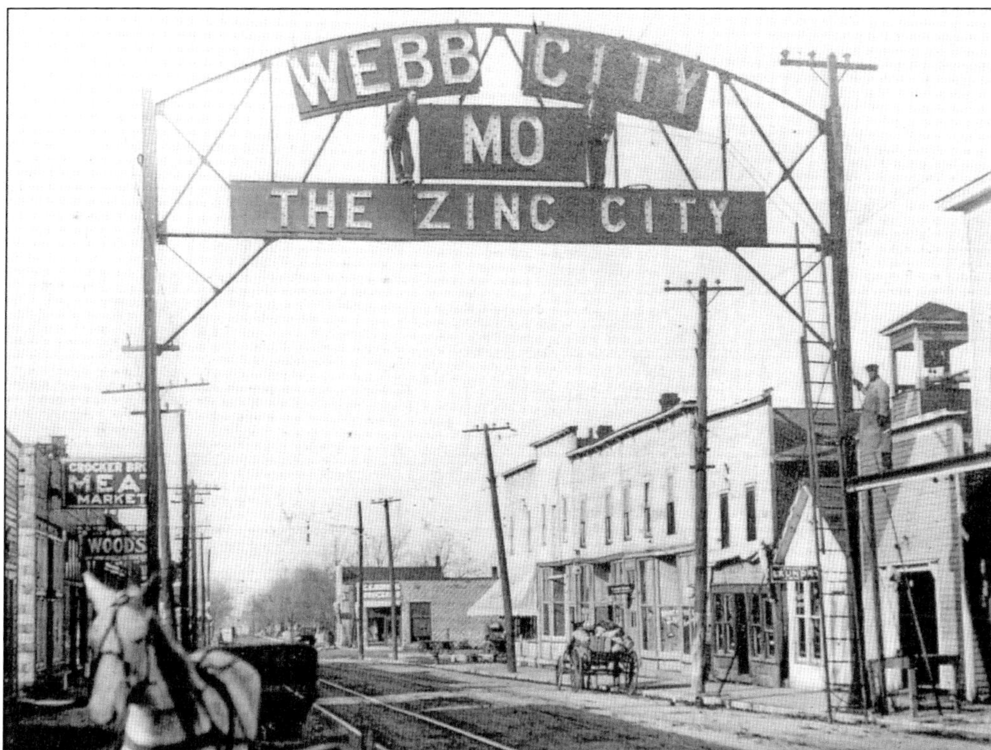


**The Zinc City Sign, 1909.** This photograph shows Daugherty Street looking east. The early growth of the city was due to the booming mine industry, earning Webb City the nickname "Zinc City." In 1926, Daugherty Street became part of the historic Route 66. (Courtesy of Webb City Public Works.)

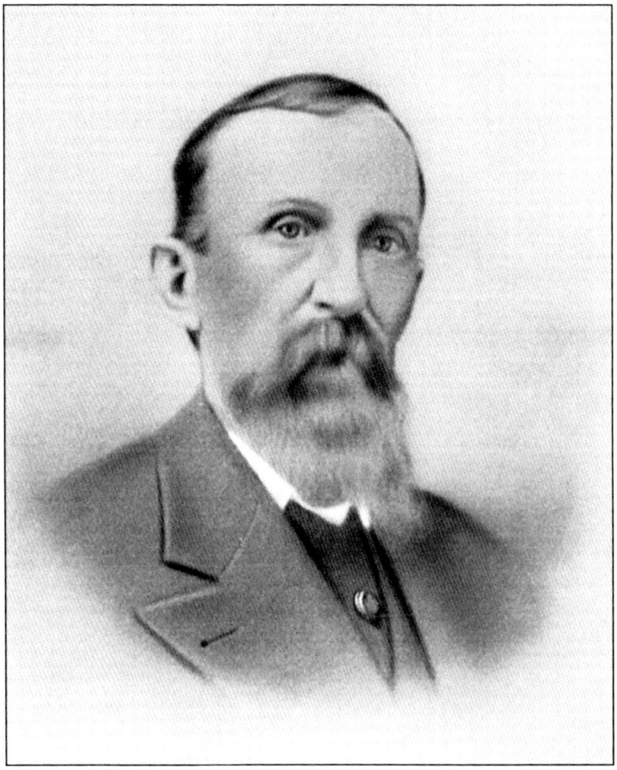

**JOHN CORNWALL WEBB.** The founder of Webb City, John Webb moved his family in 1856 from Tennessee to southwest Missouri. In 1873, while plowing his cornfield, he discovered lead lying on top of the ground. In 1875, he platted part of his original farm for the township of Webb City.

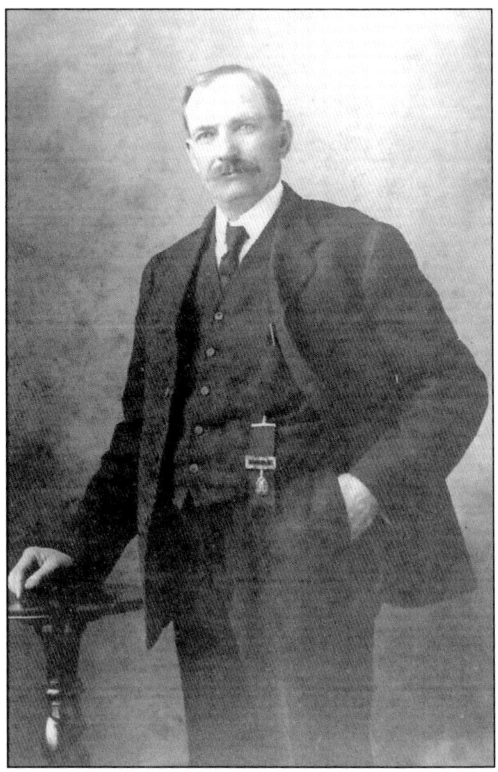

**AMOS DAVIS HATTEN.** An early-day Webb City pioneer, Hatten donated land for a football and baseball field. It became known as Hatten Athletic Field. Today, the site is home to Webb City High School.

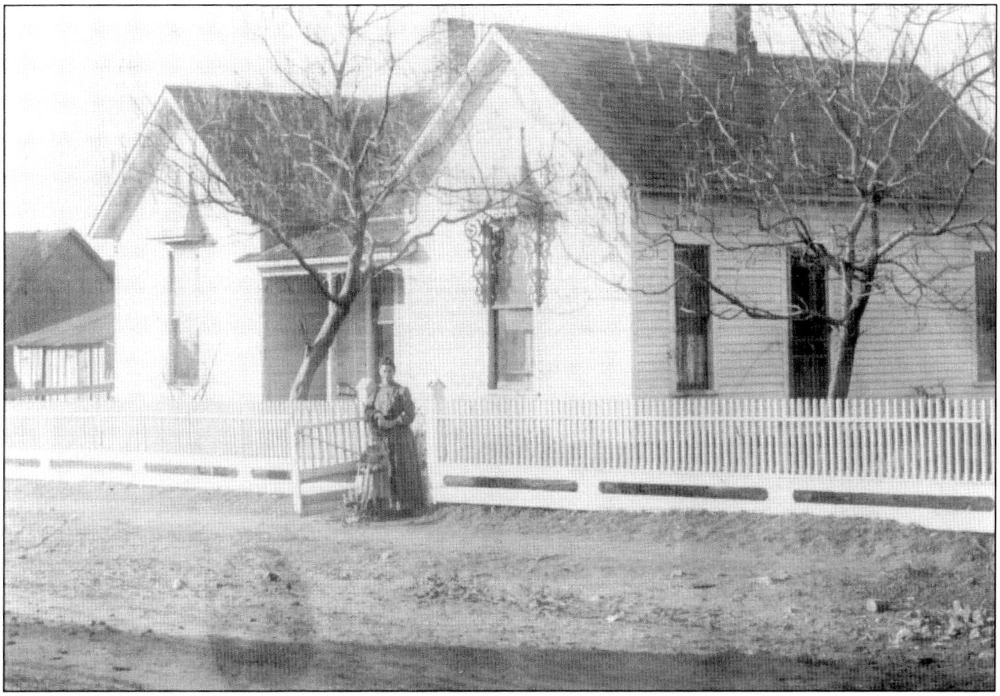

**Chapman home, 1906.** Sarah Ault Chapman and her daughter Freida Chapman stand outside their home on the corner of Prospect and Aylor Streets. (Courtesy of the Willis family.)

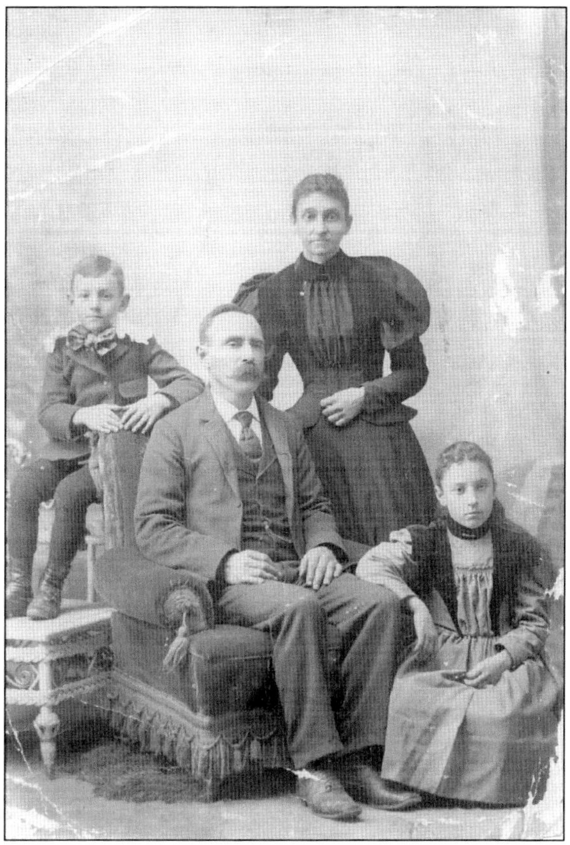

**Chapman Family, 1894.** Elza and Sarah Chapman pose for a family portrait with their children, Carl and Floy. Floy grew up and went to work for the *Daily Sentinel* when very few women were in the newspaper business. (Courtesy of the Willis family.)

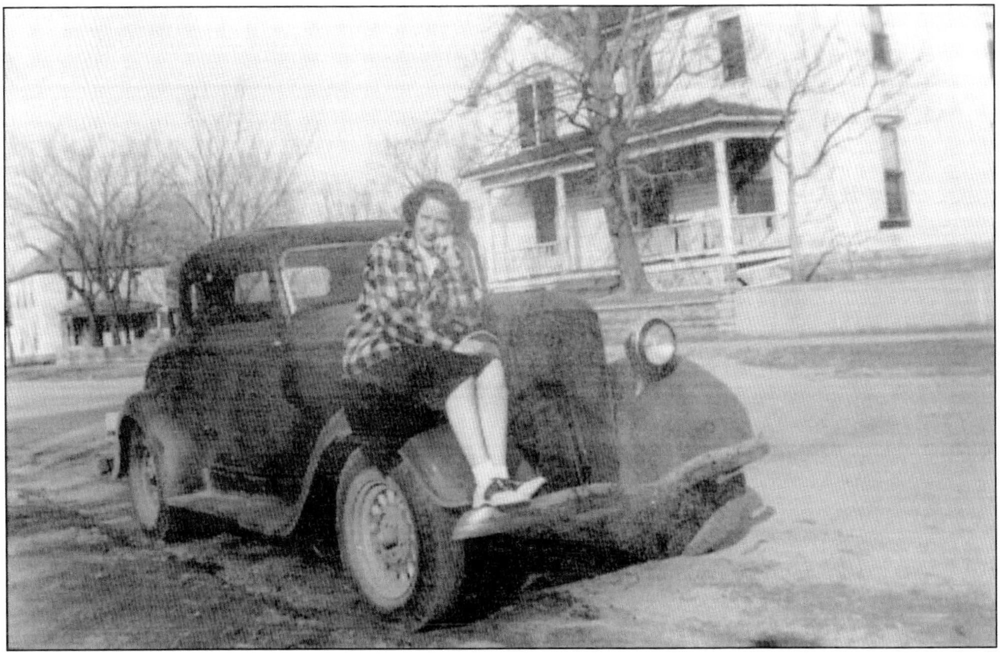

**Crystal Mills Purcell, 1944.** Sitting on the hood of her car, Purcell is a happy young girl. Her saddle Oxfords were high fashion in that era. She attended Webb City Baptist College. The daughter of Fred and Vauda Mills, she married Edward Purcell on August 10, 1947. This photograph was taken at Third and Oronogo Streets. (Courtesy of Sherry Purcell.)

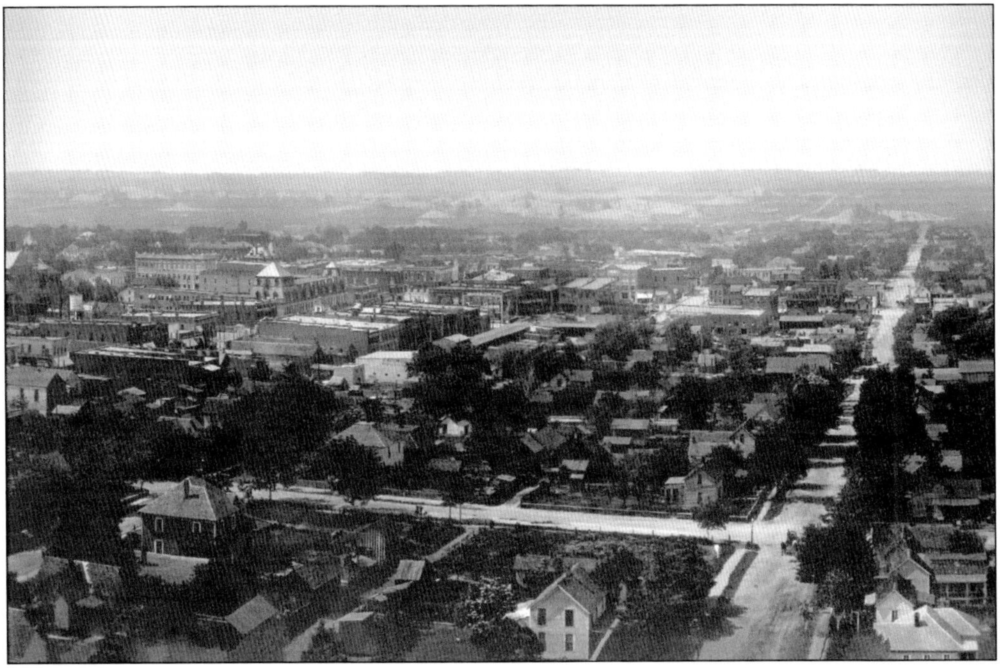

**Webb City, 1910.** This panoramic photograph was taken from the top of the water tower. The view is to the north on Tom Street. To the left are the old post office and the Newland Hotel. (Courtesy of the Bob King Collection.)

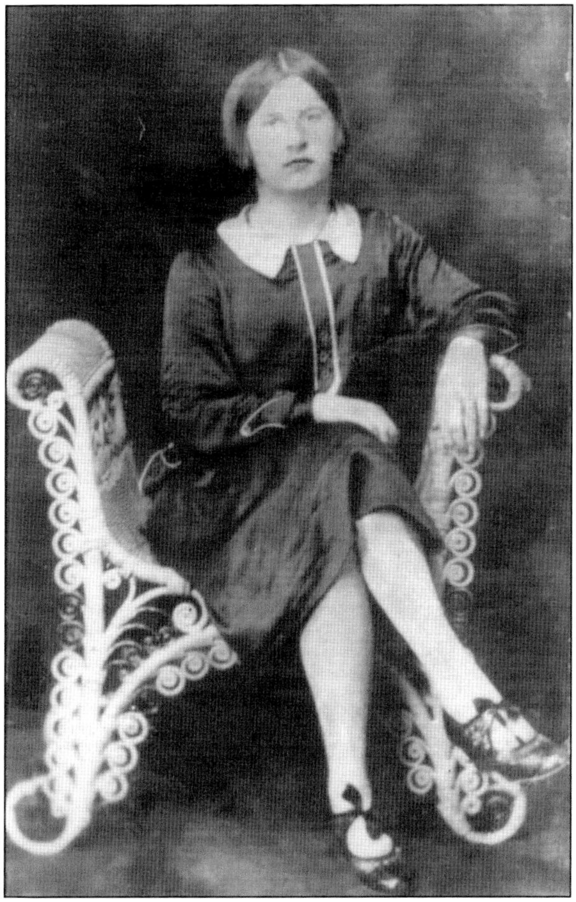

**RUBY JEWEL MARTIN-RIGGS, 1928.** The daughter of Elizabeth "Lina" and Mervin Martin, Ruby was 16 when she posed for this photograph. She married Dolphus Riggs. They were lifelong residents of the Webb City area. (Courtesy of Jim Bunch.)

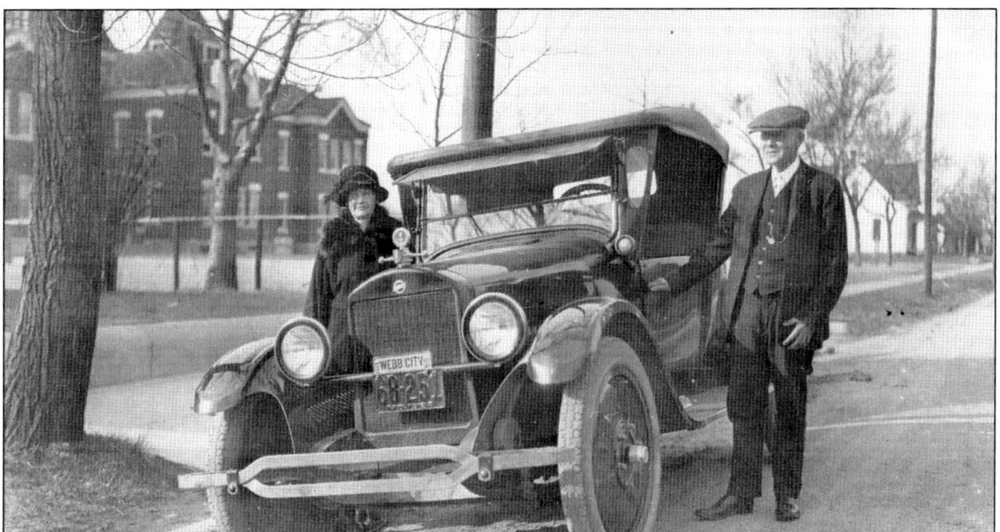


**MR. AND MRS. LAWRENCE HAVENS, 1919.** The Havens show off their new car on Liberty Street. Owning a new Model T Ford was a luxury in the early part of the 20th century. In the background at left is Webb City's Central School. (Courtesy of the Bob King Collection.)

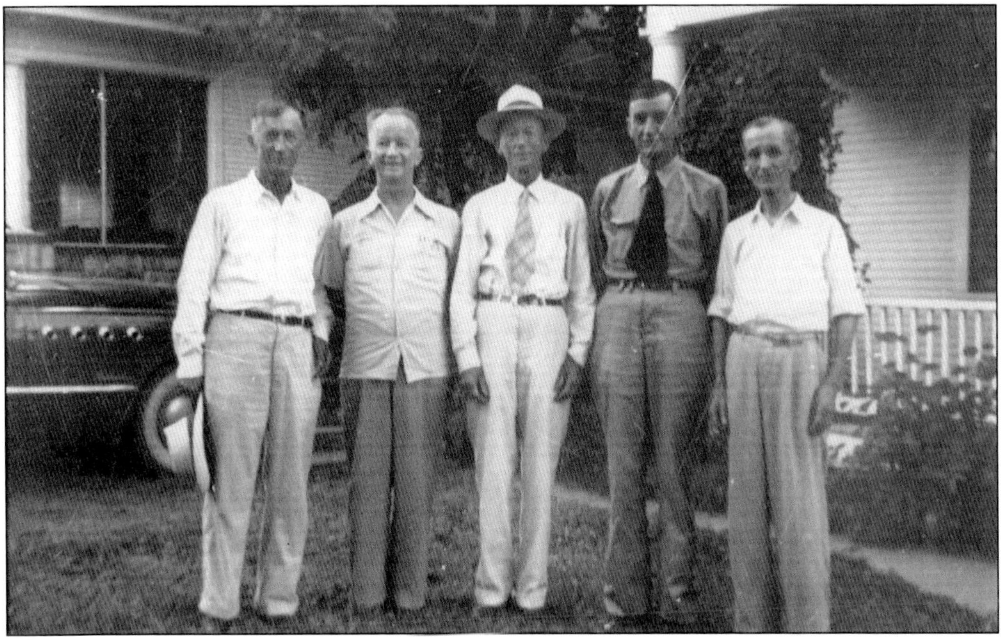

**The Five King Brothers, July 1950.** The King family are longtime residents of Webb City. Shown here are, from left to right, Ernest, Fair, Verna, Mark, and Horace King. (Courtesy of William H. King Jr.)

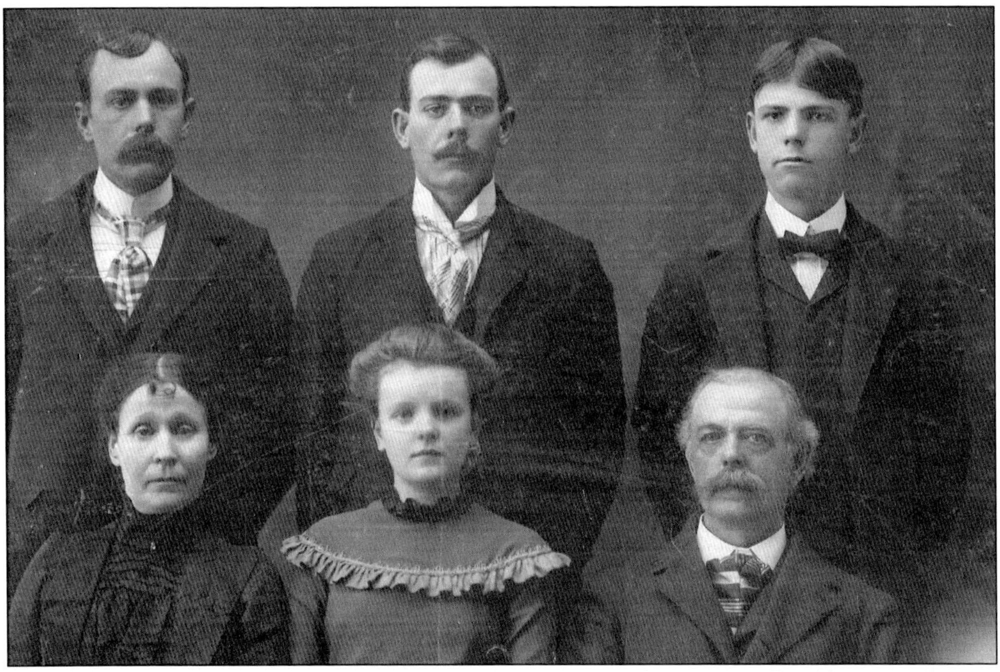

**Lofton Family Portrait, c. 1890.** The Lofton family were early pioneers of Webb City and Jasper County. From left to right are (first row) Grandma Lucinda Chappell-Lofton, Irma, and Grandpa Albartes Lofton; (second row) Lester, Guy, and Frank. The family owned many businesses in the area over the years. Grandma Lofton emigrated from England when she was young. (Courtesy of George Twigger.)

**RITA MCCALLISTER PALMER AND MUREL HAUSER, 1919.** These girls are children of Southwest Missouri Electric Railway employees. Their fine dress is an indication of the economic boom of the time. (Courtesy of the Bob King Collection.)

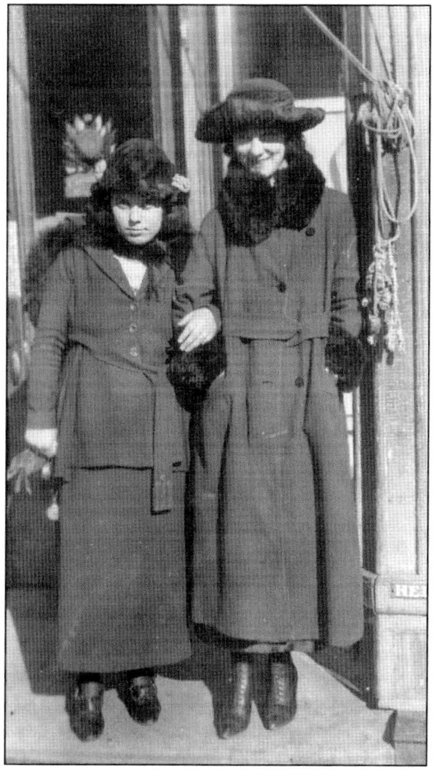

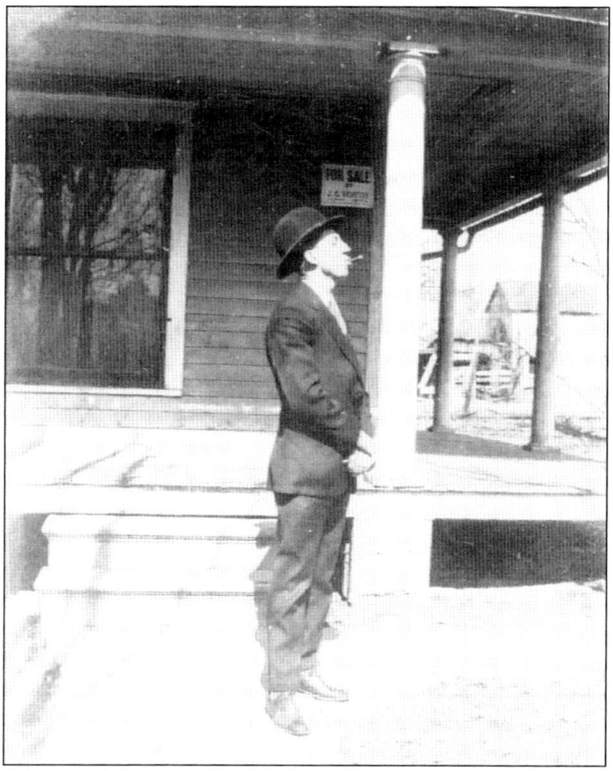


**MAN WITH CIGAR, C. 1930.** This young man looks like he is ready for someone to shoot the cigar out of his mouth. In the background, a sign on the house reads, "For Sale by J.C. Veatch." The Veatch family were early residents of Webb City and dabbled in many different businesses. (Courtesy of William H. King Jr.)

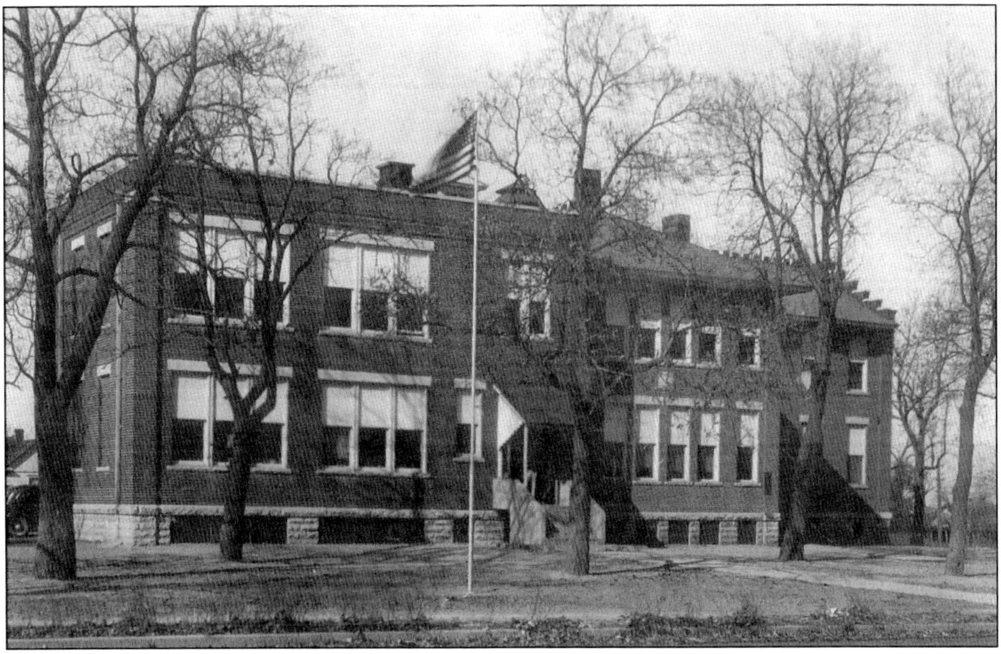

**Webster Elementary School, 1939.** The first Webster School was built in 1889 at the corner of Aylor and Allen (or Main) Streets. This is the second Webster School building. It opened for class in the fall of 1938.

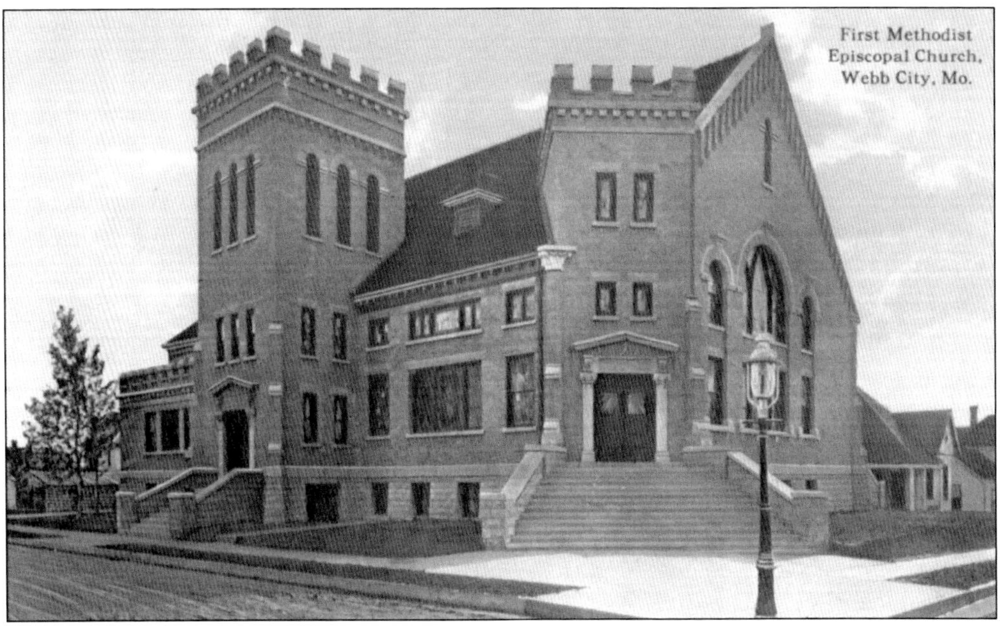


**First Methodist Episcopal Church, 1913.** The church, seen here in a postcard, is located at the corner of Second and Oronogo Streets. The land for the church was donated by John C. Webb. (Courtesy of Missouri Digital Archive.)

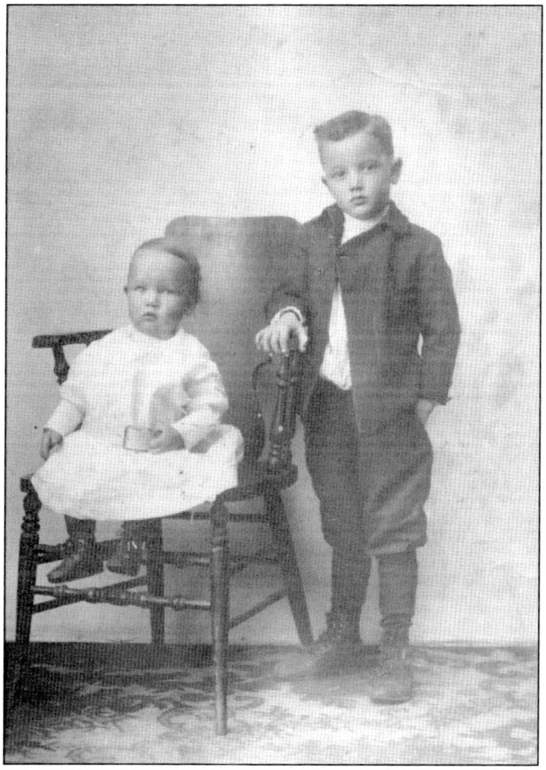

**Bibbee Boys.** On the back of this photograph, it reads, "Daisy's children, two first boys, James Devon Bibbee and Ardrian Bibbee." The photograph was taken at Commercial Studio at 211 South Allen Street in Webb City, Missouri. (Courtesy of Jasper County Record Center.)

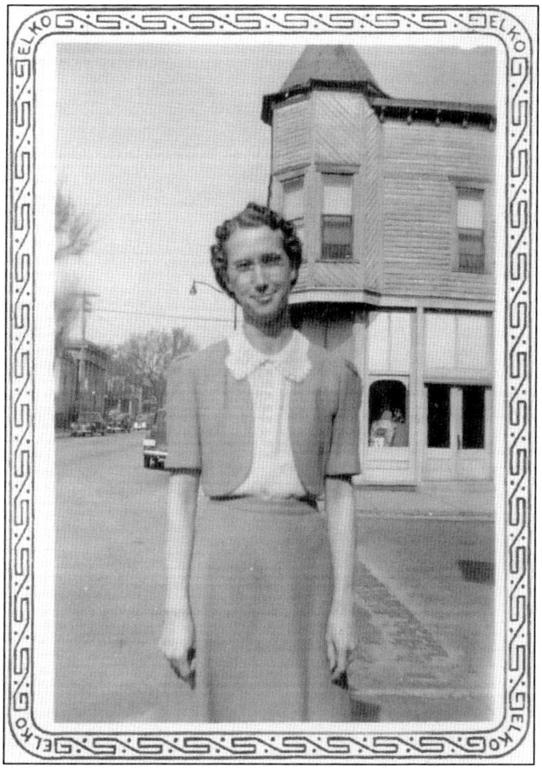

**Doxie Woodard, c. 1945.** Woodard, posing here at 207 West Daugherty Street, was a Webb City resident and businesswoman. She graduated from Joplin Business College in 1919. Spracklen's Studio is visible is in the background. (Courtesy of George Twigger.)

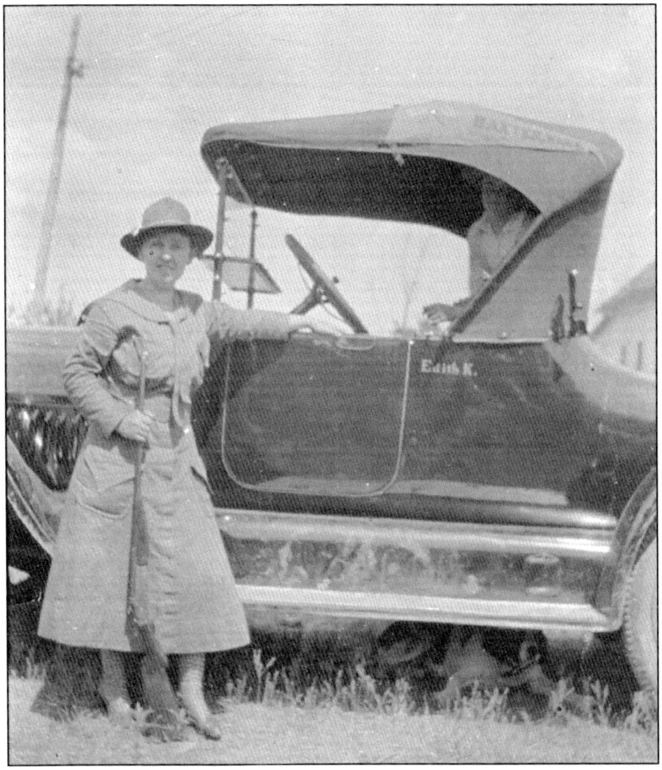

**Edith King, c. 1920.** Here, King shows off her new Model T Ford. Her name appears on the car behind the driver's-side door. The Kings were longtime residents of Webb City. (Courtesy of William H. King Jr.)

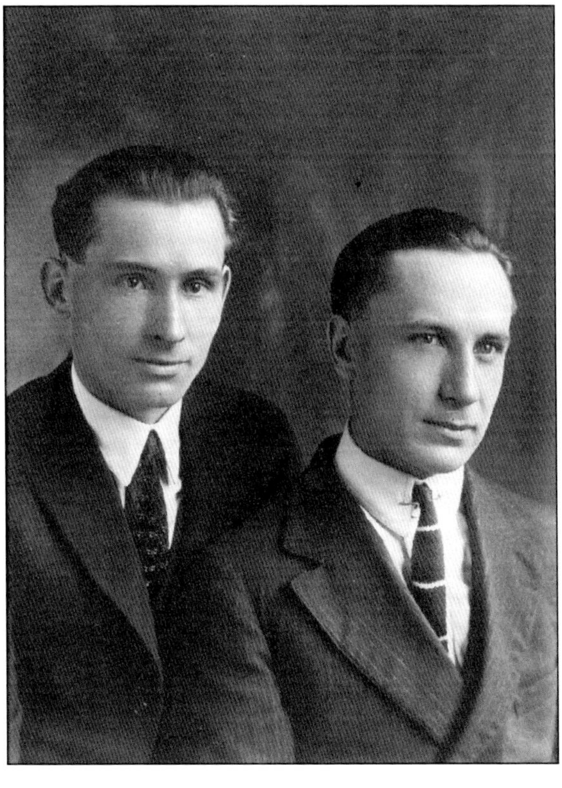

**Charles Johnson (left) and Luther Dowel, c. 1920.** The Johnson family owned Johnson Paint and Farm in downtown Webb City for many years. (Courtesy of George Twigger.)

**ARTHUR BARKER AND GUARD WILLIAM GATES, JANUARY 22, 1935.** Barker (left), a Depression-ear outlaw, was the third son of George and Arizona Donnie Barker (also known as Kate "Ma" Barker). She moved her family to Webb City in 1904. There, her two older sons graduated from grade school before the family moved to Tulsa, Oklahoma, in 1915. Arthur was arrested on July 18, 1918, for stealing a car in Joplin, Missouri. He escaped two years later. A lifelong criminal, he was killed in an attempt to escape from Alcatraz on January 13, 1936, by swimming to San Francisco. Shots fired from a patrol boat wounded him in the head; he died shortly thereafter.

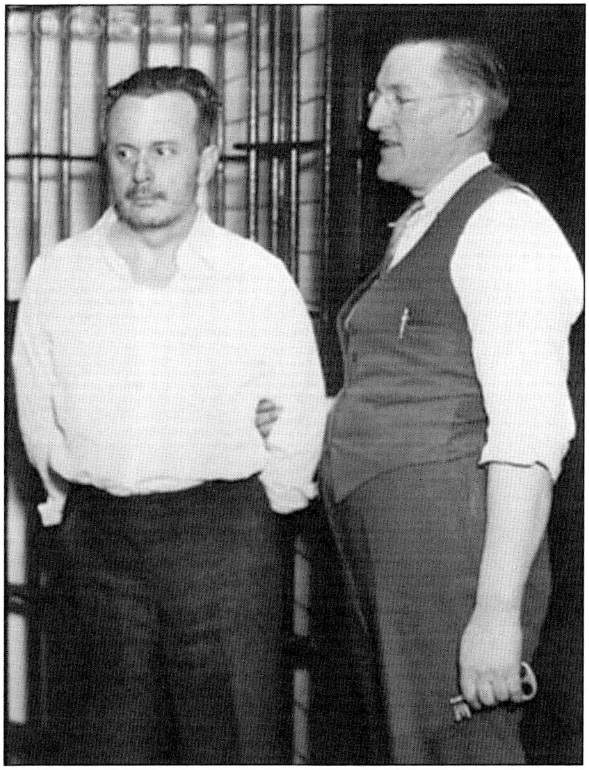

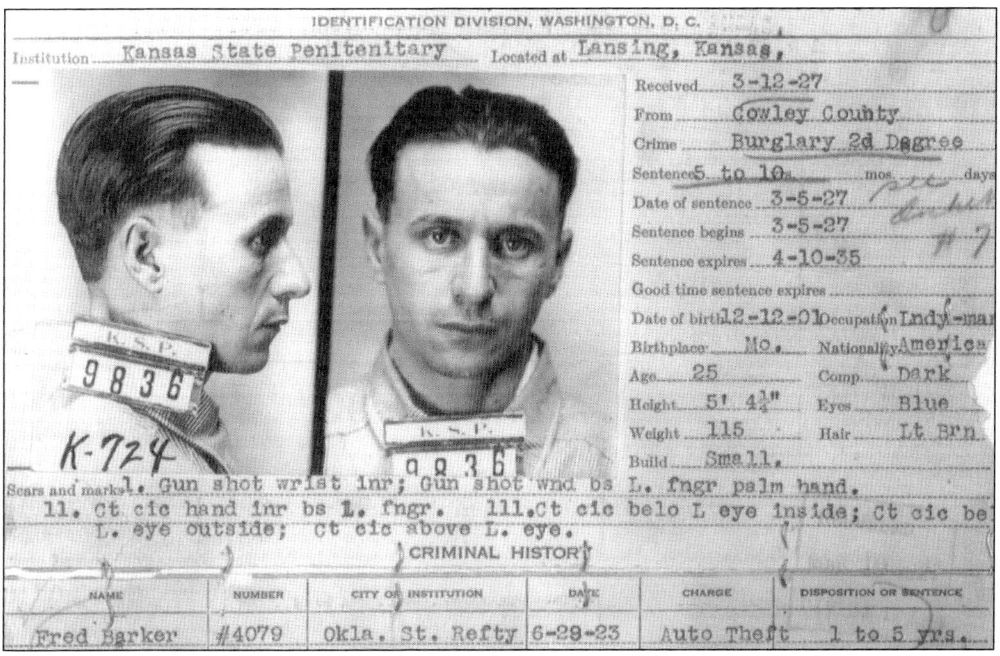

IDENTIFICATION DIVISION, WASHINGTON, D. C.

Institution Kansas State Penitentiary Located at Lansing, Kansas.

Received 3-12-27
From Cowley County
Crime Burglary 2d Degree
Sentence 5 to 10 mos. days
Date of sentence 3-5-27
Sentence begins 3-5-27
Sentence expires 4-10-35
Good time sentence expires
Date of birth 12-12-01 Occupation Indy-man
Birthplace Mo. Nationality America
Age 25 Comp. Dark
Height 5' 4¼" Eyes Blue
Weight 115 Hair Lt Brn.
Build Small.

K.S.P. 9836

K-724

Scars and marks 1. Gun shot wrist inr; Gun shot wnd bs L. fngr palm hand. 11. Ct cic hand inr bs L. fngr. 111. Ct cic belo L eye inside; Ct cic be[low] L. eye outside; Ct cic above L. eye.

CRIMINAL HISTORY

| NAME | NUMBER | CITY OR INSTITUTION | DATE | CHARGE | DISPOSITION OR SENTENCE |
|---|---|---|---|---|---|
| Fred Barker | #4079 | Okla. St. Refty | 6-29-23 | Auto Theft | 1 to 5 yrs. |

**FRED BARKER, MARCH 12, 1927.** Also a Depression-ear outlaw, Fred was the youngest son of George and Arizona "Ma" Barker. On January 16, 1935, he was killed along with his mother in a shoot-out with FBI agents. The Barkers were living in Lake Weir, Florida, at the time. Unbeknownst to the FBI, the other gang members had left three days earlier.

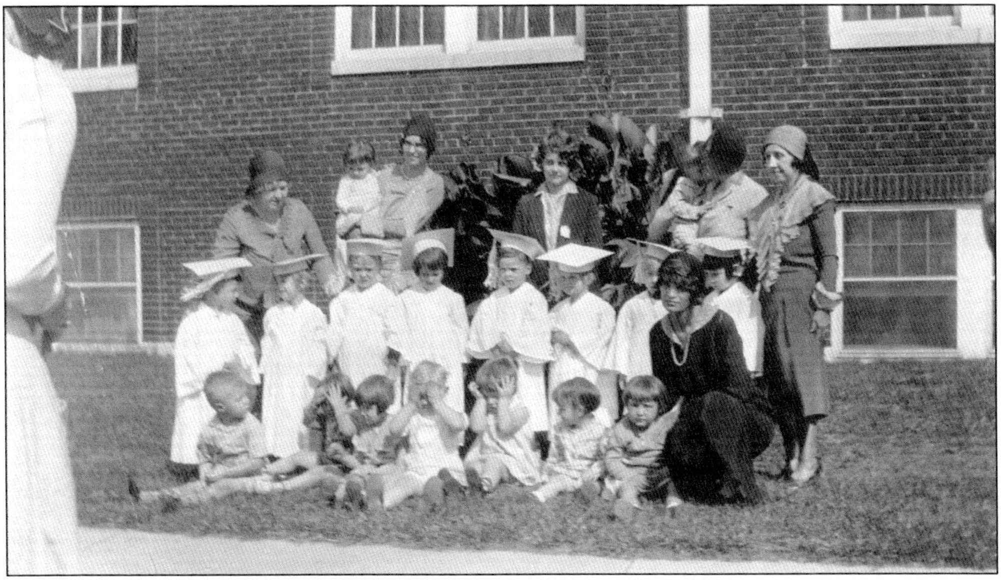

**William H. King Sr.** Little information is available about these very cute photographs. Above, the child in the second row, fifth from the left, is William King Sr. Below, he is also the fifth child from the left. It is probable that one of these ladies is his mother. The King family were early pioneers of Webb City. (Both, courtesy of William H. King Jr.)

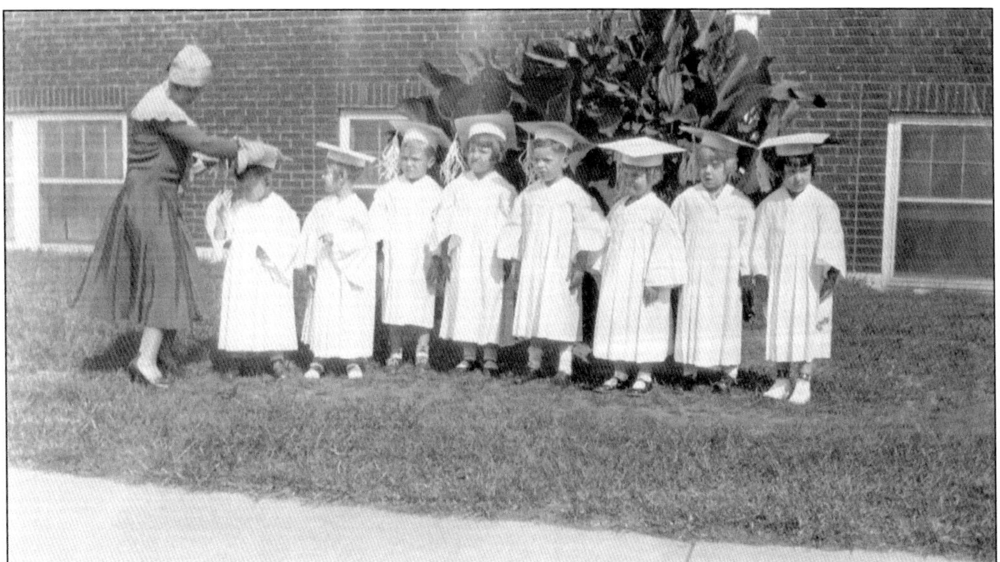

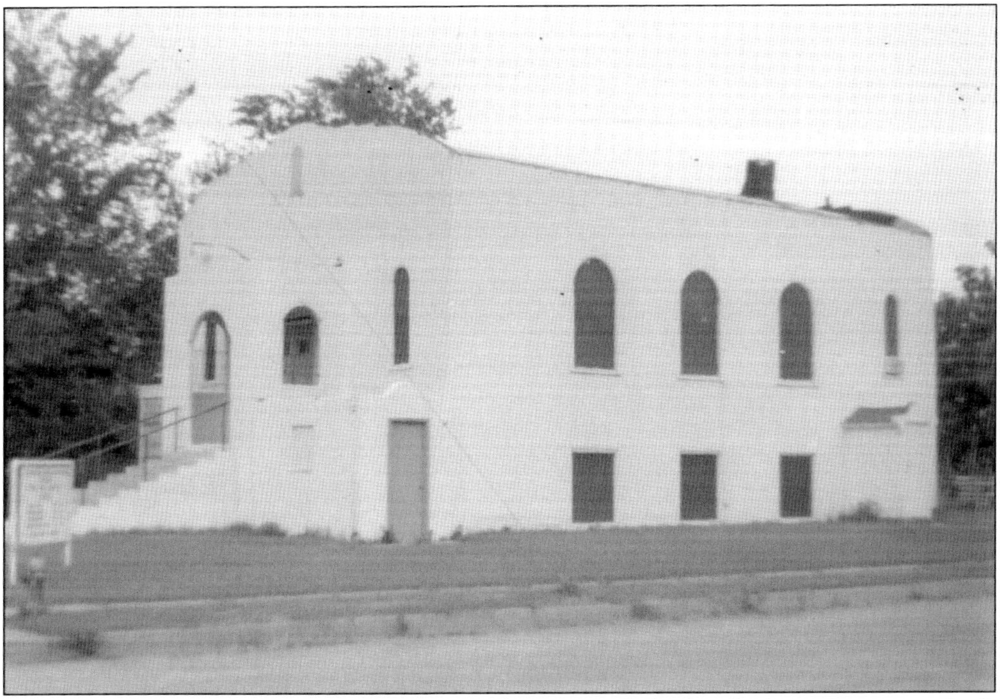

**Liberty Bible Church, 1960.** The church, on the corner of Third and Liberty Streets, was built in 1920. It was destroyed by fire on December 20, 2007. (Courtesy of William H. King Jr.)

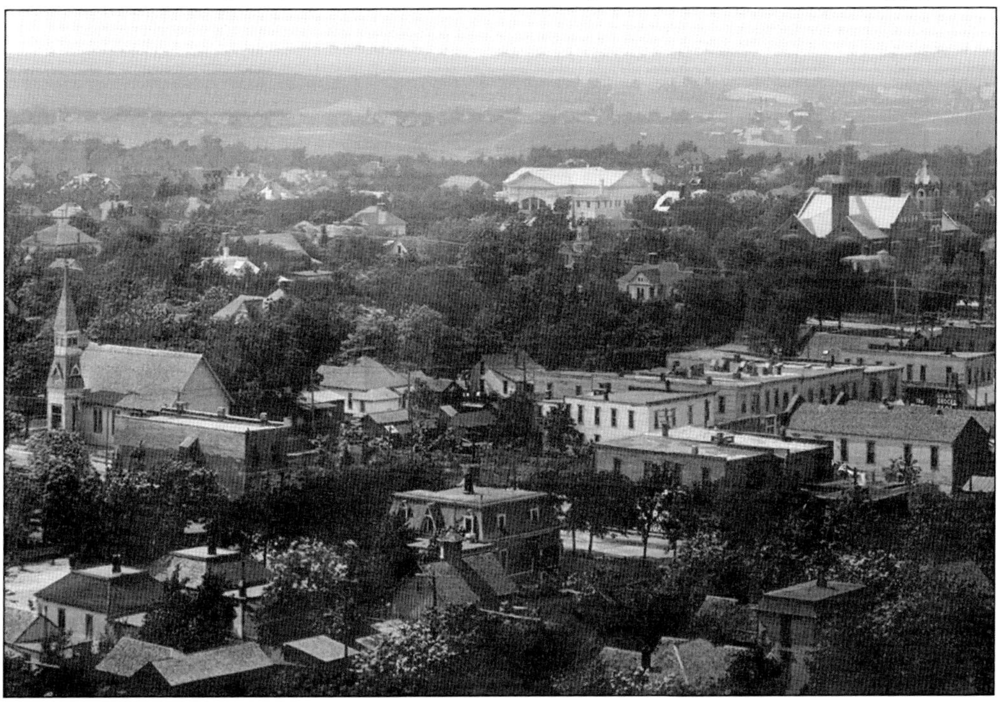

**Downtown Webb City, 1910.** On the left is First Christian Church, and in the upper center is Center Methodist Episcopal Church on Daugherty Street. In 1926, that street became Route 66. At the far right is Center School. (Courtesy of the Bob King Collection.)

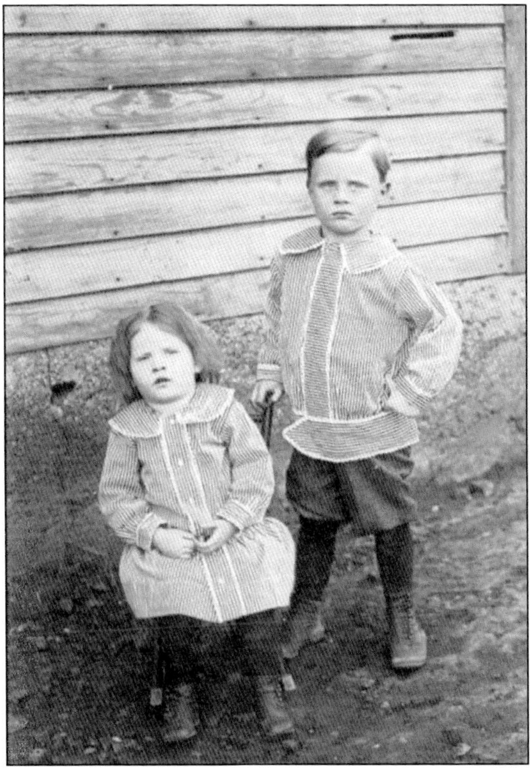

**Martin Children, 1915.** Ruby Martin Riggs (left) and Orville Martin (right) were the children of Elizabeth "Lina" and Mervin Martin. The family moved to Webb City around 1908. Orville grew up and became a member of the Webb City Fire Department. (Courtesy of the Martin family collection.)

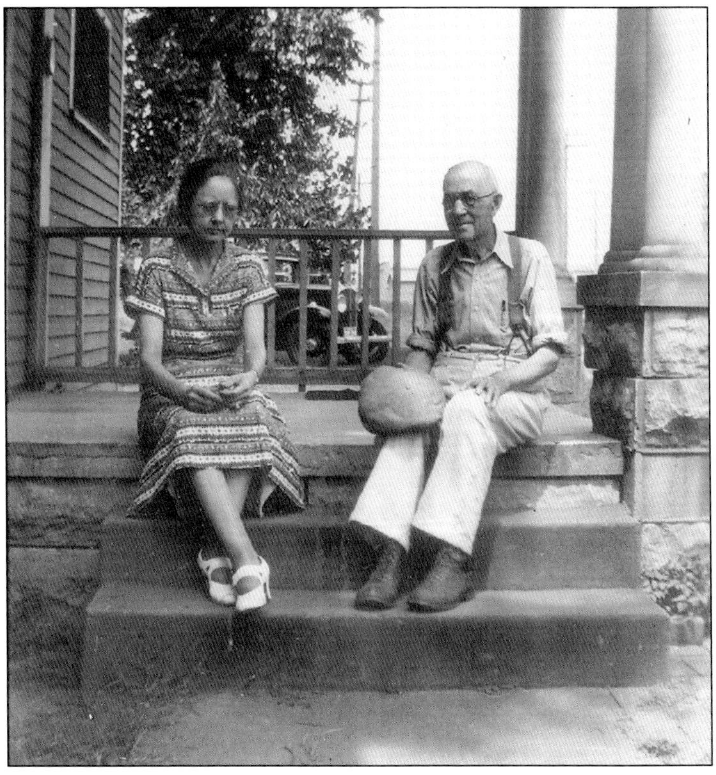

**Lura Grandstaff and Lawrence Havens, 1937.** A father and daughter sitting on the front porch, taking the time to talk, may be rare today. In the days before air-conditioning drove people inside, it was a more common sight. (Courtesy of the Bob King Collection.)

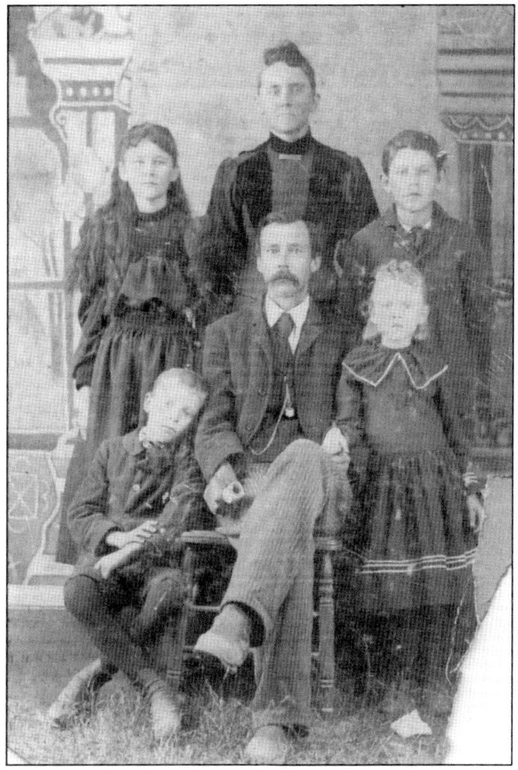

**Noel Family.** Members of the Noel family were early pioneers in the Webb City community. Sitting in the center is the father, Del Warren Noel. His wife, Mina Slankard-Noel, stands behind him. Nadine Noel-Wittich stands on the left. The Noels had four children. (Courtesy of Joseph P. Wittich Jr.)

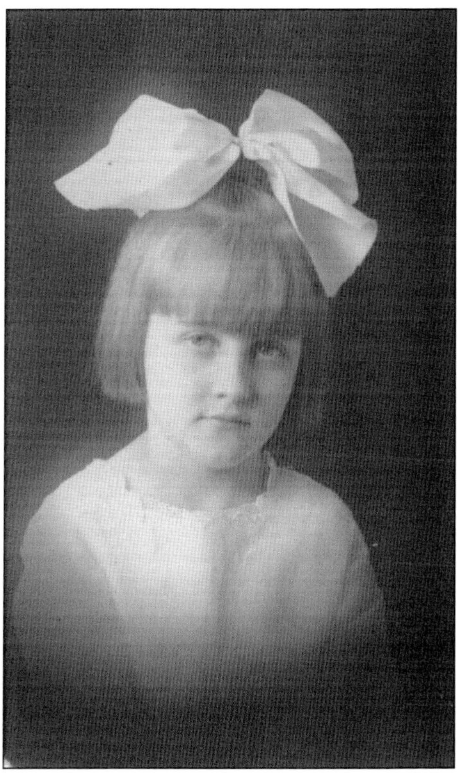

**Nadine Noel-Wittich.** Nadine, who grew up in Webb City, attended Central School. She married Joseph Porter Wittich, a columnist and sports editor for the *Joplin Globe*. (Courtesy of Joseph P. Wittich Jr.)

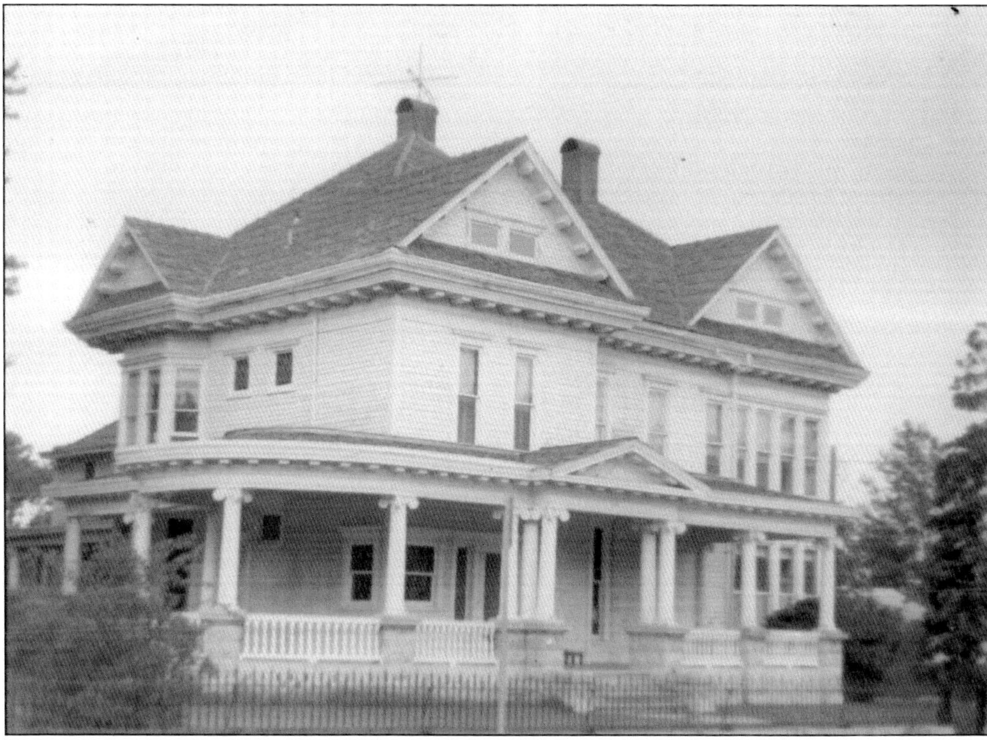

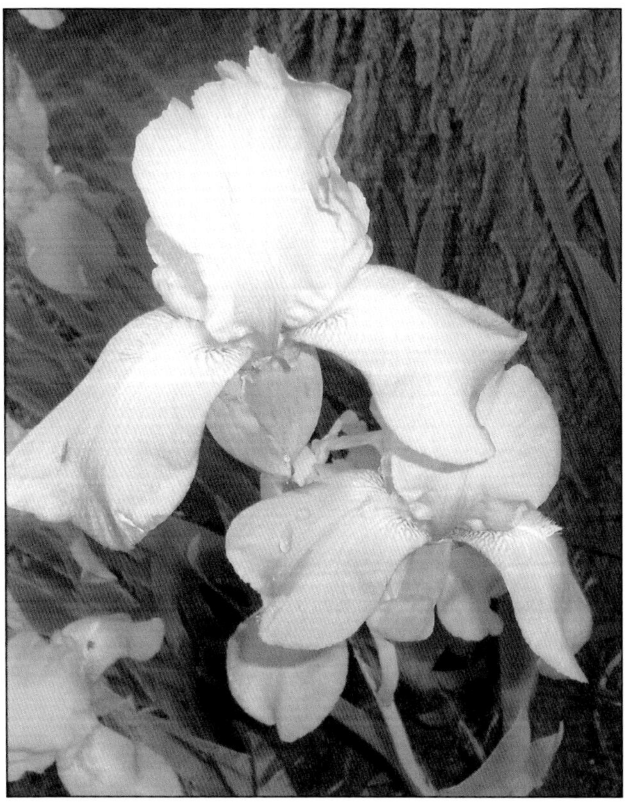

**Home of C.E. Matthew.** This home, at 221 West Second Street, today looks much like it did 100 years ago. C.E. Matthew owned Matthew Lumber Yard on Route 66 in Webb City. (Courtesy of William H. King Jr.)

**Iris.** Webb City has been called "The Friendly City of Flags on Route 66." "Flag" is an old-time name for the iris flower. At one time, Webb City had so many irises growing around town that it was nicknamed "Flag City."

# *Two*

# Community Services

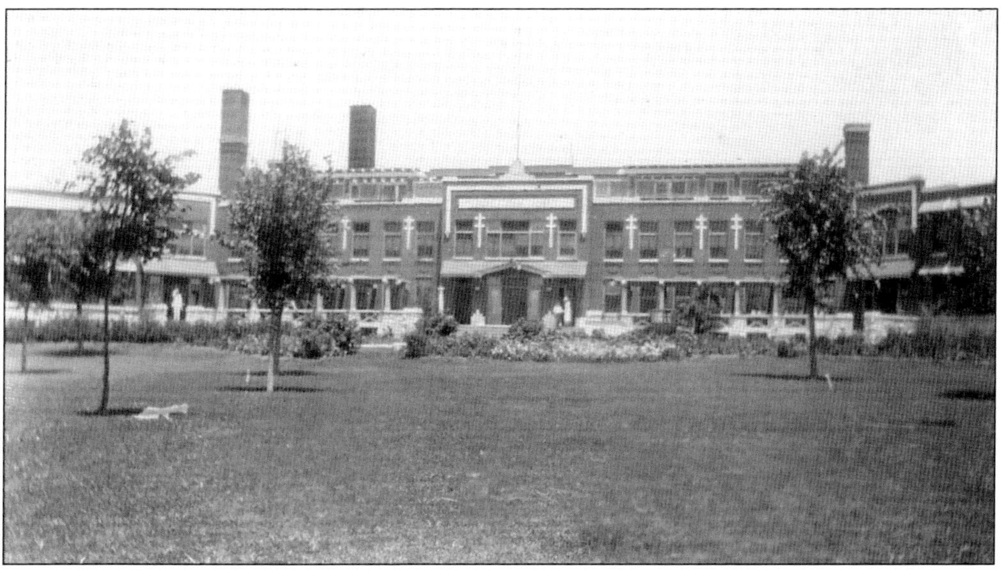

**Elmhurst Tuberculosis Hospital, 1920.** Miners of the Tri-State Mining District were plagued by silicosis, a lung disease caused from dust. It would often lead to tuberculosis. Women and children were also affected from the dust, which was brought out of the mines on the men's clothing. James A. Daugherty donated land, and the hospital opened in 1918. (Courtesy of Missouri Digital Archives.)

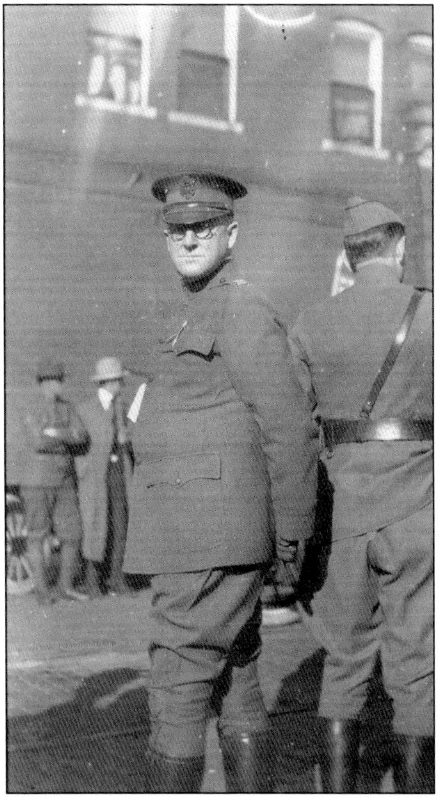

**CAPT. B.A. DUMBAULD, MD, 1918.** Dumbauld served in World War I as a member of the Medical Corps. After the war, he returned to Webb City and practiced as a physician and surgeon for more than 40 years. He was also a charter member of the Rotary Club. (Courtesy of the Bob King Collection.)

**NATIONAL GUARD ARMORY.** The Missouri National Guard was formed in 1890. The E.A. Jameson Building was the first home of B Company, 135th Heavy Tank Battalion in Webb City.

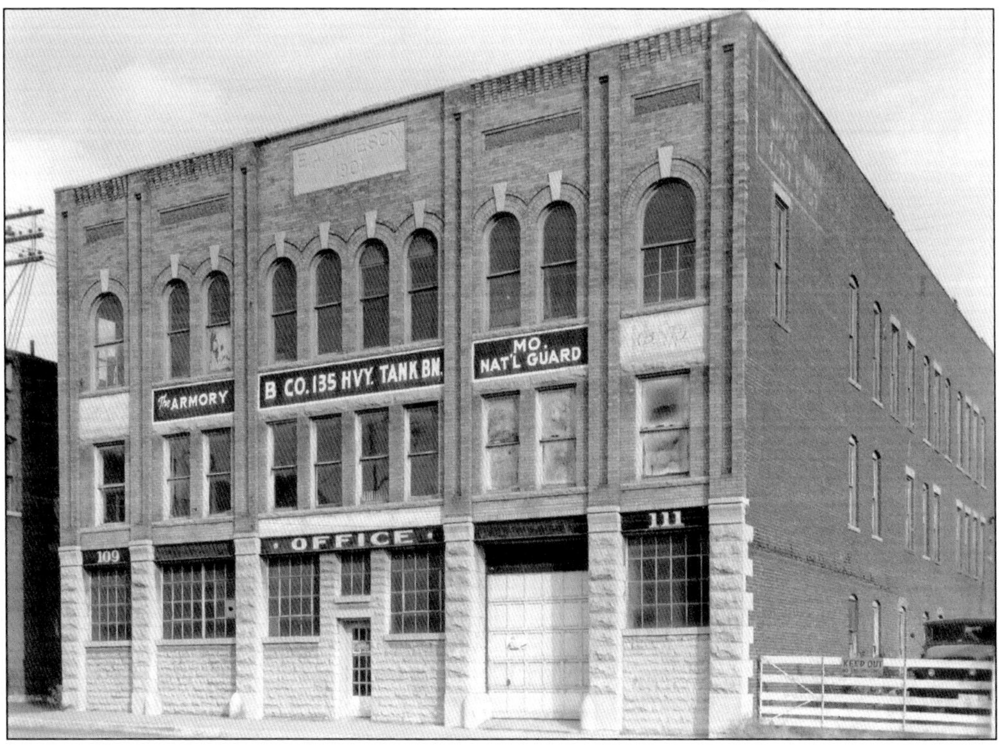

**CENTRAL ELEMENTARY SCHOOL PLAYGROUND.** The little girl in the center is Nadine Noel-Wittich. The other two little girls are unidentified. (Courtesy Joseph P. Wittich Jr.)

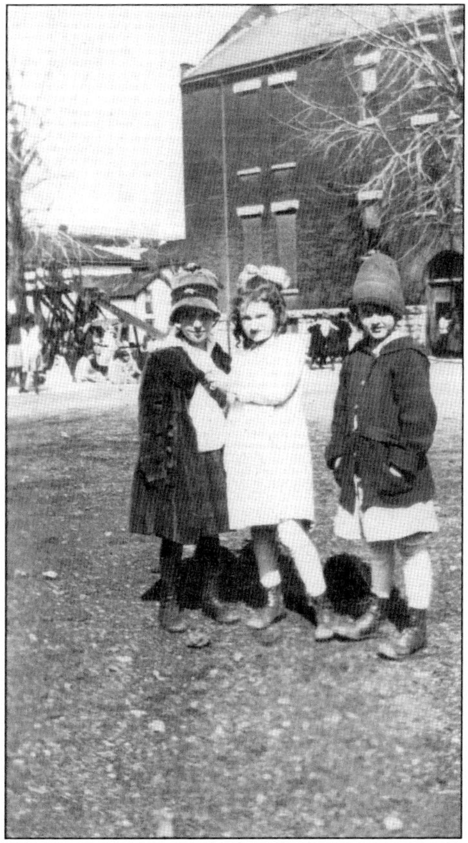

**EUGENE FIELDS ELEMENTARY SCHOOL, 1954.** The first Eugene Fields School opened in 1904. These first-graders would be attending the new school, which opened in 1954. (Courtesy of Jasper County Record Center.)

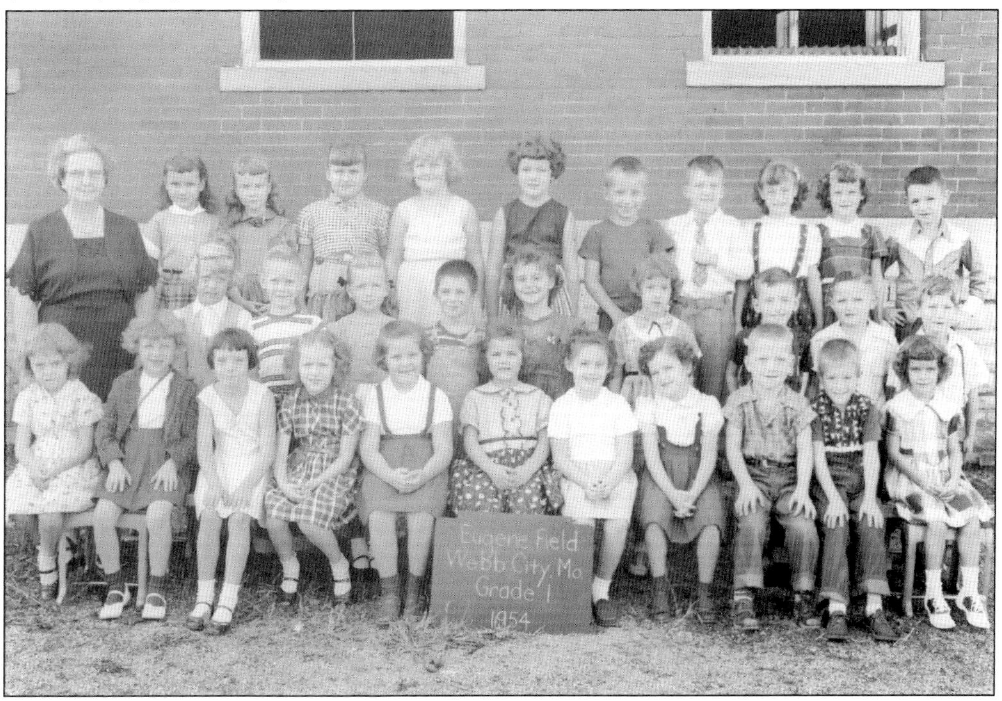

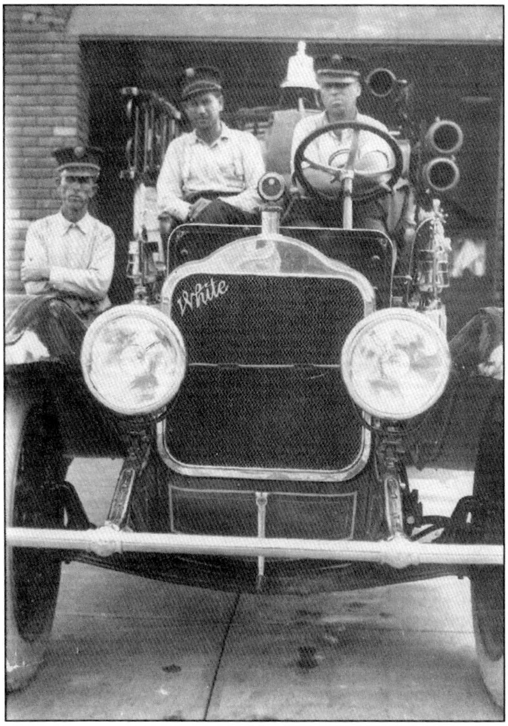


**Webb City West End Fire Department, 1919.** In 1910, residents of Webb City approved a bond issue to purchase a ladder truck and automotive fire apparatus for $10,000. At the time, this was the state of the art in fire equipment. (Courtesy of the Bob King Collection.)

**Martin Family, 1950.** Shown here are, from left to right, Roy Martin, Orville Martin (a Webb City fireman), Ruby Martin Riggs, and Dorcie Martin. The family's roots run deep in Webb City, with descendants still living in the area today. (Courtesy of Jim Bunch.)

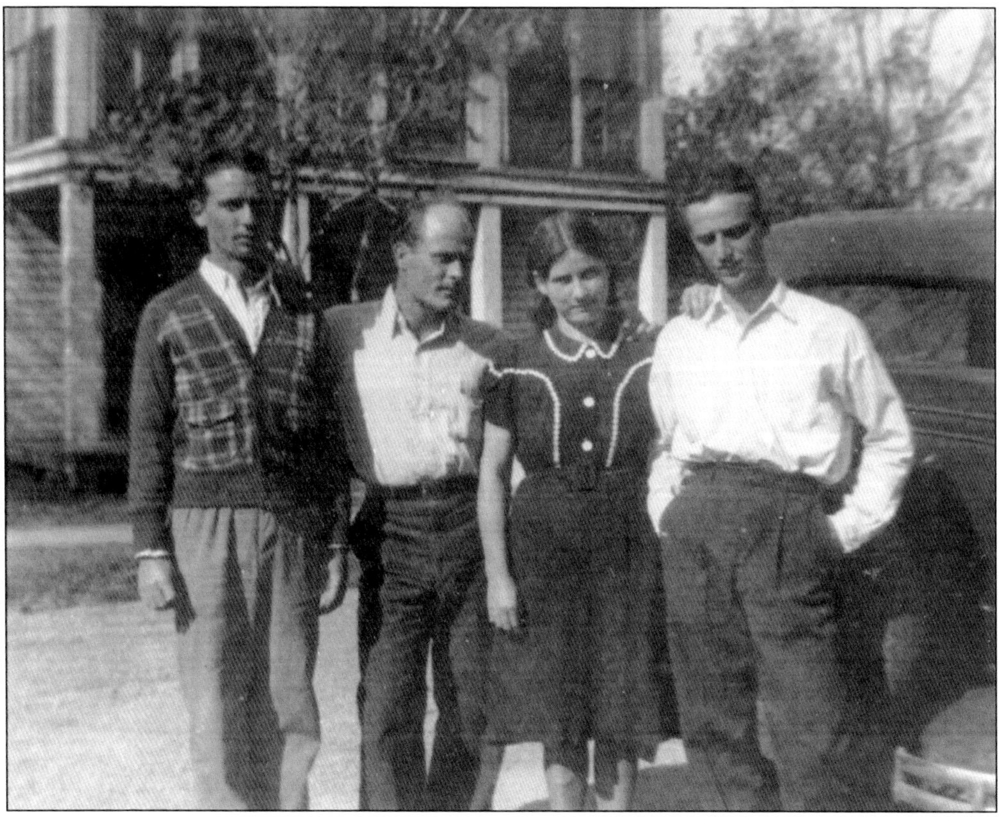

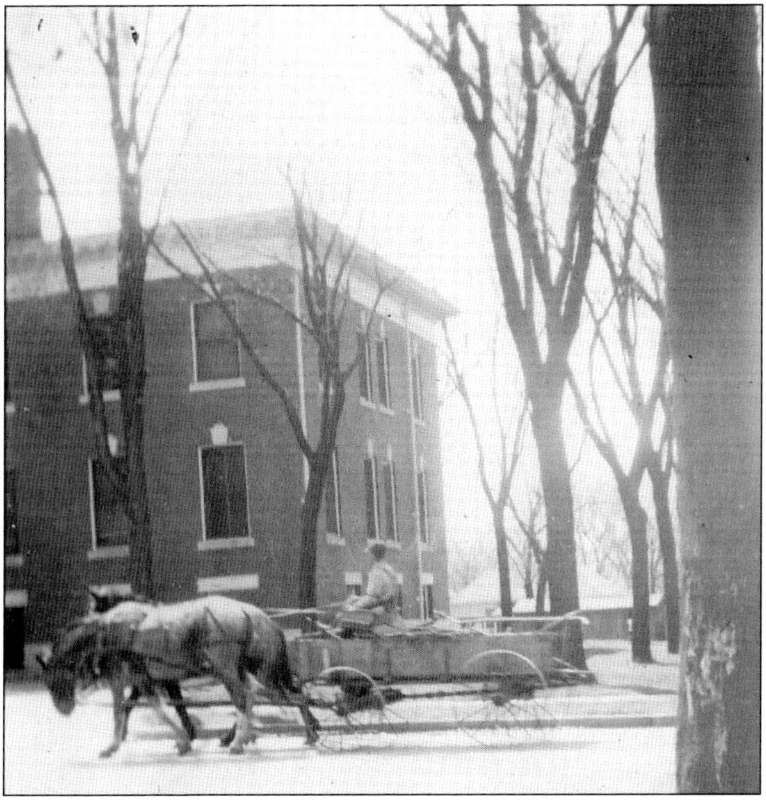

**North Side Jane Chinn Hospital.** This c. 1940 photograph, for a time lost in a family collection, shows the Jane Chinn Hospital. It is identified by its unique windows and the fact that the King family lived across the street. Note the wagon in the foreground. (Courtesy of William H. King Jr.)

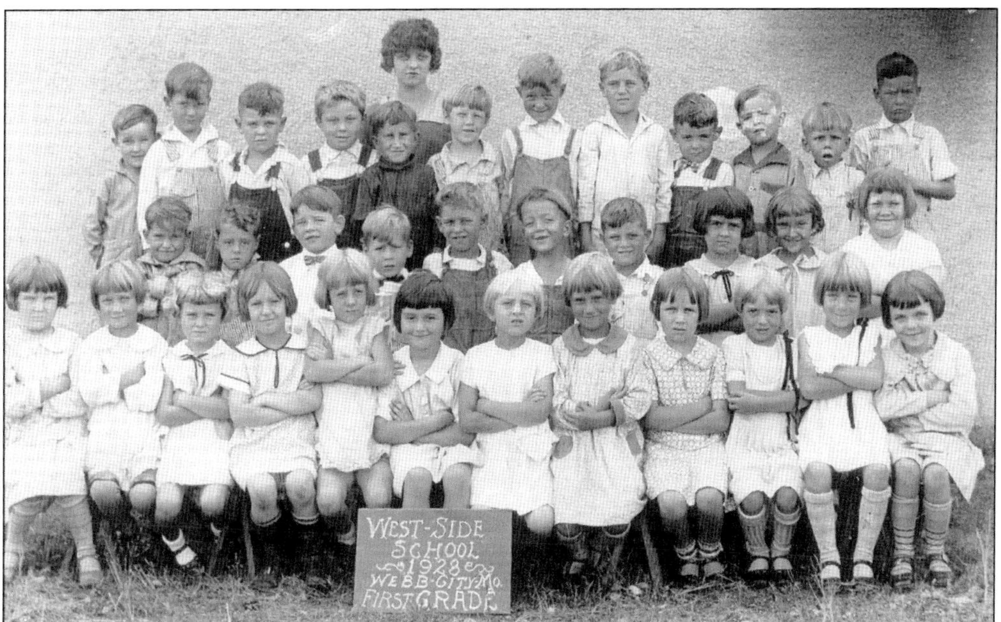


**West Side School, 1928.** These first-graders are attending the second West Side School. The first was destroyed by fire in February 1926. The school was rebuilt and ready for classes in the fall of that same year. (Courtesy of William H. King Jr.)

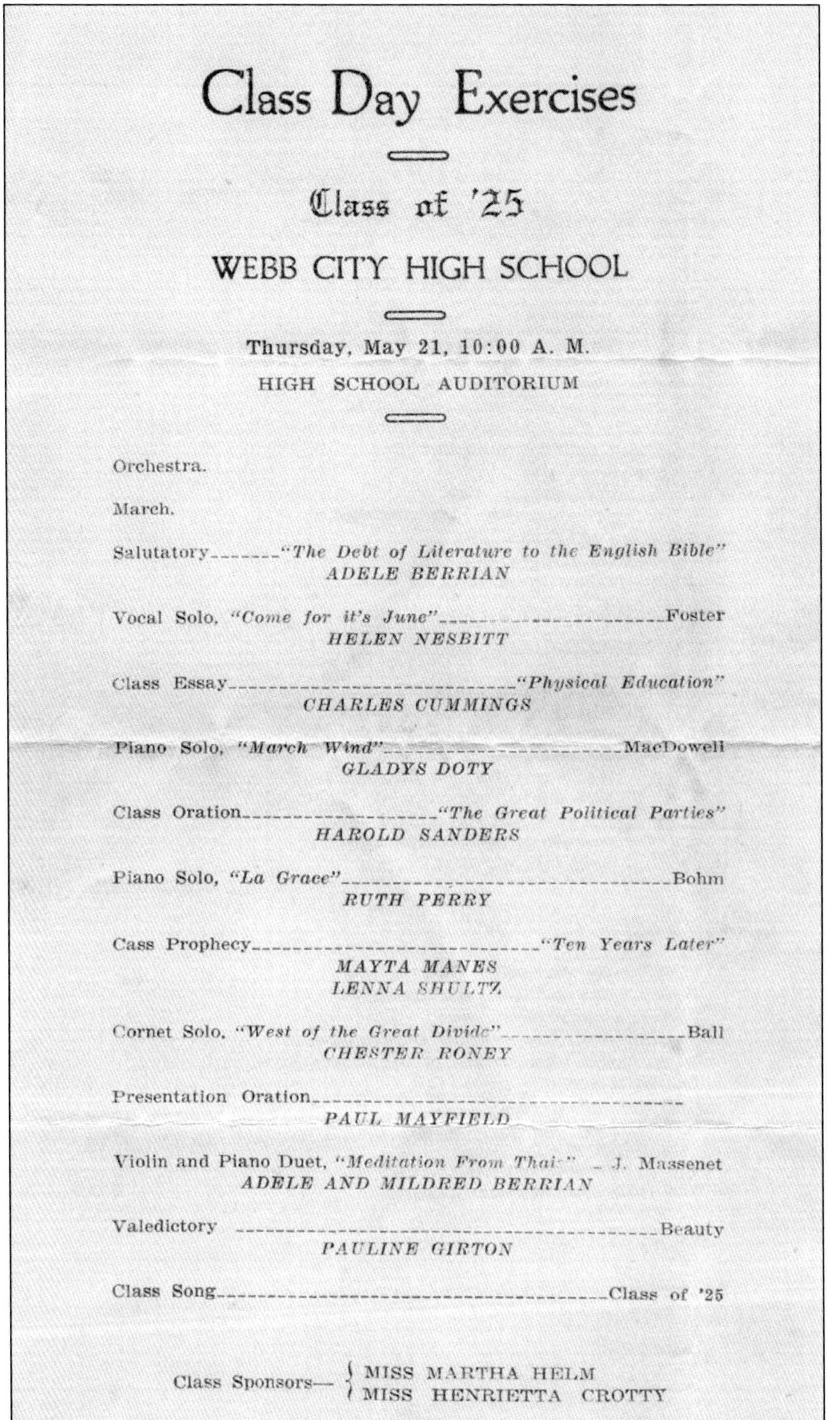

# Class Day Exercises

## Class of '25

## WEBB CITY HIGH SCHOOL

Thursday, May 21, 10:00 A. M.

HIGH SCHOOL AUDITORIUM

Orchestra.

March.

Salutatory_______*"The Debt of Literature to the English Bible"*
*ADELE BERRIAN*

Vocal Solo, *"Come for it's June"*______________________Foster
*HELEN NESBITT*

Class Essay_____________________________*"Physical Education"*
*CHARLES CUMMINGS*

Piano Solo, *"March Wind"*______________________MacDowell
*GLADYS DOTY*

Class Oration____________________*"The Great Political Parties"*
*HAROLD SANDERS*

Piano Solo, *"La Grace"*__________________________________Bohm
*RUTH PERRY*

Cass Prophecy___________________________*"Ten Years Later"*
*MAYTA MANES*
*LENNA SHULTZ*

Cornet Solo, *"West of the Great Divide"*_________________Ball
*CHESTER RONEY*

Presentation Oration_____________________________________
*PAUL MAYFIELD*

Violin and Piano Duet, *"Meditation From Thai-"* _ J. Massenet
*ADELE AND MILDRED BERRIAN*

Valedictory _________________________________________Beauty
*PAULINE GIRTON*

Class Song_____________________________________Class of '25

Class Sponsors— { MISS MARTHA HELM
MISS HENRIETTA CROTTY

**GRADUATION COMMENCEMENT PROGRAM, 1925.** This is the 1925 graduation-day exercises program for Webb City School. The names on the program reflect the names of founders and early businesspeople. (Courtesy of the Jasper County Record Center.)

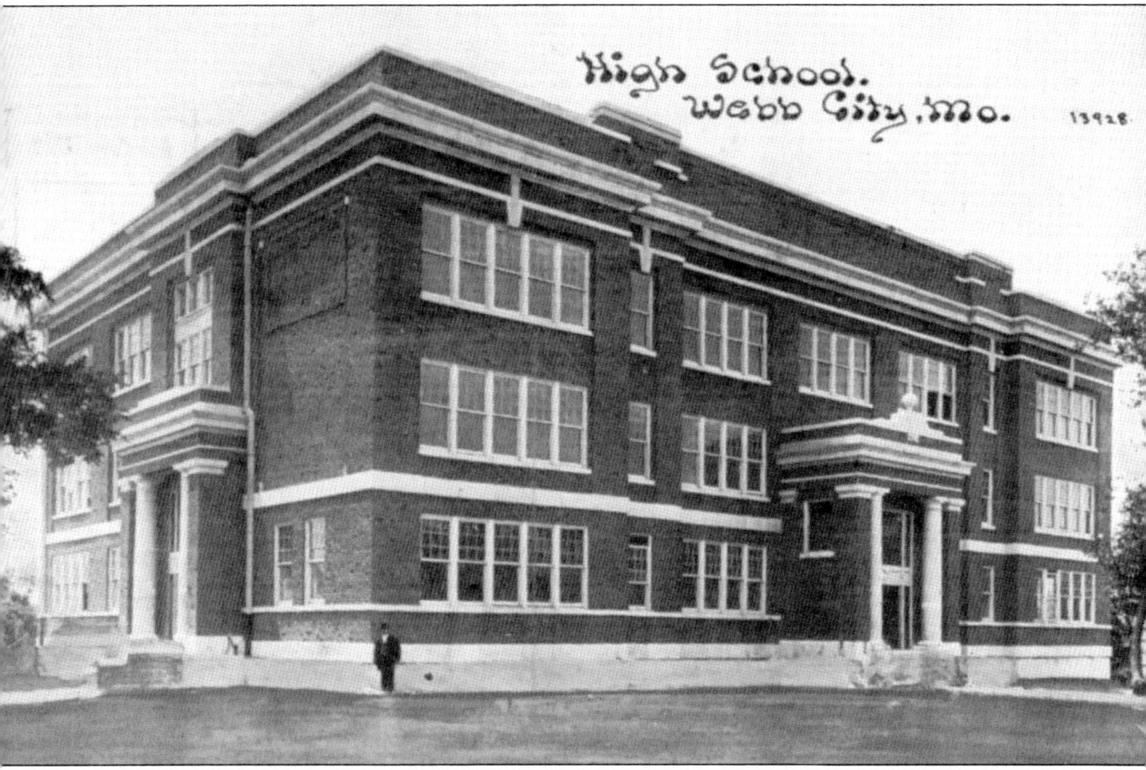


**Webb City Senior High School.** The school, seen here in a postcard, opened for classes in 1911. It was demolished in September 1974. The building stood on the corner of Washington and Broadway Streets. (Courtesy of Missouri Digital Archive.)

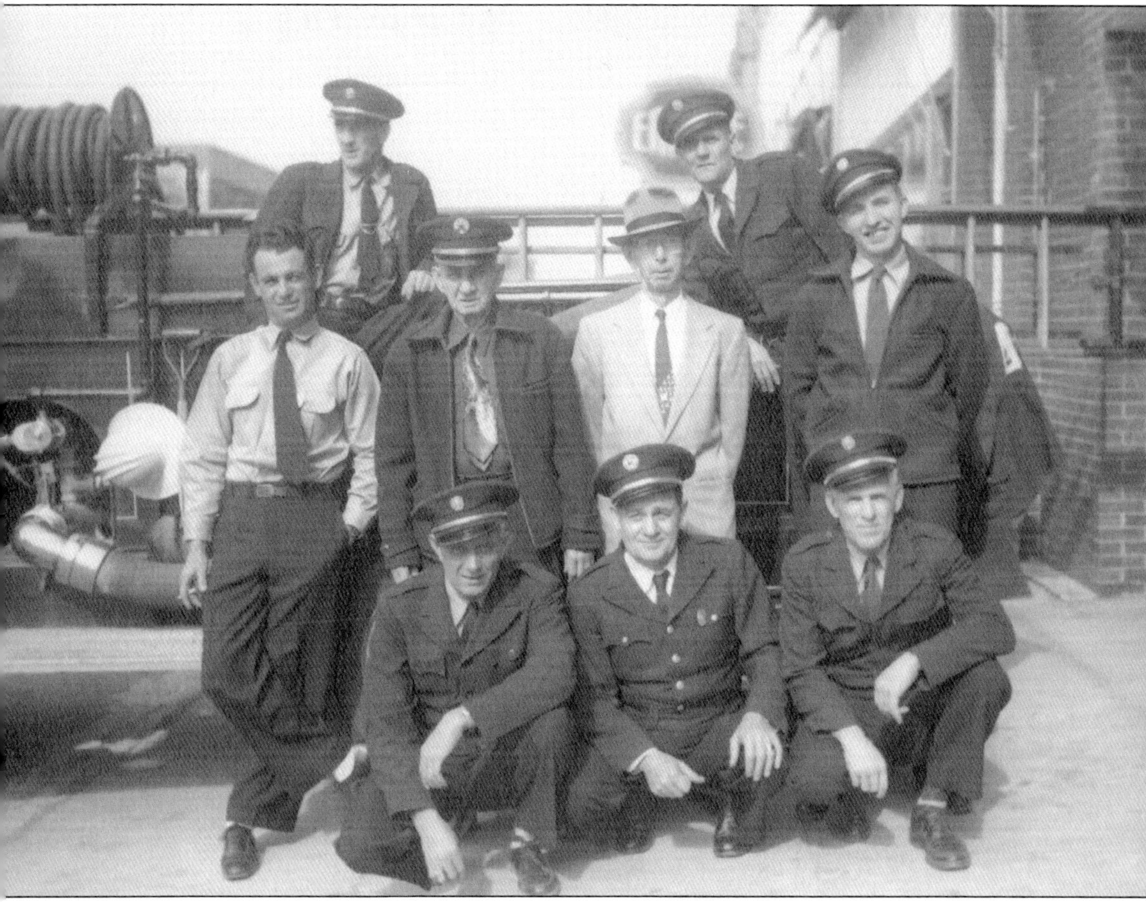

**WEBB CITY FIRE DEPARTMENT, 1952.** The man in the light-colored coat in the second row is Mayor Clarence Fly. (Courtesy of Webb City Police Department.)

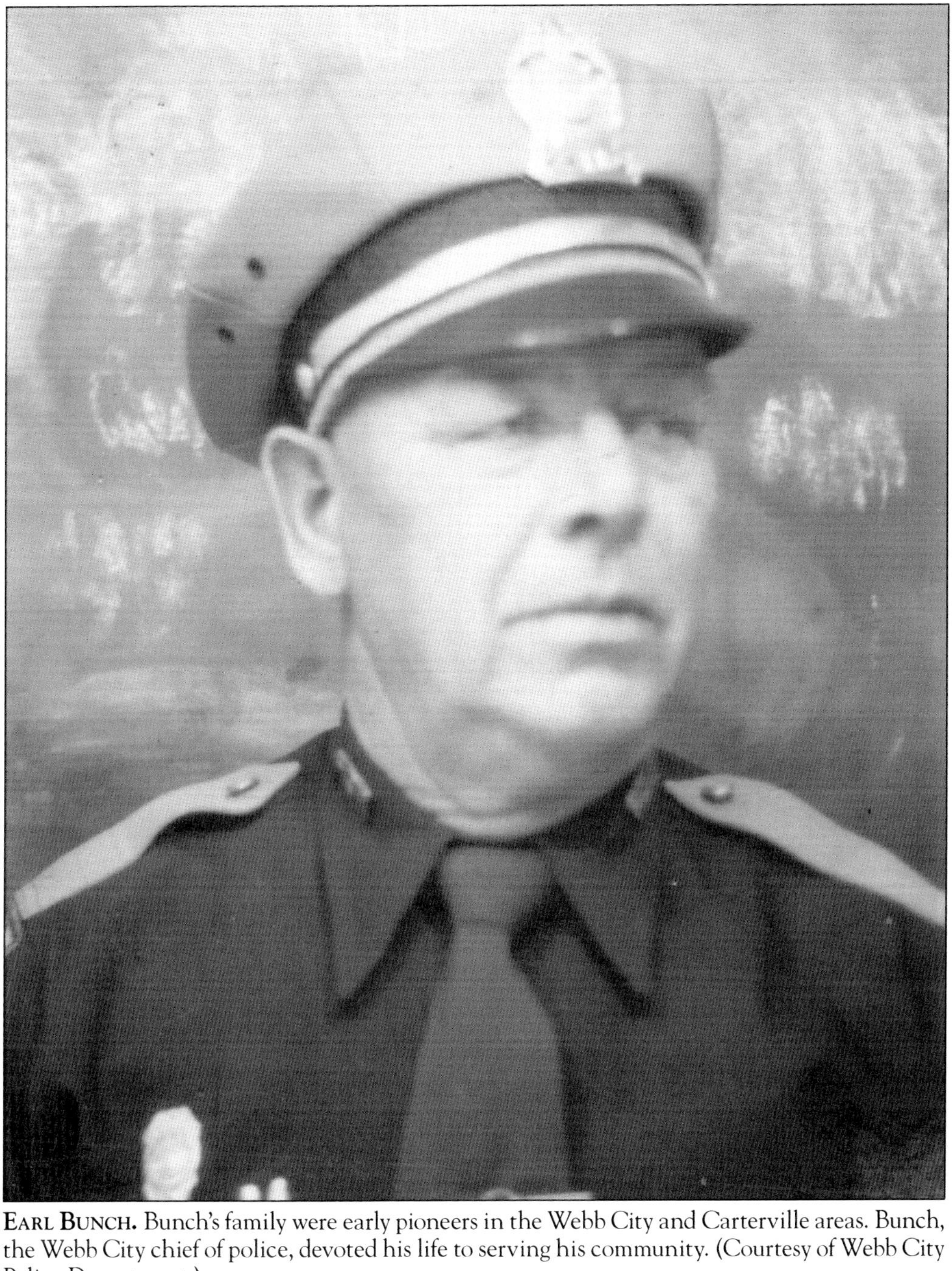

**EARL BUNCH.** Bunch's family were early pioneers in the Webb City and Carterville areas. Bunch, the Webb City chief of police, devoted his life to serving his community. (Courtesy of Webb City Police Department.)

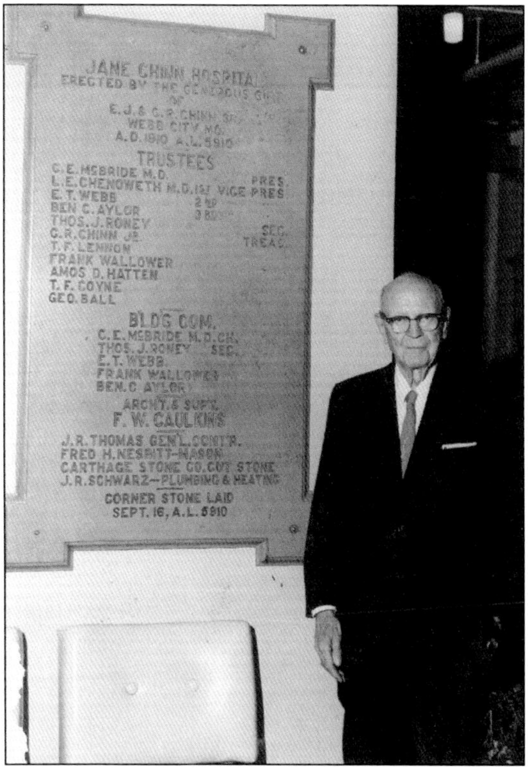


**Frank Wallower at Jane Chinn Hospital.** Wallower, a hospital trustee, stands beside a dedication plaque on which his name is engraved. (Courtesy of Missouri Digital Archive.)

**Jane Chinn Hospital.** Because of their love for Webb City and the recognition of the need for a hospital, Jane and Charles Chinn donated the money to build a hospital and to supply equipment. (Courtesy of Webb City Police Department.)

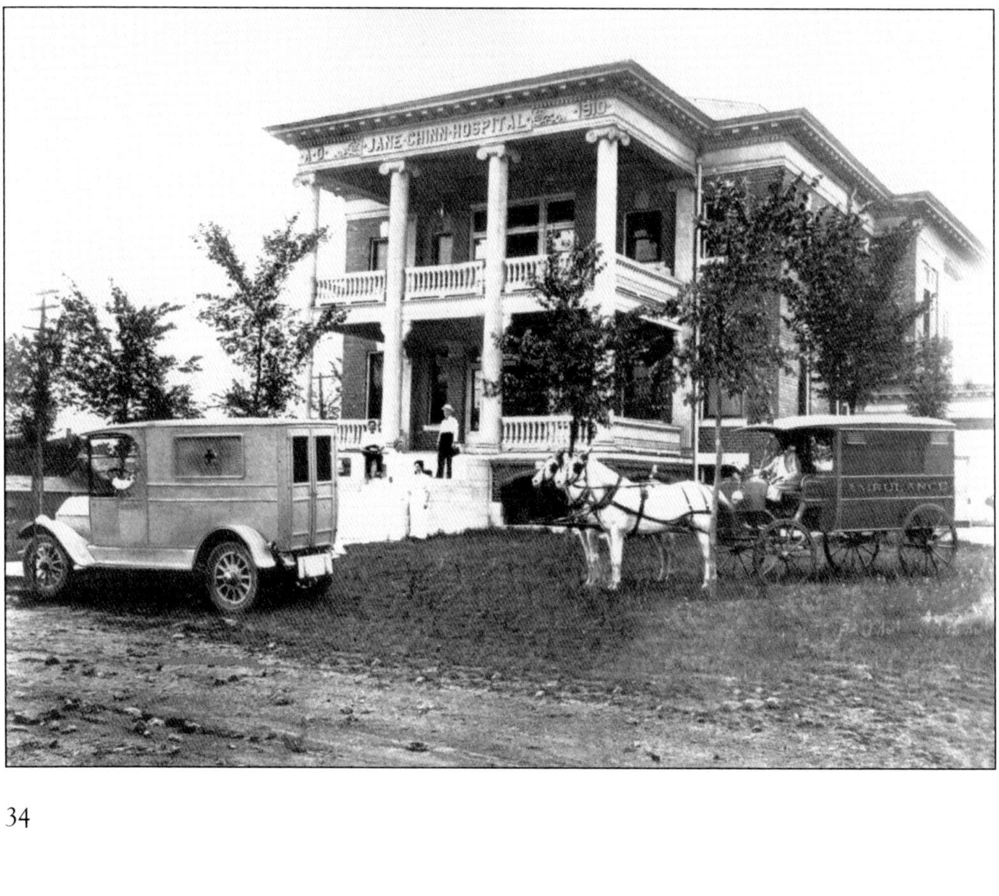

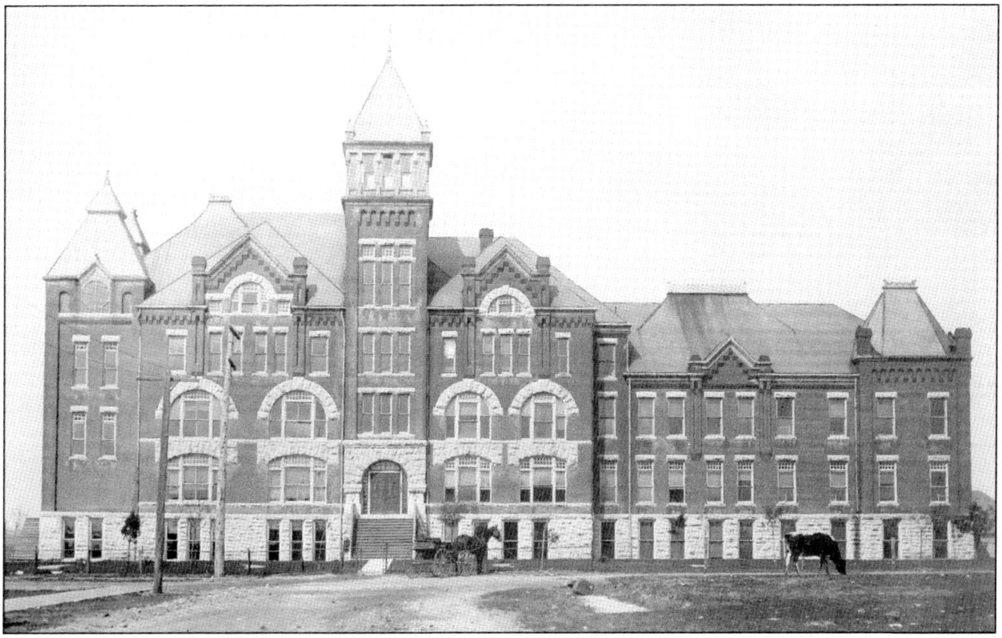

**Webb City Baptist College.** The school opened for classes on September 15, 1896, as a coeducation institution. It shortly thereafter changed to a school for young ladies. Its doors closed in 1909 after summer school classes for teachers. In subsequent years, the building was used as an apartment house, an orphanage, and a doctor's office. In 1936, the building was demolished. The bricks were salvaged, and the land was sold to Amos Hatten. (Courtesy of Bradbury Bishop Deli and Route 66 Diner.)

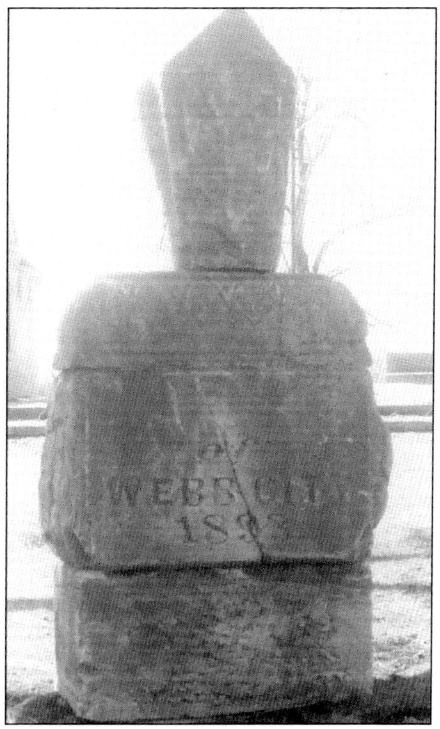


**Cornerstone, Webb City Baptist College, 2013.** At first, it was believed that this cornerstone had been lost. It was finally located at the intersection of College Avenue and Austin Street in 1978 and placed at the entrance to Hatten Park. The land for the park was donated to the city on May 1, 1933, by Amos Hatten. During the WPA era, a swimming pool and a bathhouse were built inside the park.

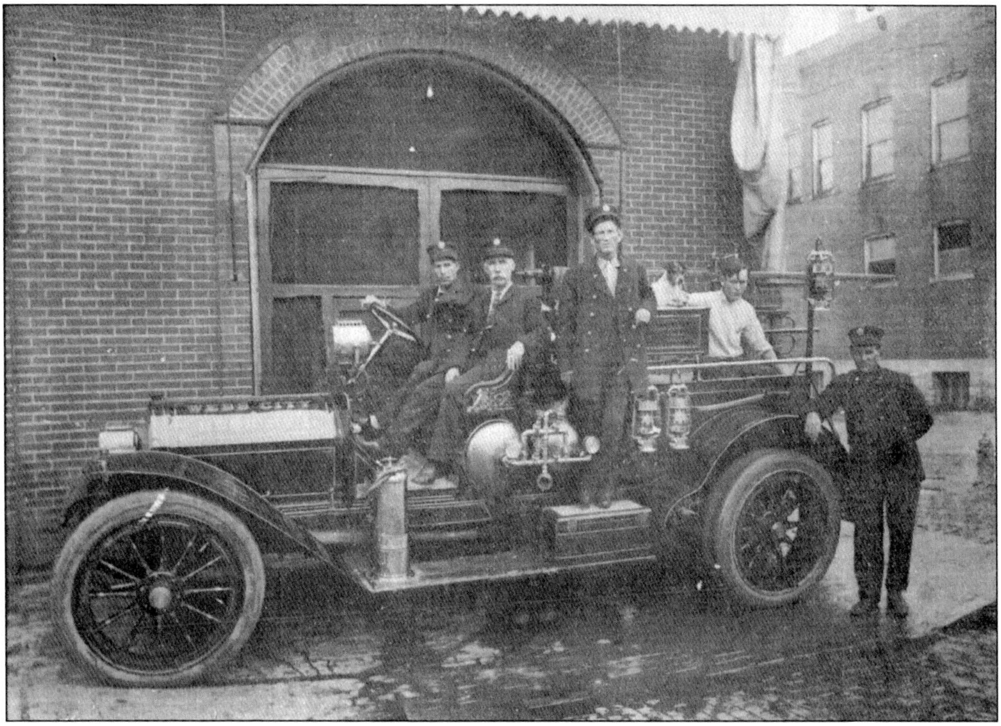

**Webb City Firefighters.** Members of the Webb City Fire Department pose with their mascot in front of the fire station at 209 West Broadway Street. Prior to the construction of the fire station, this was the location of the Home Telephone Company. Built in 1907, today the structure houses the Webb City Police Department. (Courtesy of Webb City Police Department.)

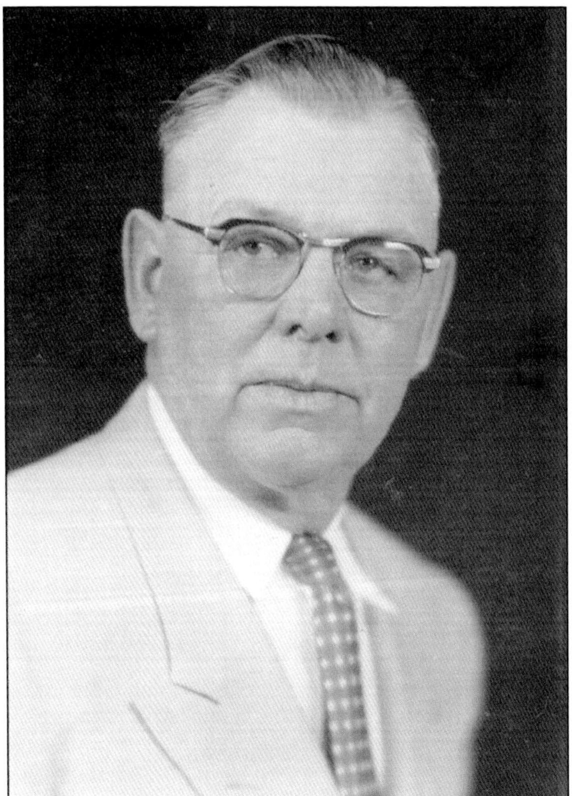

**Earl Bunch, April 20, 1953.** When Bunch served as chief of police, it was an elected position. Today, the chief is hired by the city council. He married Rachel Laughlin, and they were both lifelong residents of Webb City. (Courtesy of Webb City Police Department.)

**Central School, c. 1890.** The first Central School was built in 1877 and opened in April of that year. With an influx of miners and their families, the four-room school on Broadway Street soon became overcrowded. It was replaced in 1894 with a larger brick structure in the photograph below.

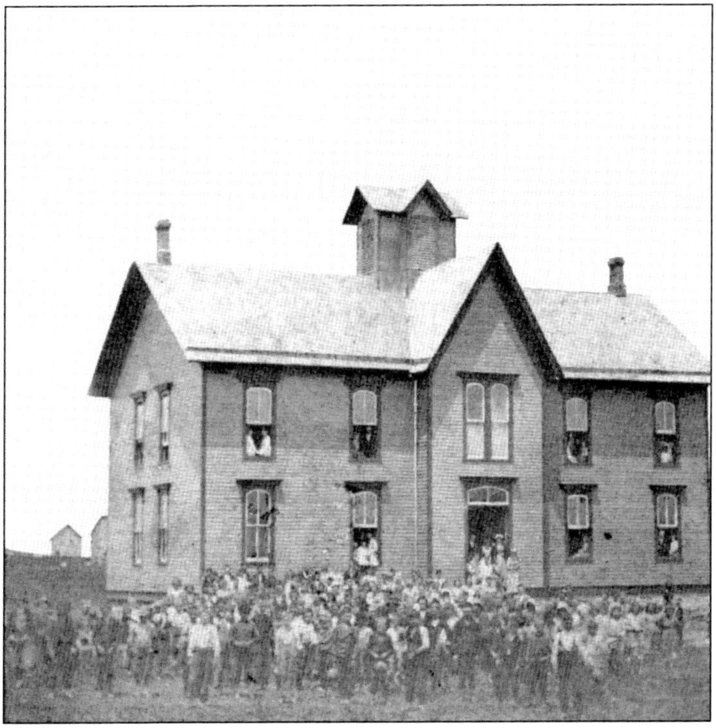

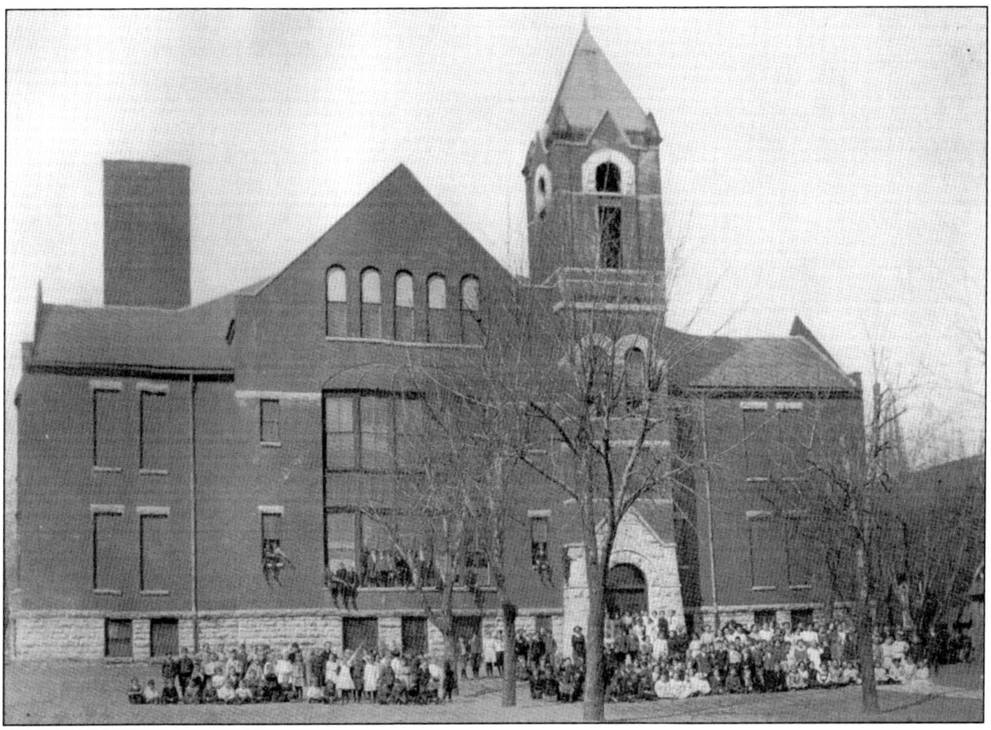

**Webb City Junior High School, c. 1920.** This building initially served as Webb City's Central School, constructed in 1894. In 1920, the seventh and eighth grades were relocated to this school in order to establish a program similar to that of the high school.

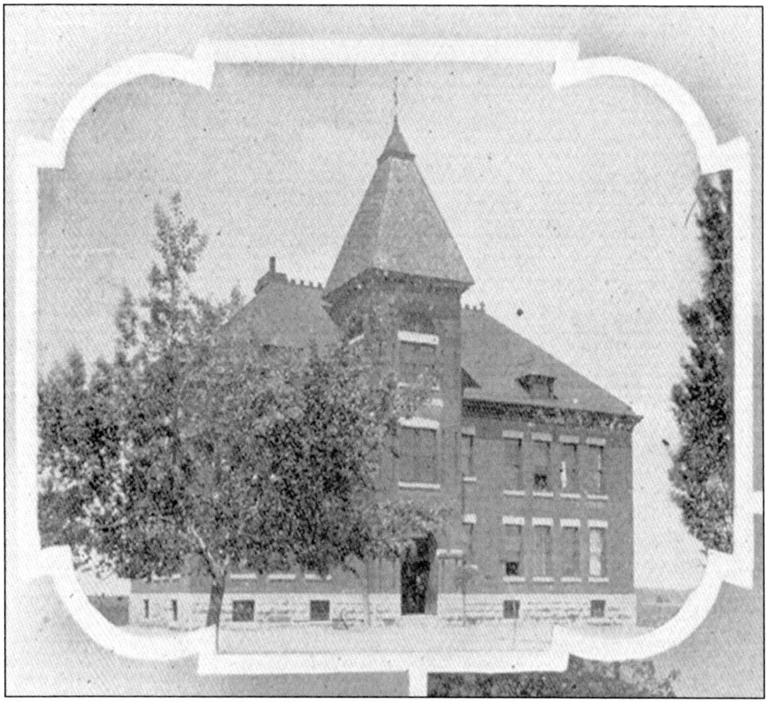

**WEST SIDE SCHOOL, 1907.** The six-room West Side School, seen here in a postcard, was built in 1892. It was destroyed by fire on February 22, 1926. A defective flue was believed to be the cause of the fire. A bond issue was then passed by Webb City voters to rebuild the structure.

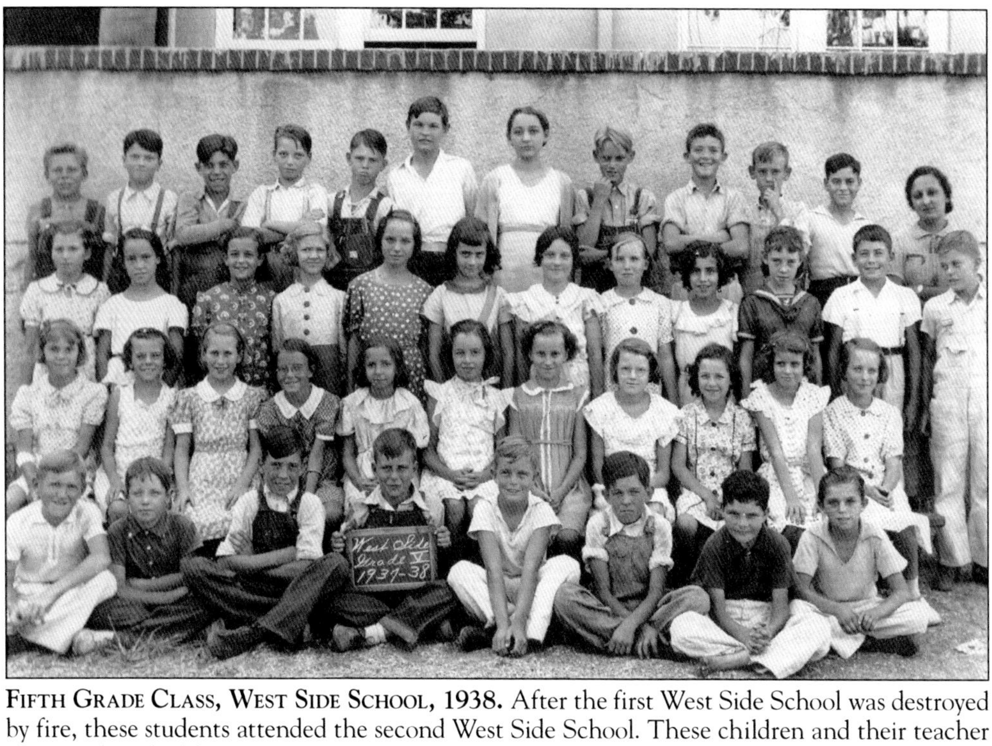


**FIFTH GRADE CLASS, WEST SIDE SCHOOL, 1938.** After the first West Side School was destroyed by fire, these students attended the second West Side School. These children and their teacher are not identified (Courtesy of William H. King Jr.)

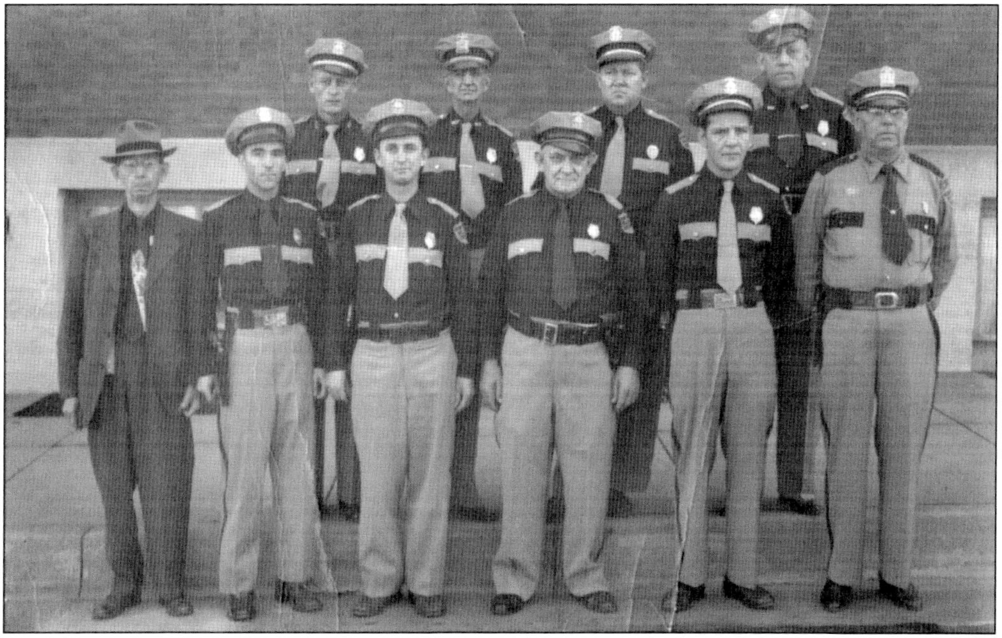

**Webb City Police Department, 1953.** Shown here are, from left to right, (first row) Mayor Clarence Fly, Robert Freeze, Dallas Simpson, William Morgan, Walter Rich, and Chief Earl Bunch; (second row) Assistant Chief Carl Woolsey, L.A. "Tex" Beeson, L.E. Vaughn, and Glen Woolsey. (Courtesy of Webb City Police Department.)

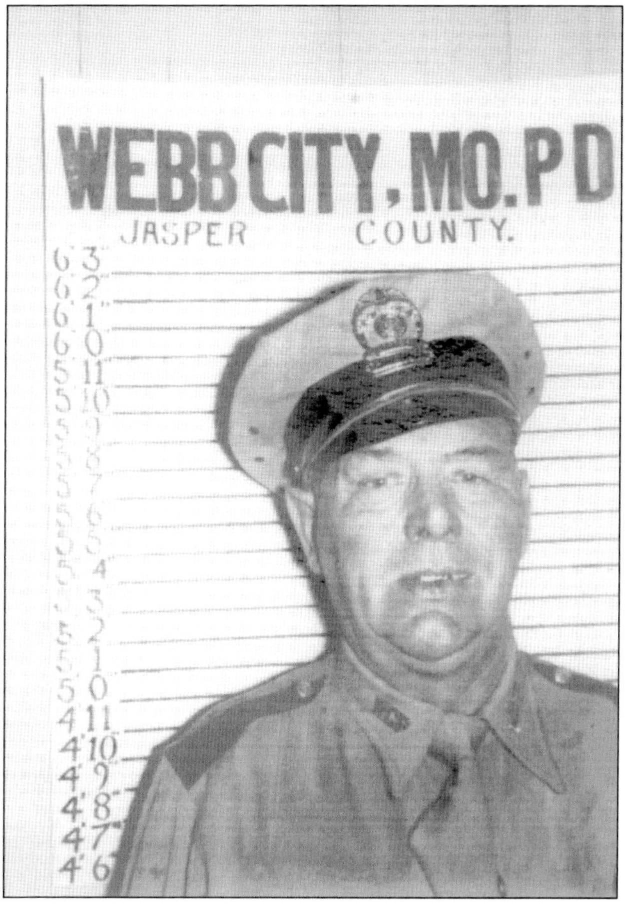


**Joking Around.** Chief Earl Bunch, here pretending to be a suspect, was highly respected and ran for office more than once. He was reelected on April 20, 1953. The position of chief of police is no longer elected, but is rather filled by the city council. (Courtesy of Webb City Police Department.)

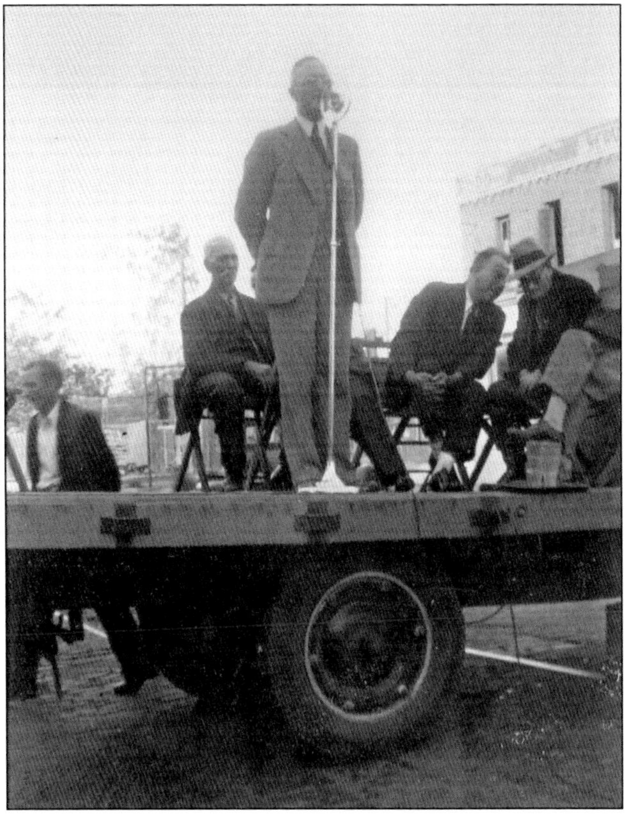

**Harry S. Truman, 1934.** Before he became president, Harry Truman was a senator from Missouri. Here, he makes a campaign speech from a wagon bed in Webb City. (Courtesy of Missouri Digital Archive.)

**Sound Car, Truman Campaign, 1934.** This sound car was used in the senatorial campaign of Harry Truman when he came to Webb City. (Courtesy of Missouri Digital Archive.)

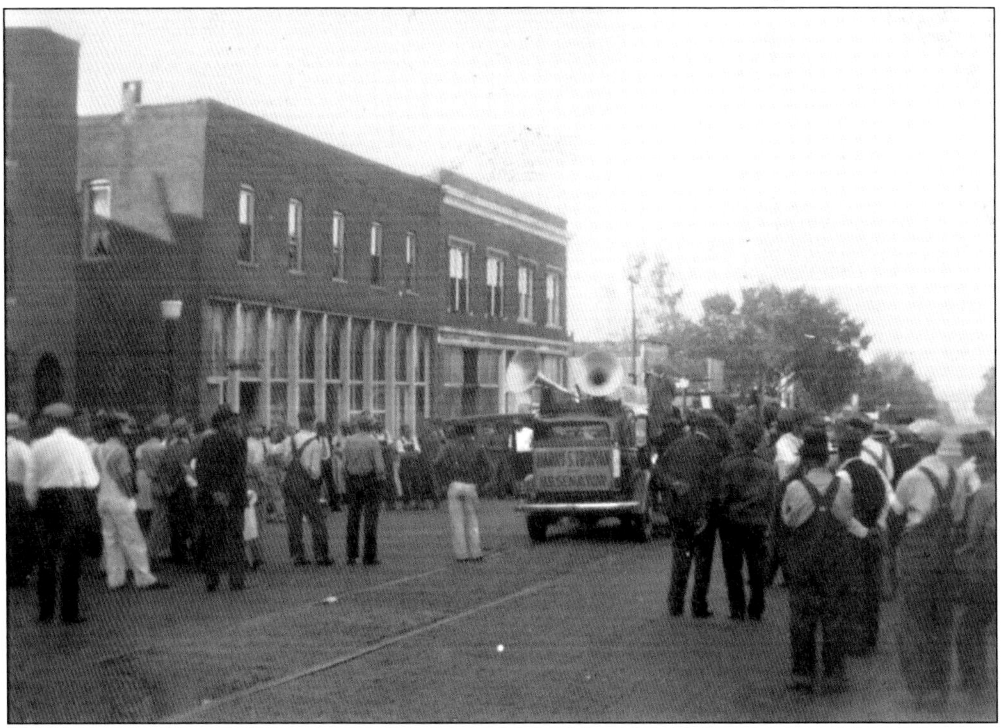

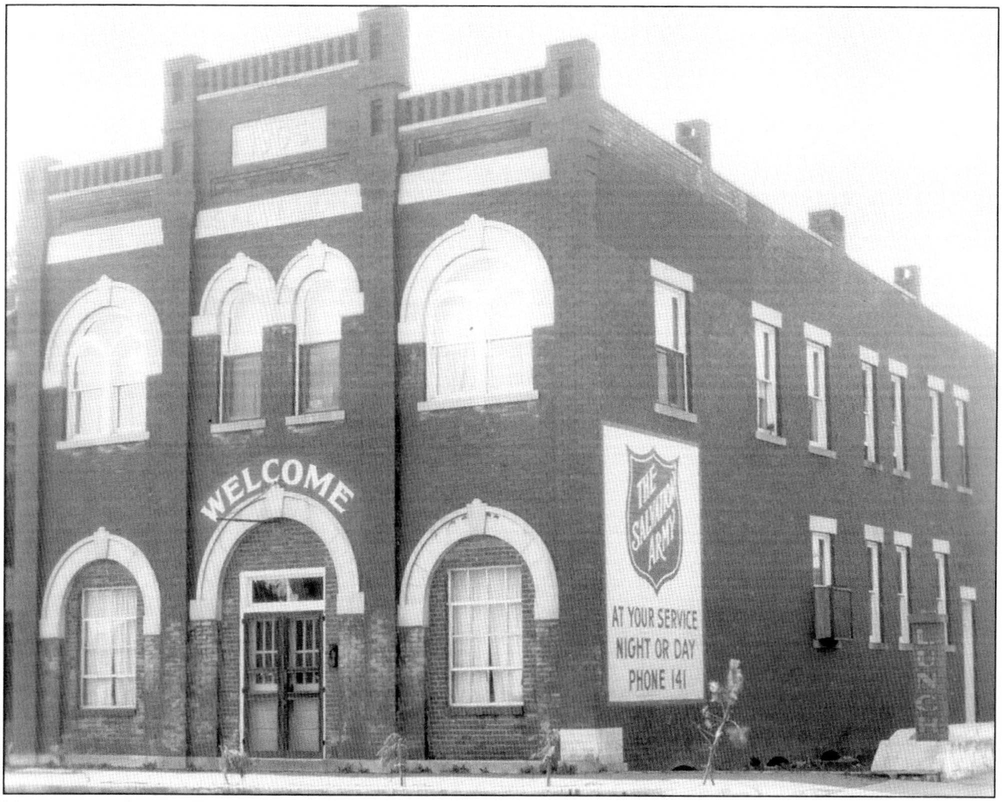


**SALVATION ARMY, EAST MAIN STREET.** The Salvation Army was started in England around 1865. The plight of miners brought the organization to Webb City. It established a hospital in 1905. The Salvation Army later moved to Joplin.

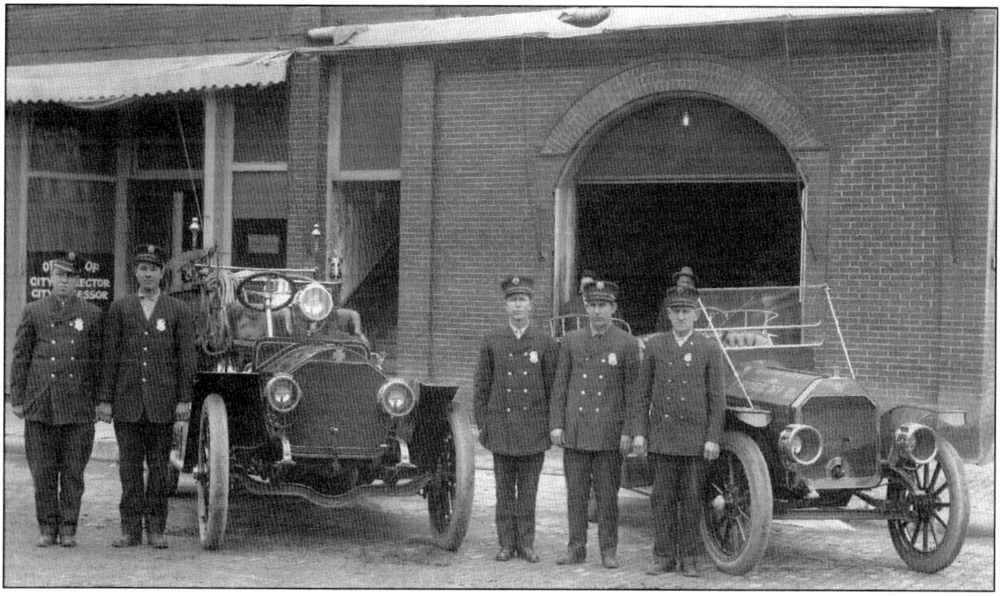

**WEBB CITY FIRE DEPARTMENT, 1920.** An all-volunteer fire department was established in 1889. It would be 10 years before firemen were paid for their services.

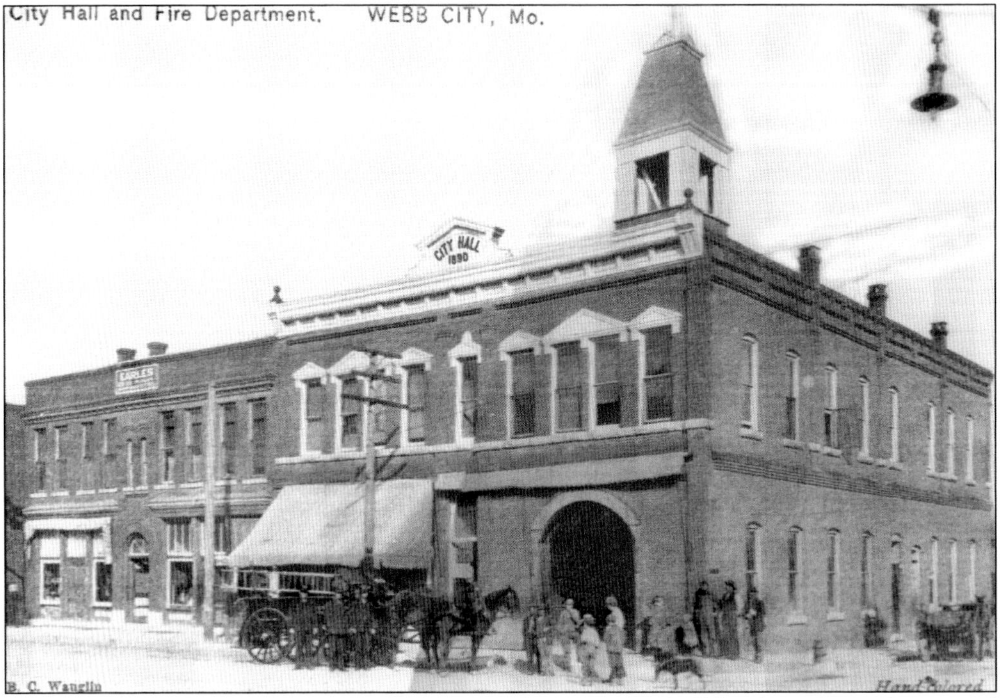


**City Hall and Fire Department, 1905.** Over the years, city hall has been located at several places in town. The location seen in this postcard is the corner of First and Allen Streets.

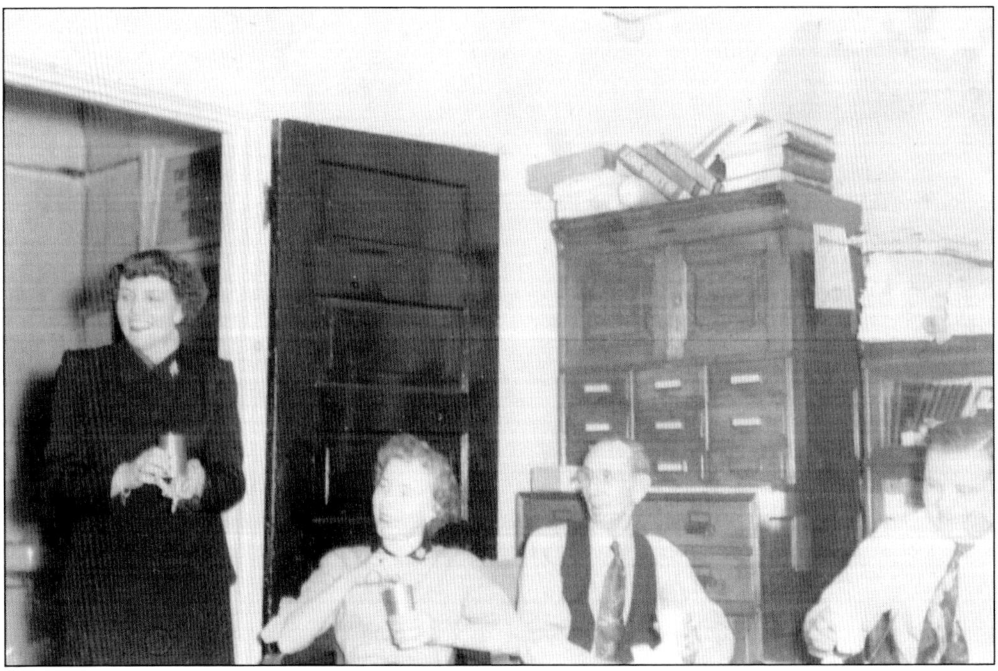

**Clarence S. Fly, c. 1950.** Fly (second from right) served as a councilman for Webb City's Third Ward. He became mayor pro-tern on November 19, 1951, and continued in the office until he was elected mayor in April 1952 for a full two-year term. (Courtesy of George Twigger.)

# *Three*

# LEISURE

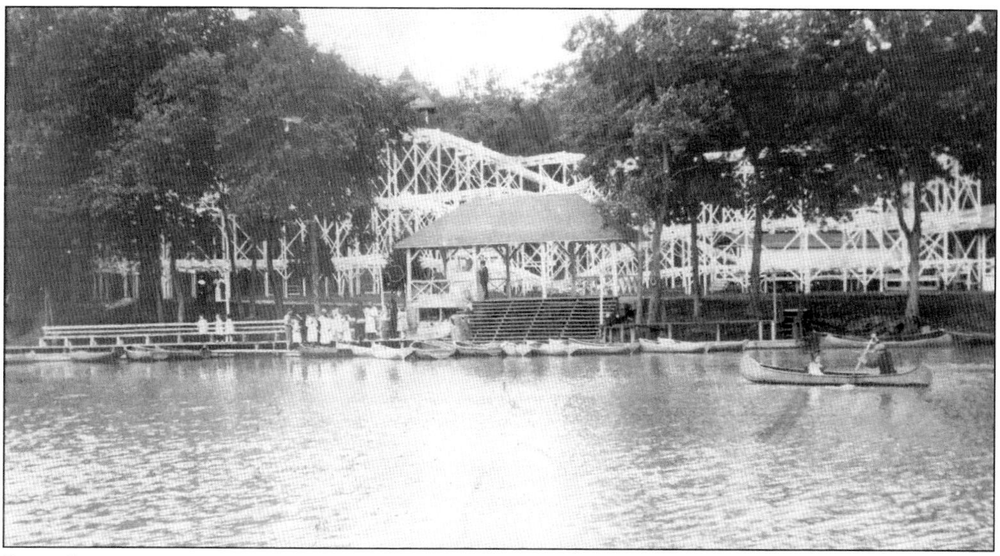

**BOAT LANDING AT LAKESIDE PARK, JUNE 1, 1919.** Lakeside Park was located between Webb City and Carthage on Center Creek. The creek was dammed to create a lake. In addition to the figure-eight roller coaster seen here, the park had a baseball field, hotel, and swimming pool. It was owned by the Southwest Missouri Electric Railway Company. Today, the lake and dam are all but gone. (Courtesy of the Bob King Collection.)

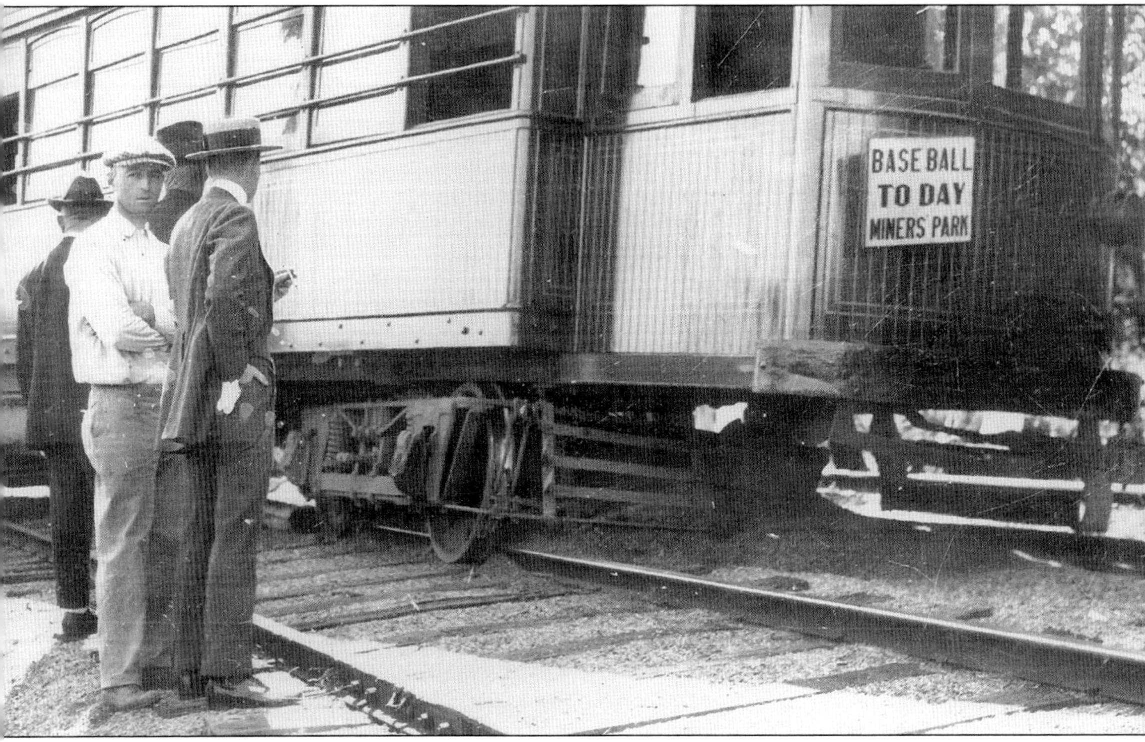


**BASEBALL ADVERTISEMENT, 1919.** Games, parades, celebrations, dances, and other upcoming events were advertised on the front of streetcars. The car seen here was derailed when it broke a flange. (Courtesy of the Bob King Collection.)

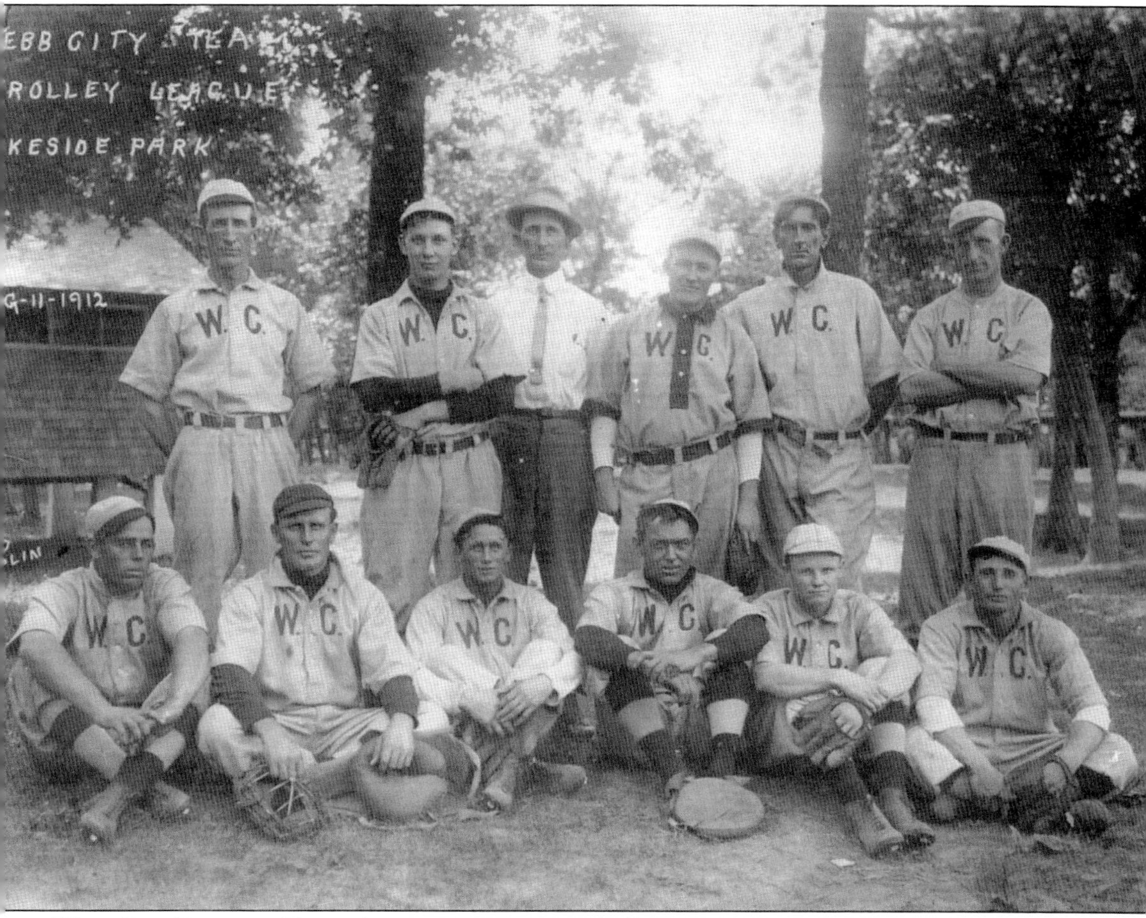


**Webb City Baseball Team, August 11, 1912.** Baseball, America's pastime, was one of the ways that miners let off steam on the weekends. This Webb City team was part of the Trolley League. Its games were played at the ballpark in Lakeside Park.

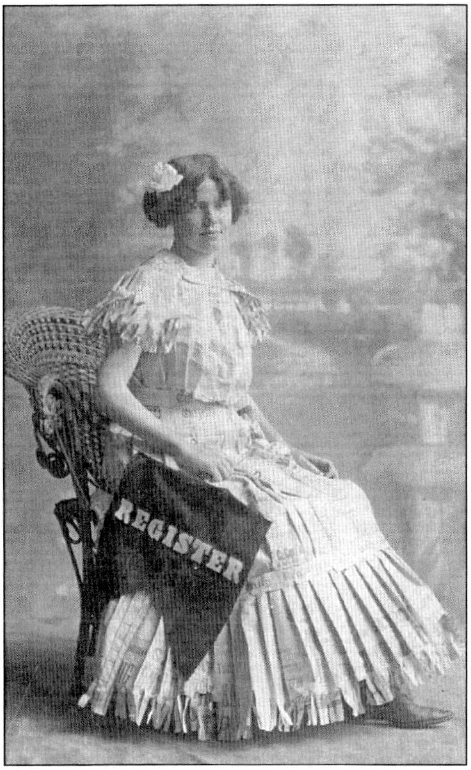


**Girl in Dress Made from Newspaper.** The dress worn by this unidentified girl is made of sections of the *Daily Register*. The family of George Armstrong, a journalist who worked at the paper, found the photograph in his personal belongings after his death. The *Daily Register*, established in 1891, continued publishing under the name the *Webb City Daily Register* until 1917. (Courtesy of Willis family.)

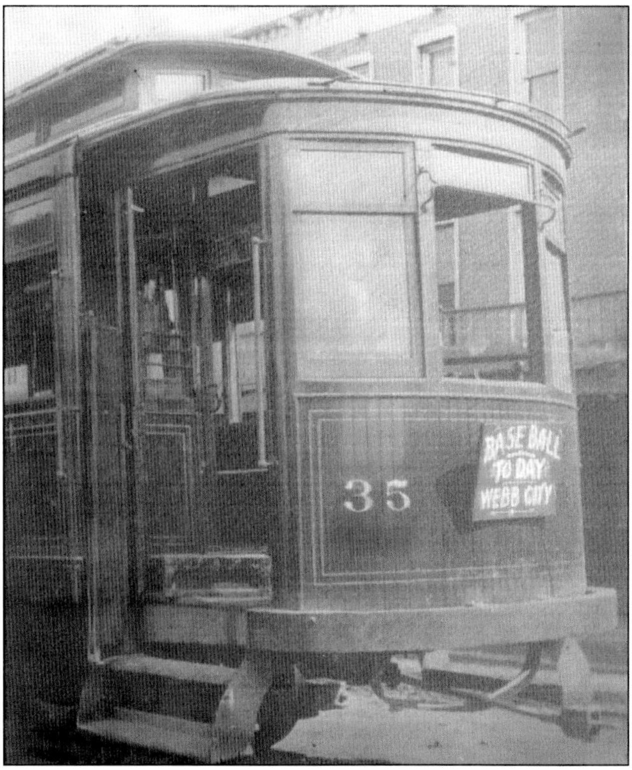


**Trolley Advertising, 1919.** Streetcars were the major means of transportation for the Webb City community. The front of a trolley was a good place to promote upcoming events, such as baseball games. (Courtesy of the Bob King Collection.)

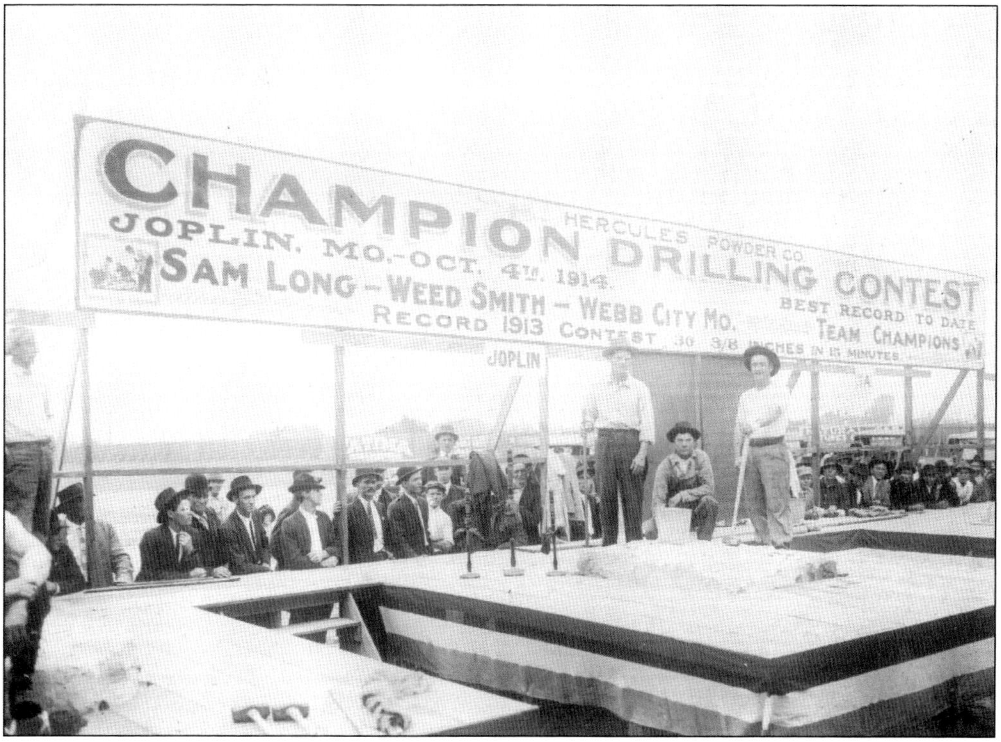


**DRILLING CONTEST, OCTOBER 4, 1914.** In a contest sponsored by Hercules Powder Company, Sam Long and Weed Smith from Webb City drilled a record 30.75 inches in 15 minutes in 1913. Pictured here a year later at the contest are, from left to right, H. Haines, Weed Smith, and Edward Haines from the Beulah S. Mine in Webb City. (Courtesy of Missouri Digital Archive.)

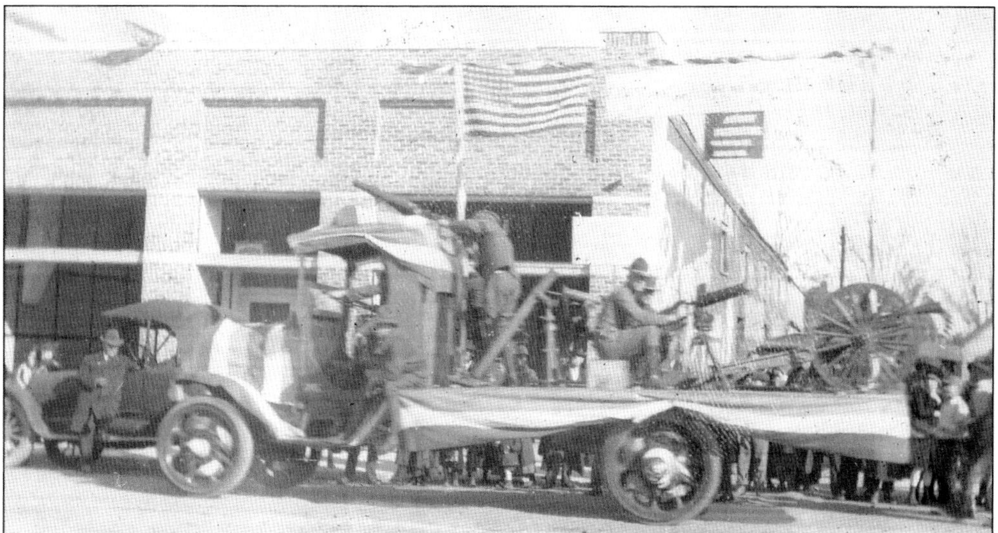

**PARADE FLOAT, NOVEMBER 11, 1919.** This float had taken part in an Armistice Day Parade in Joplin and here has returned to Webb City. The long banner across the top reads, "Men and Guns That Won the World War." (Courtesy of the Bob King Collection.)

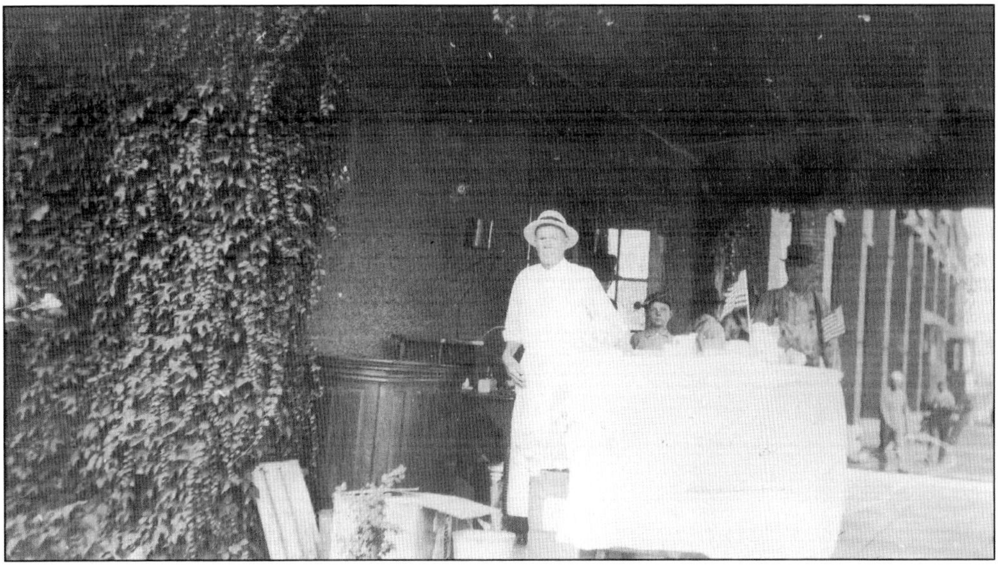

**Railway Employees' Clubhouse, July 4, 1919.** Holidays did not stop the streetcars from running. Employees working on holidays were provided with lunch at the Southwest Missouri Electric Railway Clubhouse. (Courtesy of the Bob King Collection.)

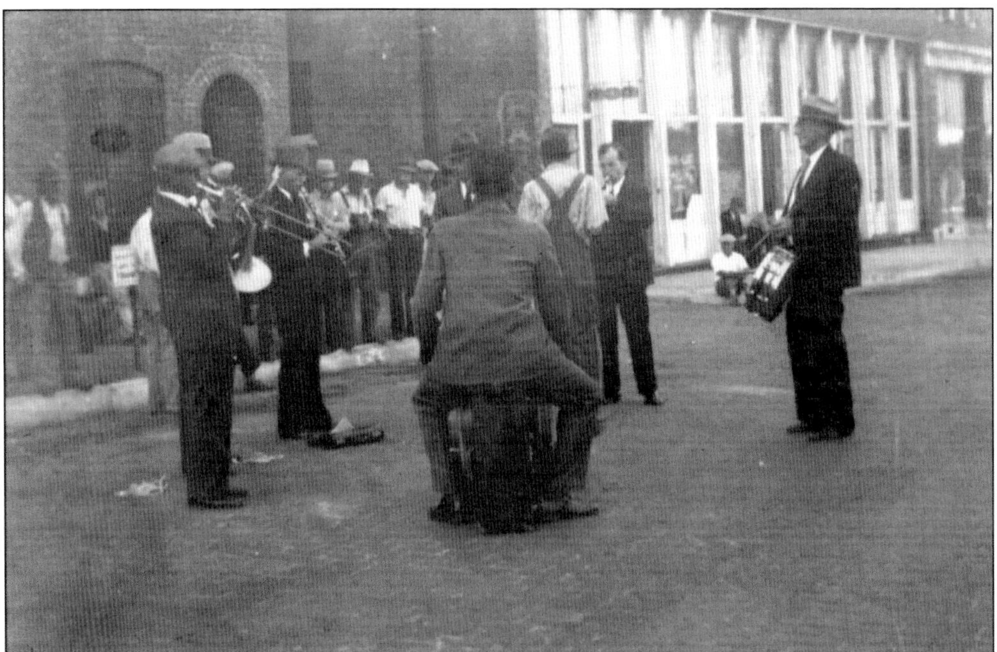

**Street Band, 1934.** A street band provided entertainment when Harry S. Truman came to Webb City to campaign for the US Senate. (Courtesy of Missouri Digital Archive.)

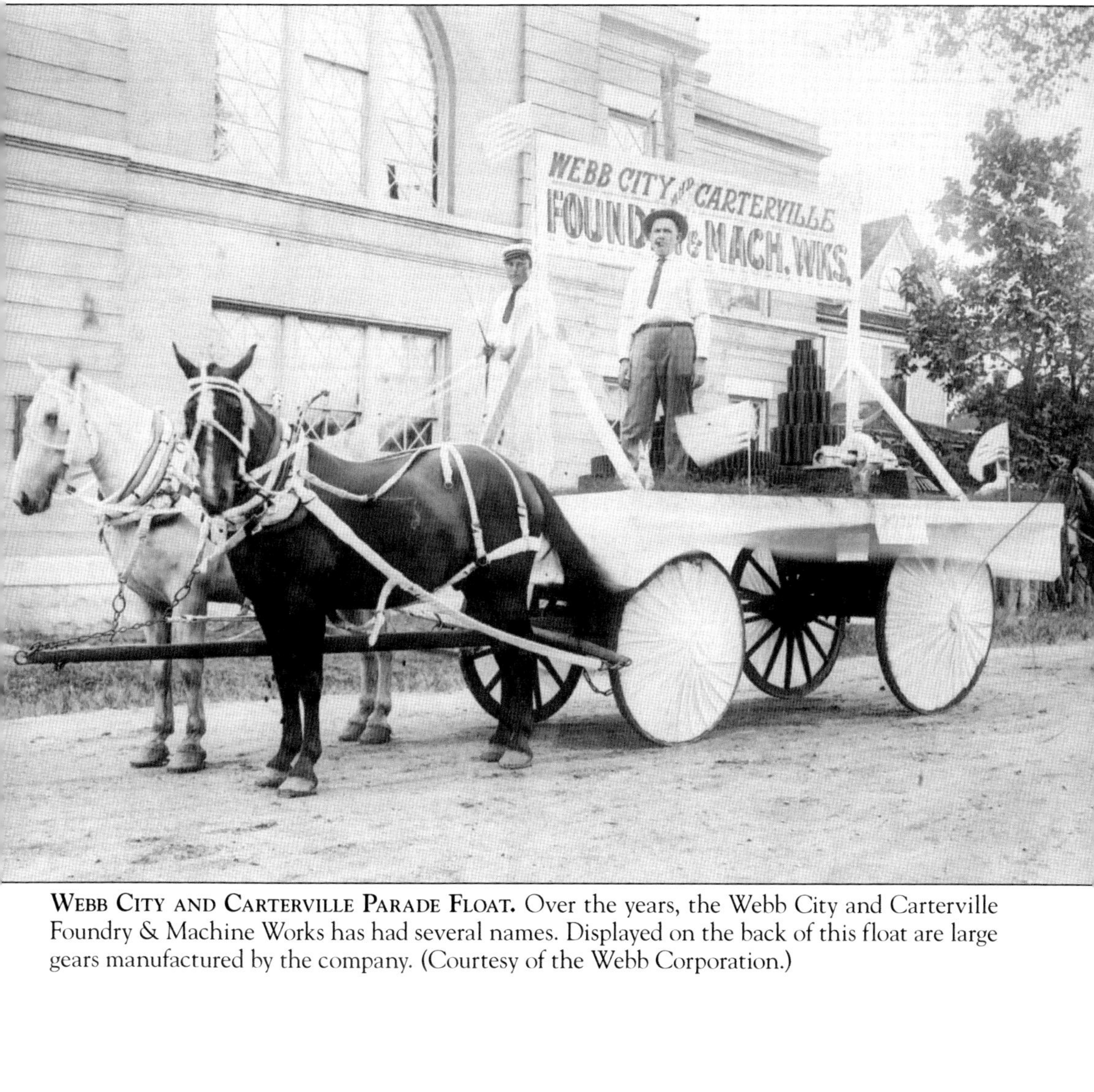


**WEBB CITY AND CARTERVILLE PARADE FLOAT.** Over the years, the Webb City and Carterville Foundry & Machine Works has had several names. Displayed on the back of this float are large gears manufactured by the company. (Courtesy of the Webb Corporation.)

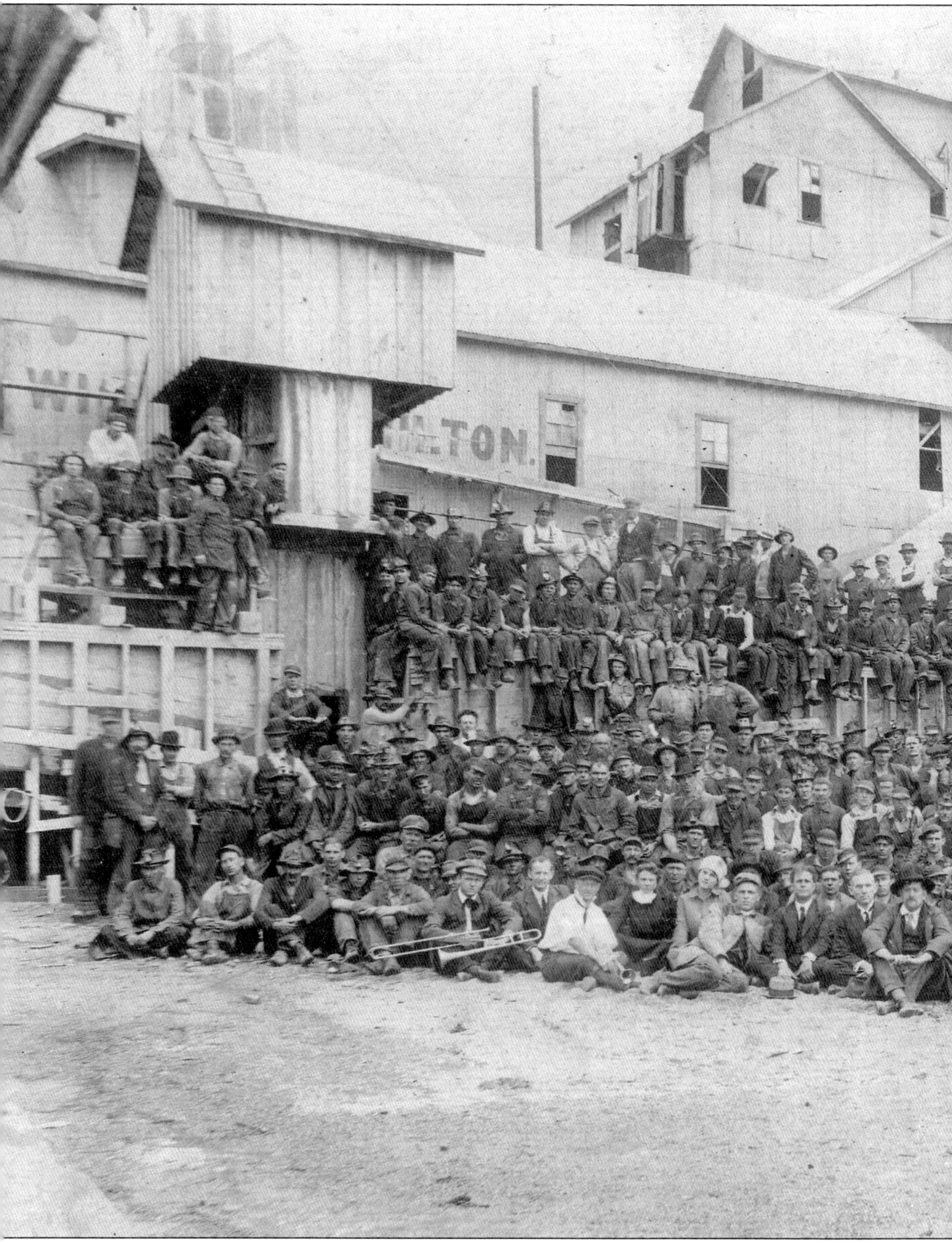


**WINGFIELD MINE, OCTOBER 12, 1915.** An evangelistic meeting with the miners was held by Charles Scoville after the accidental death of a coworker. T.C. Palmer, a shoveler at the Wingfield

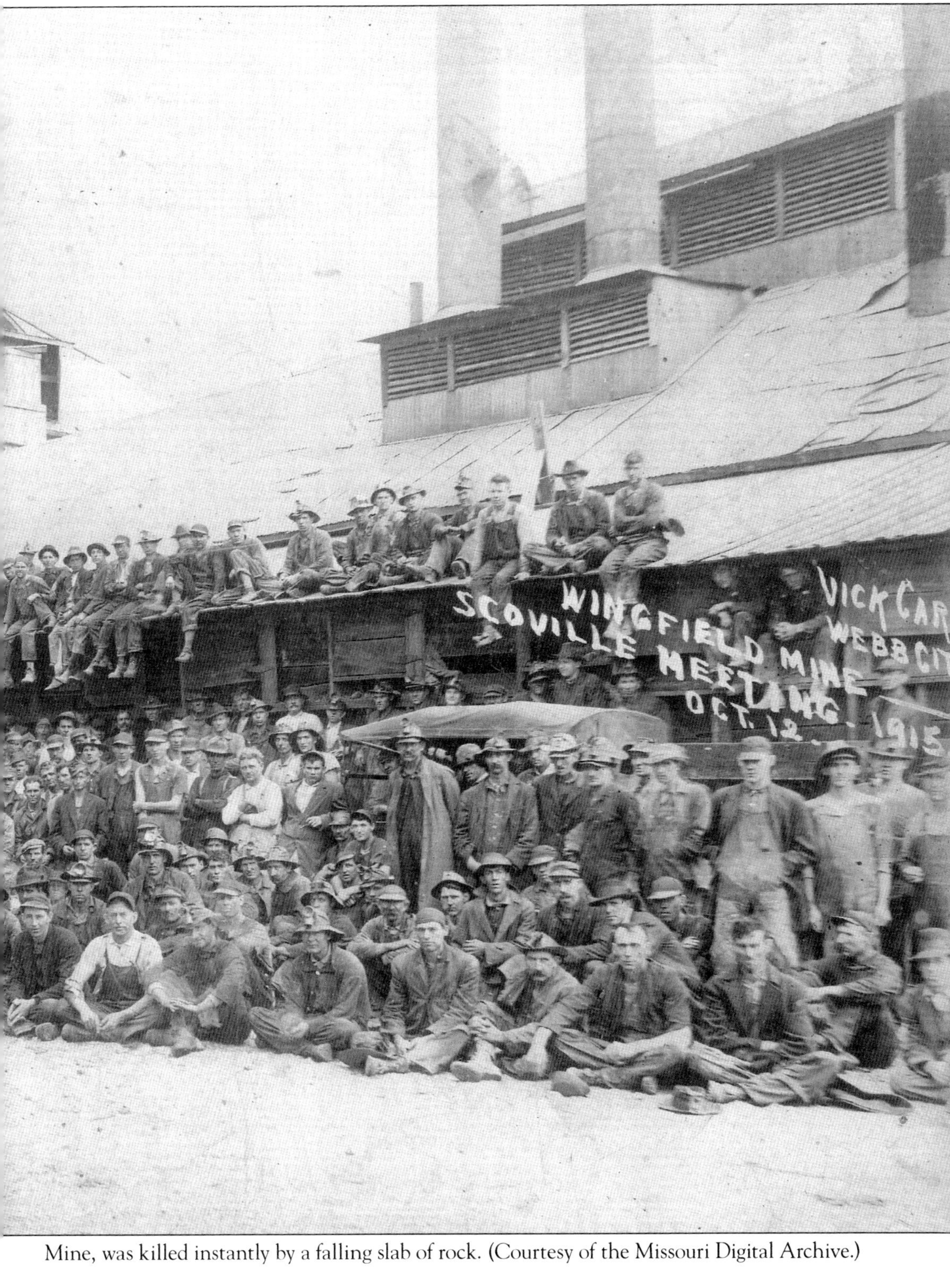


Mine, was killed instantly by a falling slab of rock. (Courtesy of the Missouri Digital Archive.)

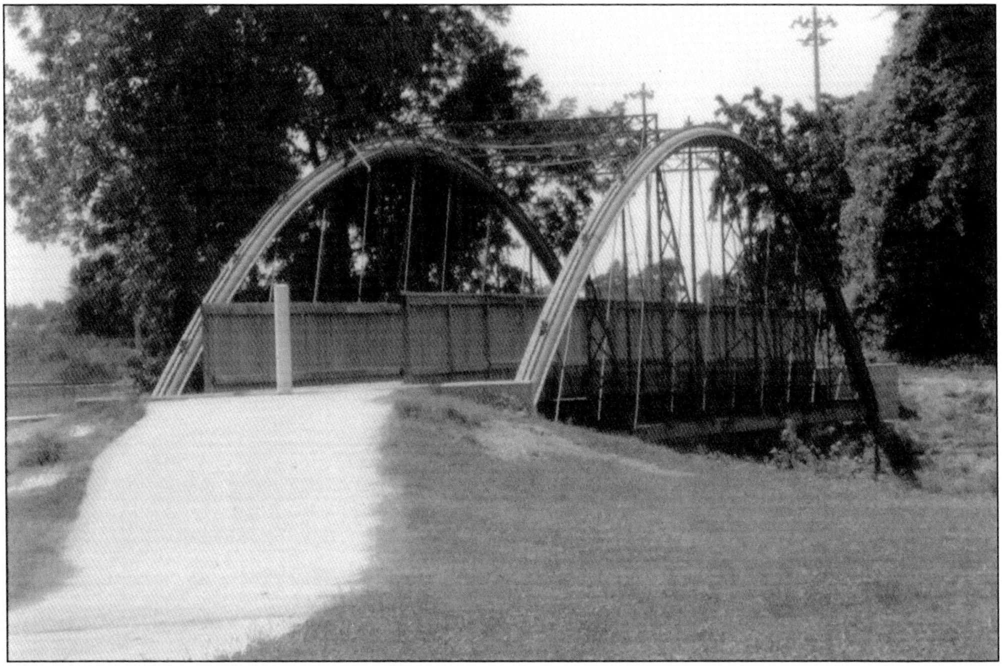

**GEORGIA CITY BRIDGE, 2009.** This bridge, built in 1871, was first located over Spring River in Georgia City, Missouri. Due to its poor condition and the danger of it being destroyed in a flood, the bridge was moved to King Jack Park. The oldest extant all-metal bridge in Missouri, it has a one-span bowstring arch truss.

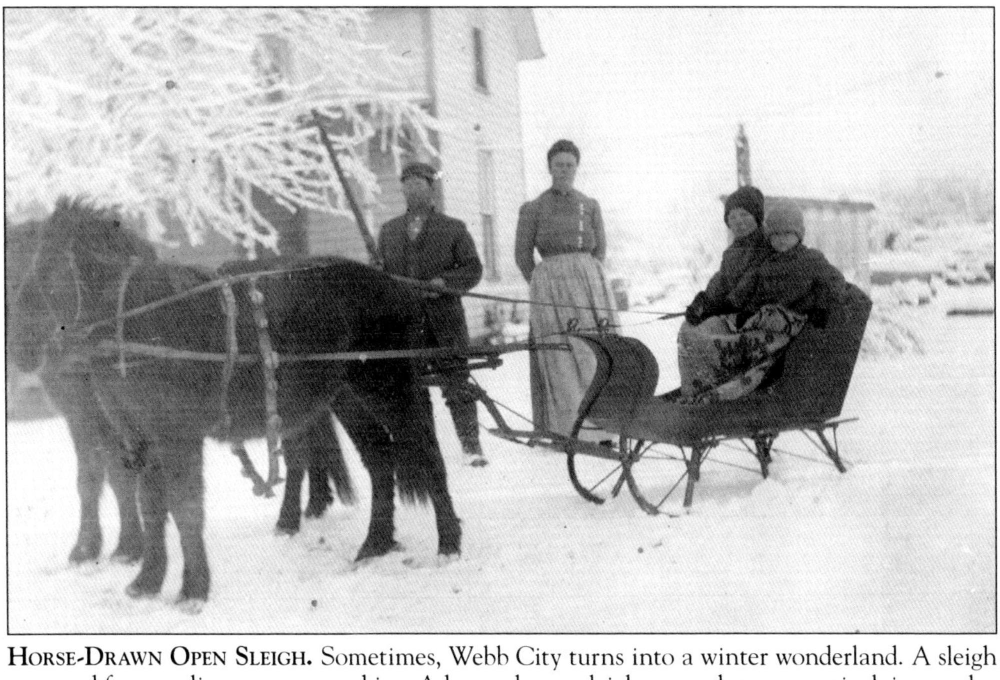

**HORSE-DRAWN OPEN SLEIGH.** Sometimes, Webb City turns into a winter wonderland. A sleigh was used for traveling on snow and ice. A horse-drawn sleigh not only was practical, it was also fun. (Courtesy of William H. King Jr.)

**Goldie Watkins, 1920.** Owning a camera was a luxury that not everyone could afford. The camera Watkins is holding was state-of-the-art technology for its day. (Courtesy of the Bob King Collection.)

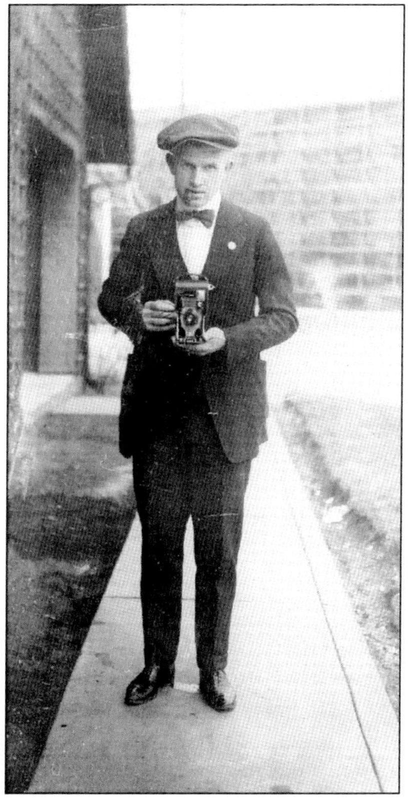

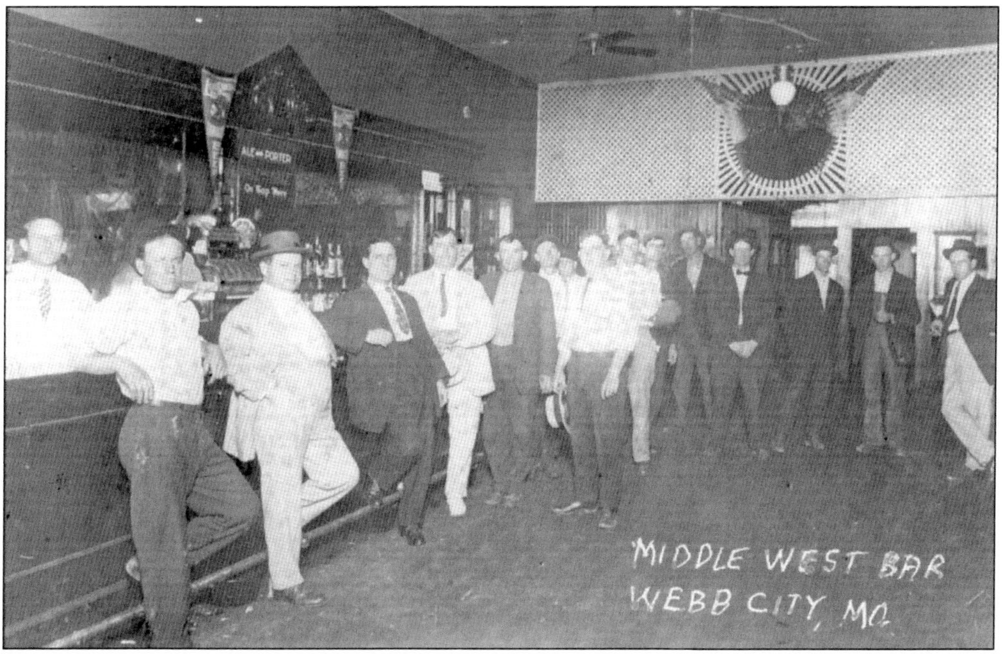


**Middle West Bar.** The year of this photograph is not known, but it is believed to have been taken in the Depression era. Like most boomtowns, Webb City had its rowdy side, including one or two "ladies of the evening." Drinking in the local bar was one way the miners spent their free time.

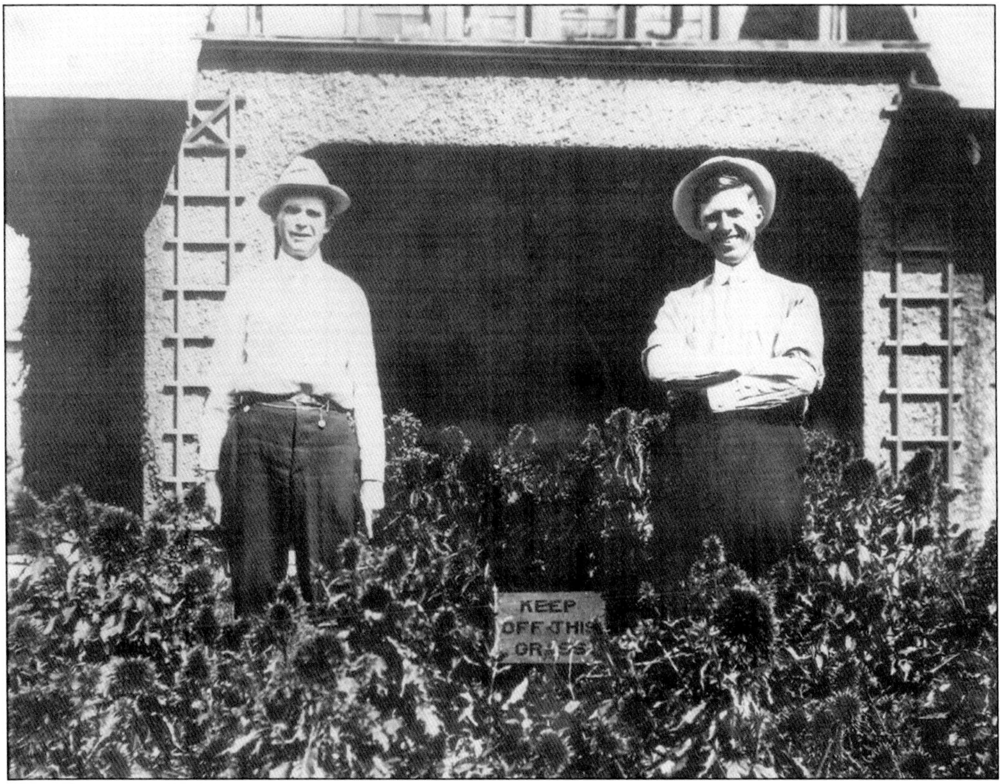


**SOUTHWEST MISSOURI ELECTRIC RAILWAY CLUBHOUSE, 1919.** The employee clubhouse gave workers a place to rest and to pass time between shifts. It was equipped with beds, showers, and both pool and card tables. (Courtesy of the Bob King Collection.)

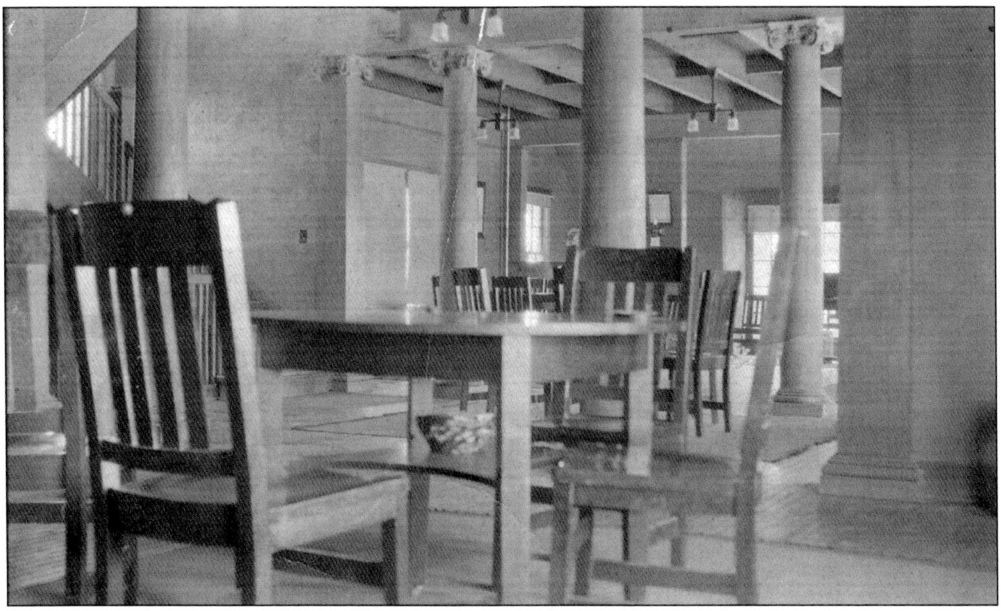

**INTERIOR OF RAILWAY EMPLOYEES' CLUBHOUSE, 1919.** Here, card tables are seen inside the Southwest Missouri Electric Railway clubhouse. (Courtesy of the Bob King Collection.)

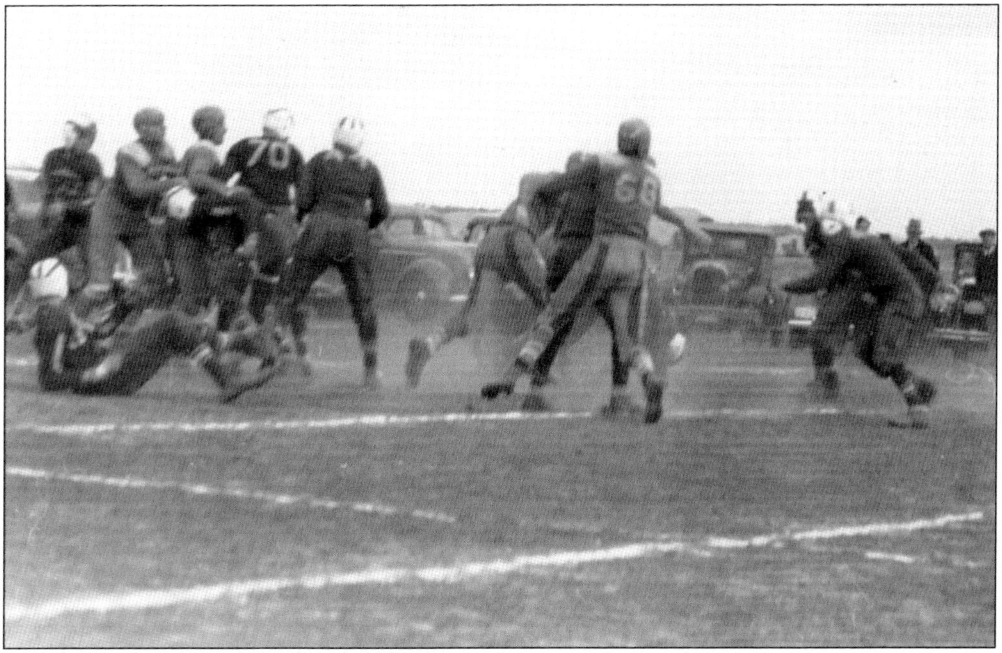

**Hatten Athletic Field.** Webb City's high school football team is a source of pride for the community. The team enjoys fan support that is only equaled by that of the National Football League.

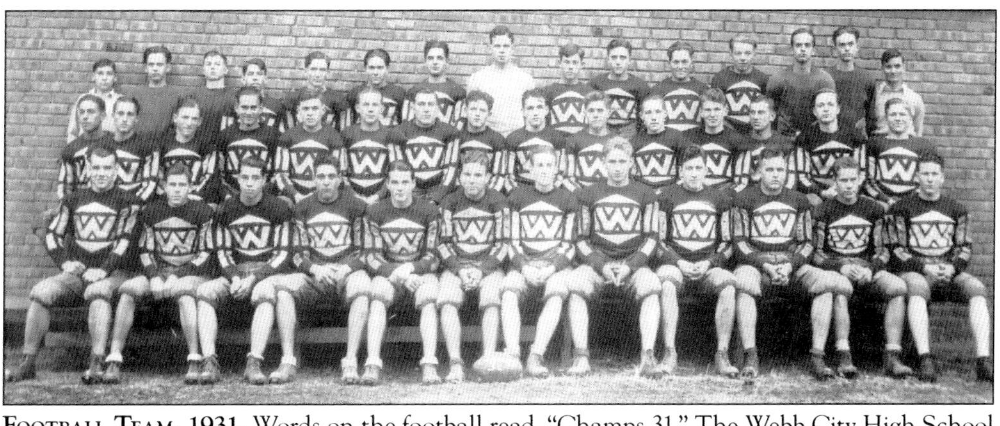

**Football Team, 1931.** Words on the football read, "Champs 31." The Webb City High School football teams have a winning record dating back to 1907.

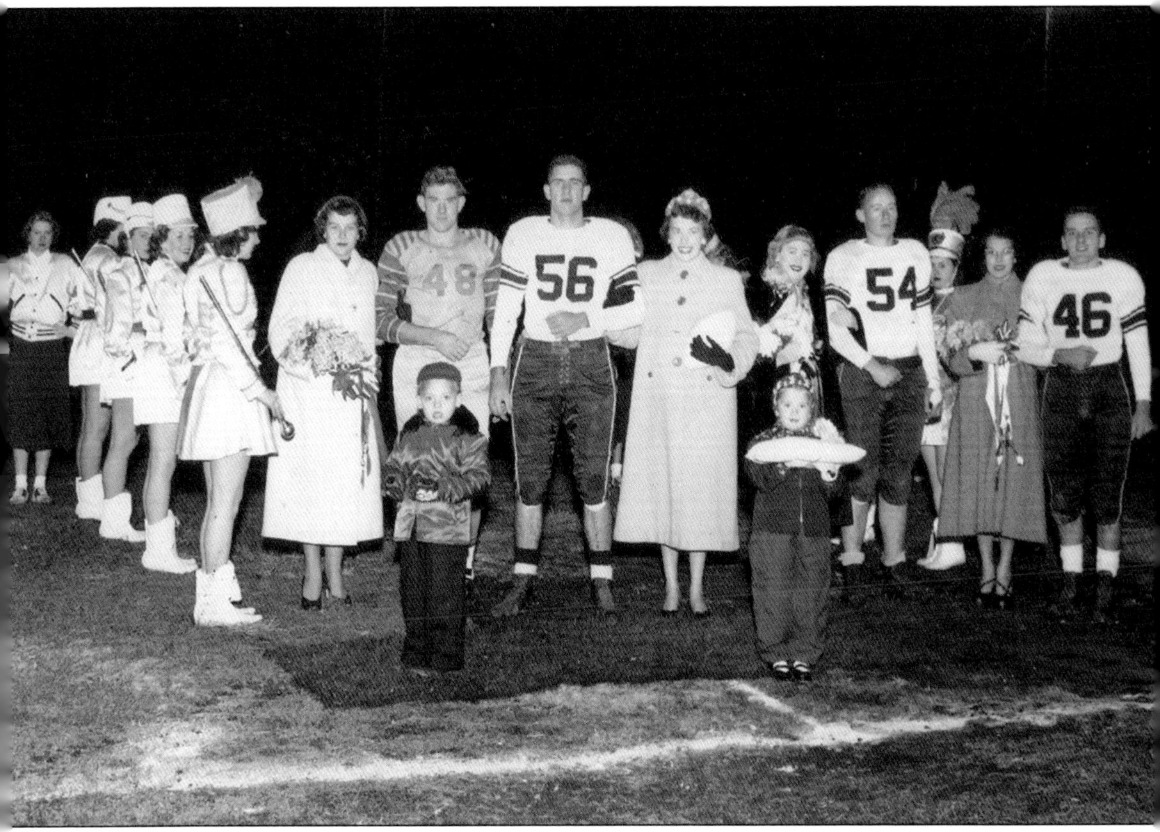

**HOMECOMING QUEEN'S COURT, 1951.** Webb City High School football is full of traditions, and the homecoming queen is one of them. The Queen's Court includes, from left to right, attendant Missy Grayston and her unknown escort, Gary Sampson accompanying Queen Barbara Knost, 1950 Queen Bobbie Laster and her escort James Jones, and attendant Barbara Miller and her escort Richard Bellairs. The children are Bobby Chancellor and Susie Benson.

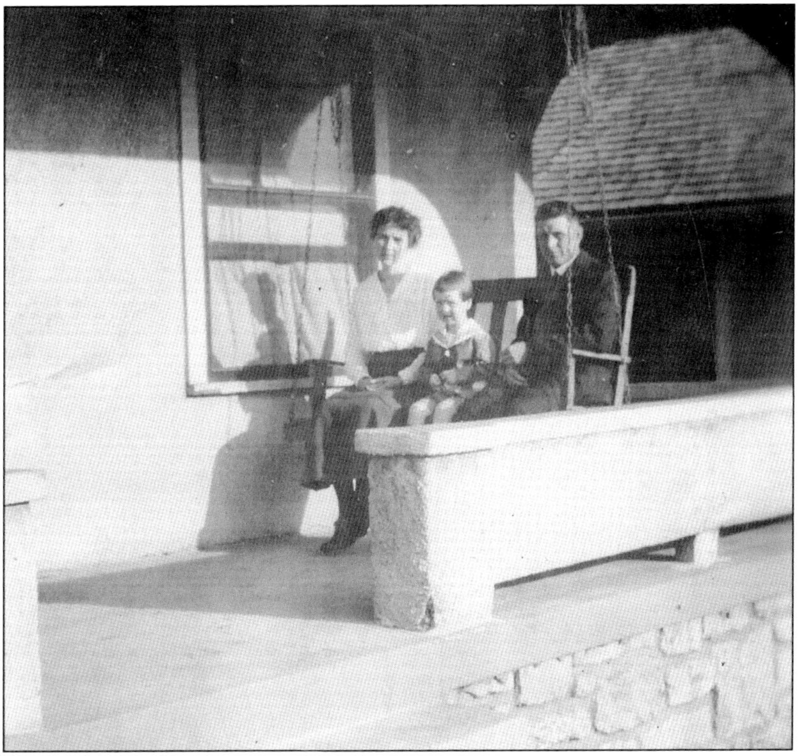

**Wolfe Family, 1920.** This family is enjoying one of the favorite activities people did with their leisure time. From left to right they are Hazel, Dick Jr., and Dick Sr. They are sitting in the swing on their front porch. (Courtesy of the Bob King Collection.)

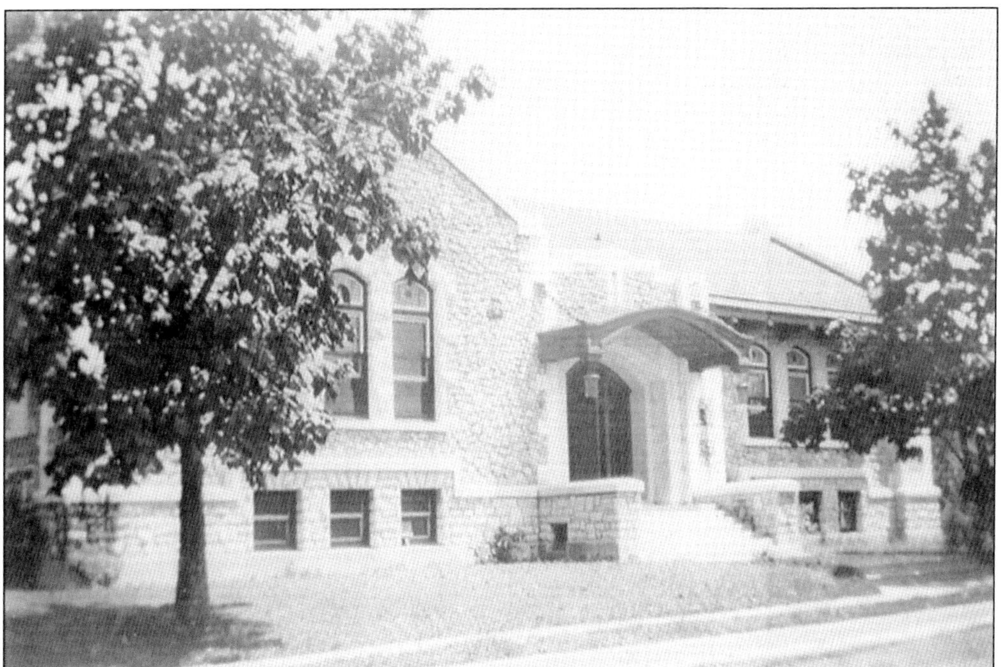

**Webb City Library, c. 1930.** Reading always has been and always will be a good way to spend leisure time. This library, at 101 South Liberty Street, was established in 1914, and the building was remodeled in 2005.

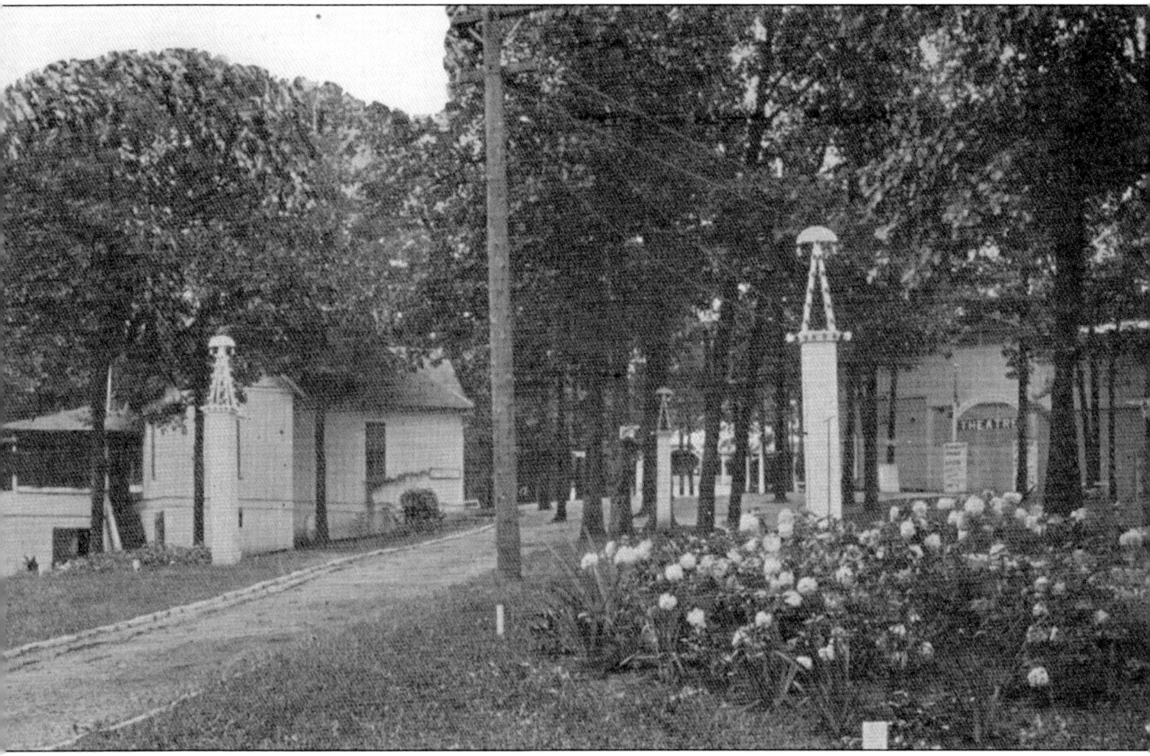


**Lakeside Park.** In the summer, the park provided many actives for the residents of Webb City and the surrounding area. The park was owned and operated by Southwest Missouri Electric Railway, which had its home in Webb City.

# *Four*

# INDUSTRY AND BUSINESS

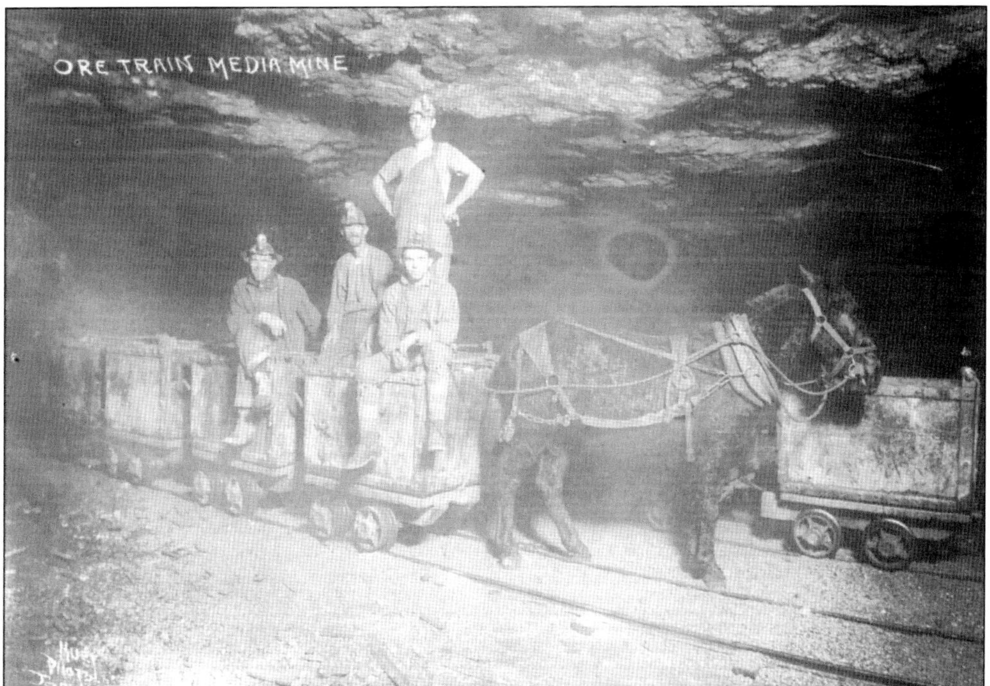


**ORE TRAIN AT MEDIA MINE, 1920.** Here, a mule pulls self-dumping square ore cars. These cars were not common to the Tri-State Mining District. (Courtesy of Missouri Digital Archive.)

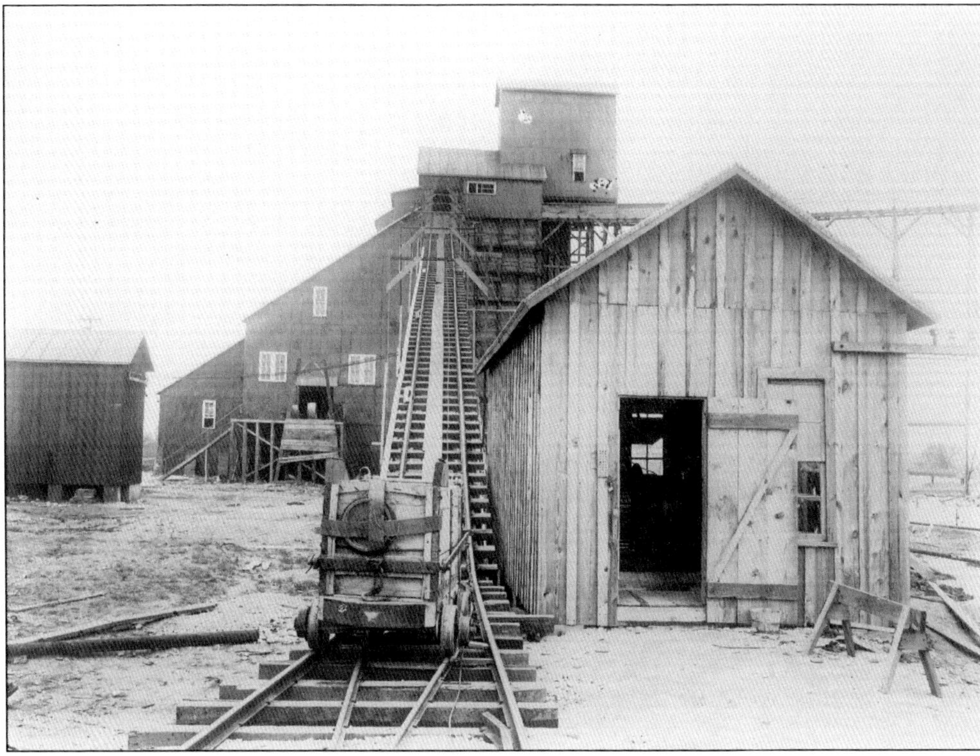

**YELLOW DOG MINE, 1910.** Tramcars, such as this one, hauled ore from the field shaft up the tracks or "tramway" to the mill. Miners were sometimes also transported by this method. (Courtesy of Missouri Digital Archive.)

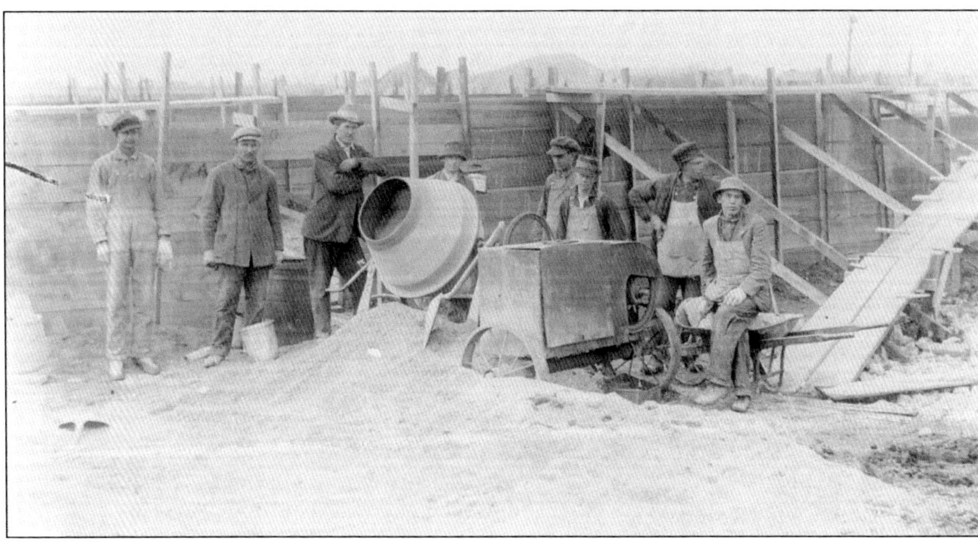

**CONSTRUCTION CREW, CISCO MINE NO. 3, 1910.** To build a mill, the foundation needed to be supported by concrete. Today, concrete ruins are scattered over the Tri-State Mining District. The Environmental Protection Agency has projects in place to clean up this old concrete. (Courtesy of Missouri Digital Archive.)

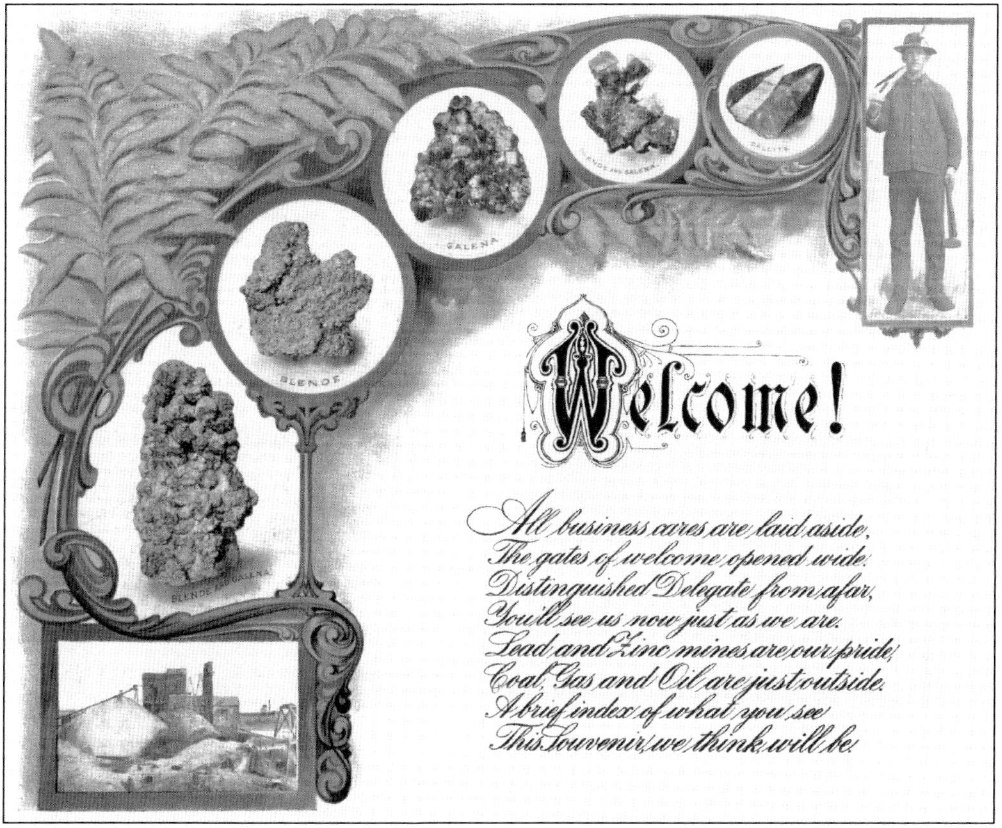


**Mining District Souvenir Book, 1907.** This is the welcome page from the 1907 souvenir book for the Missouri, Kansas, Indian Territory, Arkansas Mining District. The book is titled *The World's Greatest Zinc and Lead District as Seen through the Camera.*

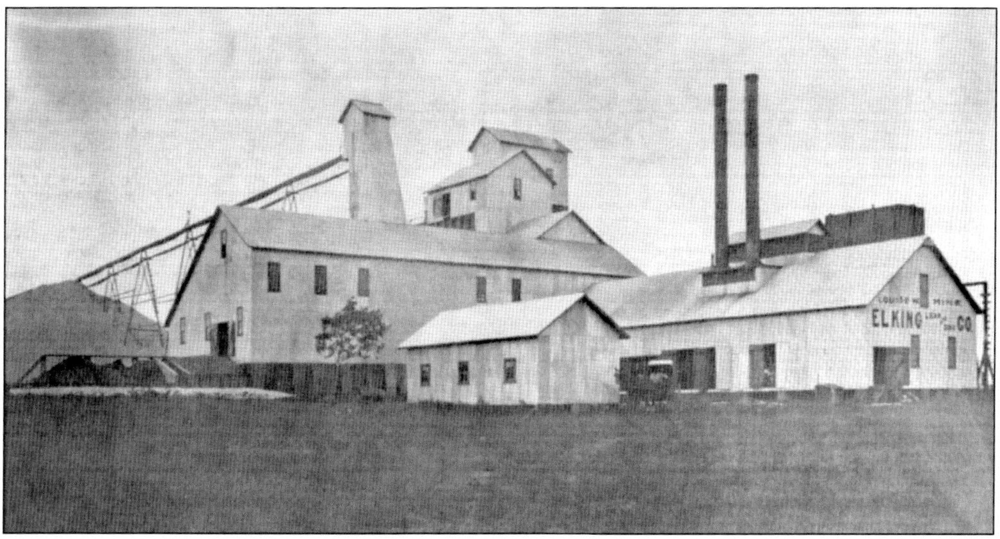


**Louis W. Mine, 1907.** This mine, of the Elking Lead and Zinc Company, was one of many mines featured in the 1907 souvenir book *The World's Greatest Zinc and Lead District as Seen through the Camera.*

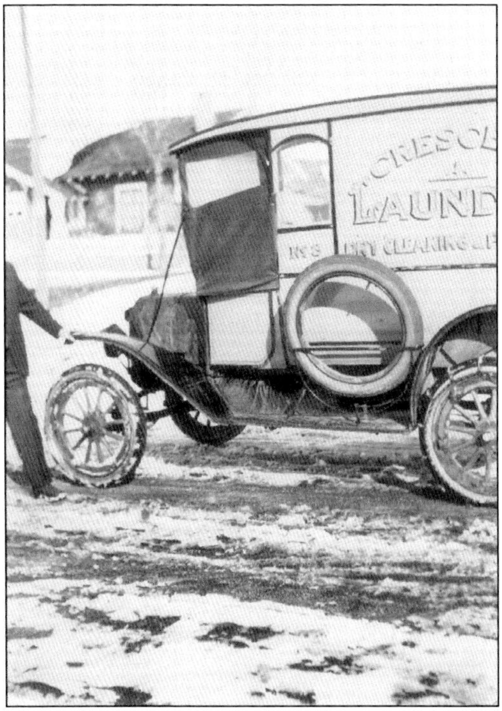


**CRESCENT LAUNDRY TRUCK, 1915.** Businesses both large and small thrived in Webb City during the days of the mining boom. (Courtesy of the Bob King Collection.)

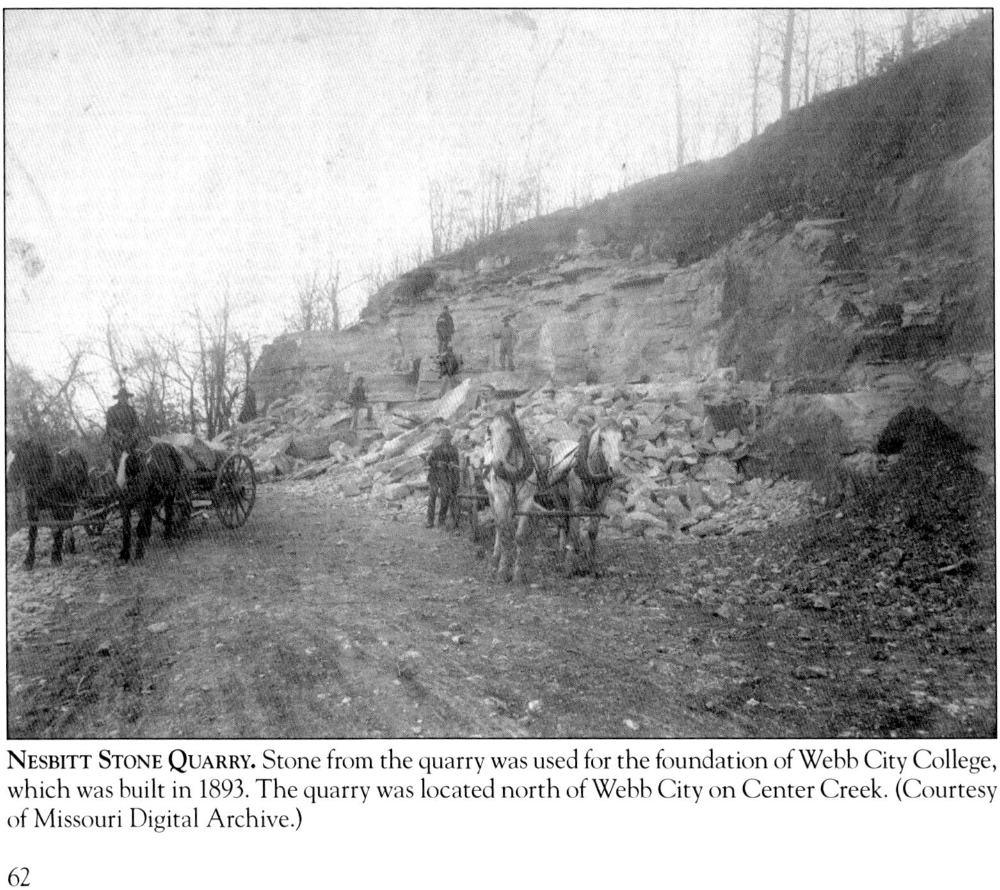

**NESBITT STONE QUARRY.** Stone from the quarry was used for the foundation of Webb City College, which was built in 1893. The quarry was located north of Webb City on Center Creek. (Courtesy of Missouri Digital Archive.)

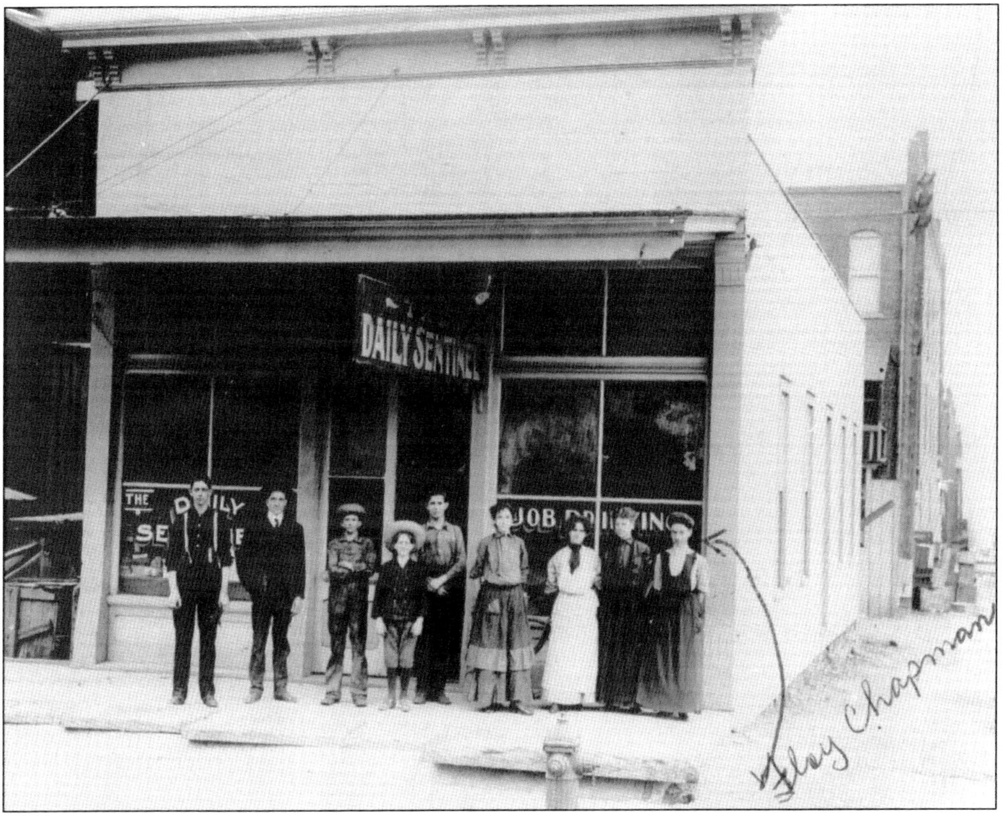


**Webb City *Daily Sentinel* Staff, 1925.** Floy Chapman is the staff member standing on the far right. The *Webb City Daily Sentinel* was established in 1890 and continued operations until 1961, when it became the *Webb City Sentinel*, a weekly newspaper. Floy Chapman is also seen in the photograph below. (Courtesy of the Willis family.)

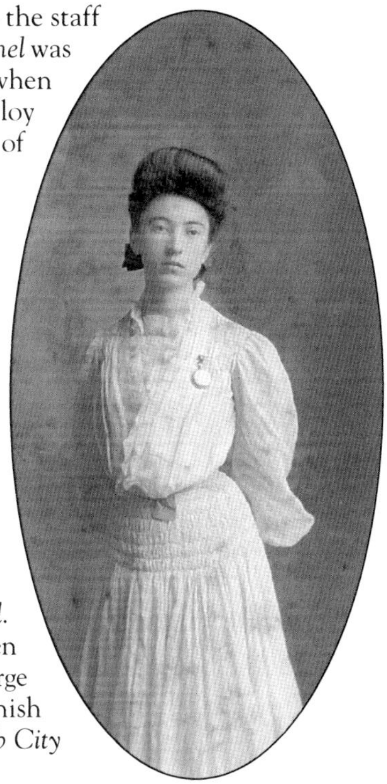

**Floy Chapman.** An employee at the *Webb City Daily Sentinel*. She went to work for a newspaper at a time when few women did. She was the second wife of Oklahoma newspaperman George Armstrong. Floy left six children when she died from Spanish influenza in 1918. Today, the publication is called the *Webb City Sentinel*, a weekly newspaper. (Courtesy of the Willis family.)

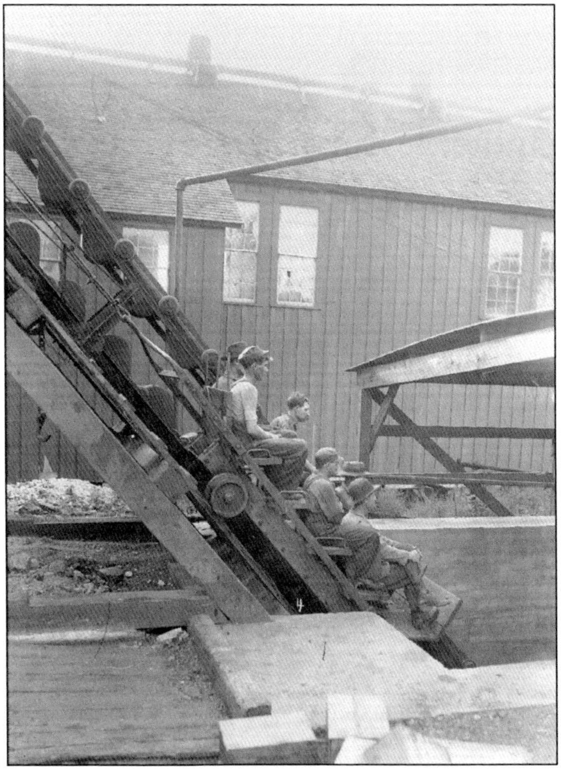

**Yellow Dog Mine, 1910.** The largest mining operation in the Tri-State Mining District, this facility employed over 400 workers. (Courtesy of Missouri Digital Archive.)

**Portland Mine, 1908.** Workers pose in front of the operation's mill building. In the background is a gentleman seated in a buggy. (Courtesy of Missouri Digital Archive.)

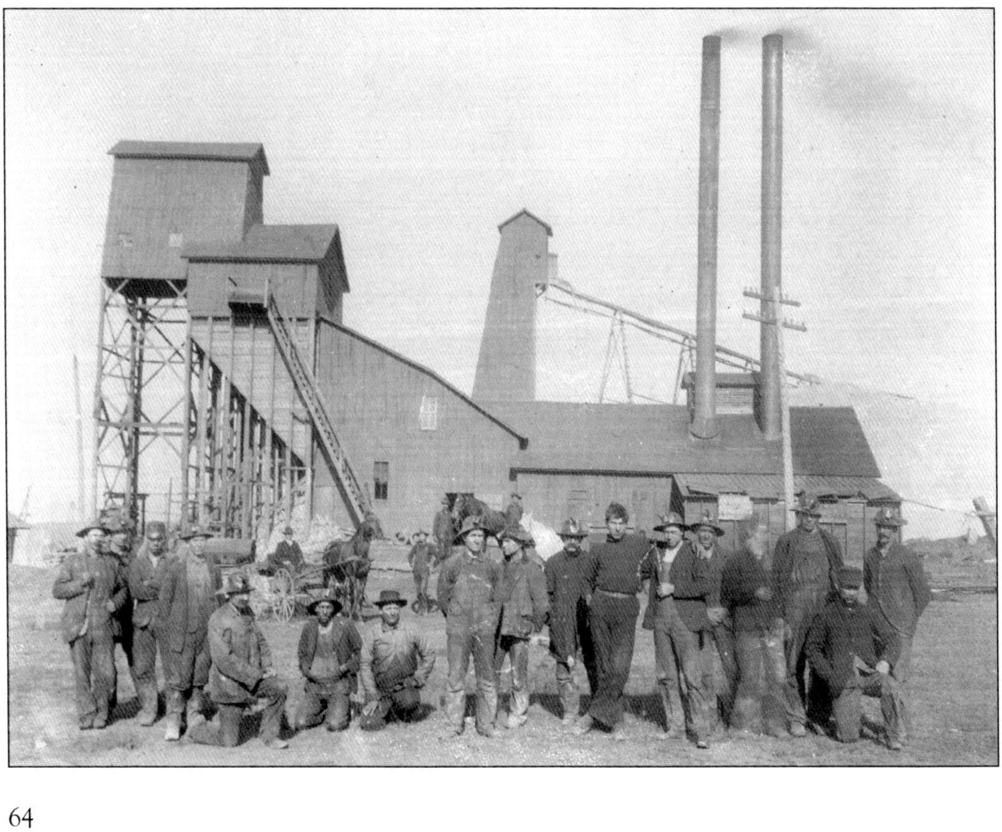

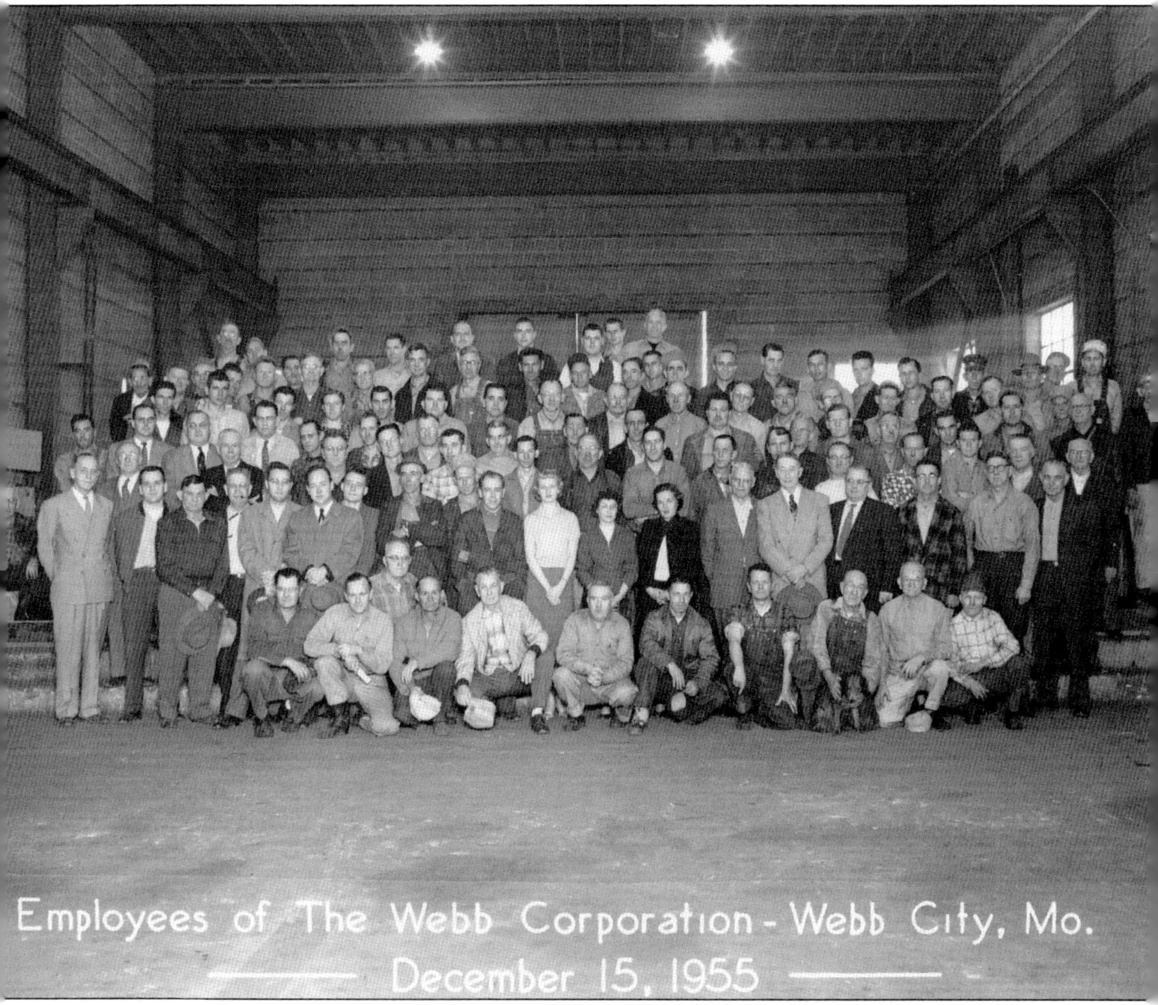


**WEBB CORPORATION CHRISTMAS PARTY, DECEMBER 15, 1955.** Shown here is an employee holiday party during Webb City's manufacturing era. The corporation is still doing business in the same location and is one of Webb City's oldest companies. (Courtesy of William H. King Jr.)

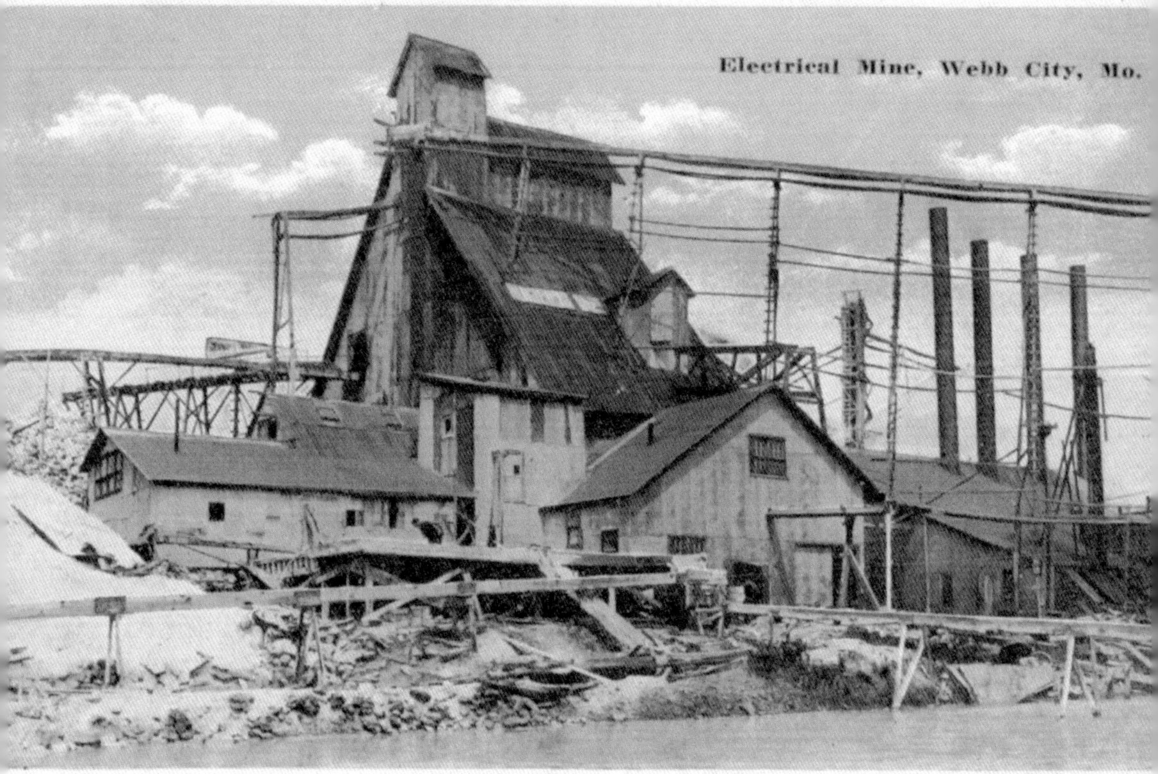


**ELECTRICAL MINE.** Electricity was such a luxury that companies often used the word "electric" in their titles. Positive mine names were considered good luck. (Courtesy of Missouri Digital Archive.)

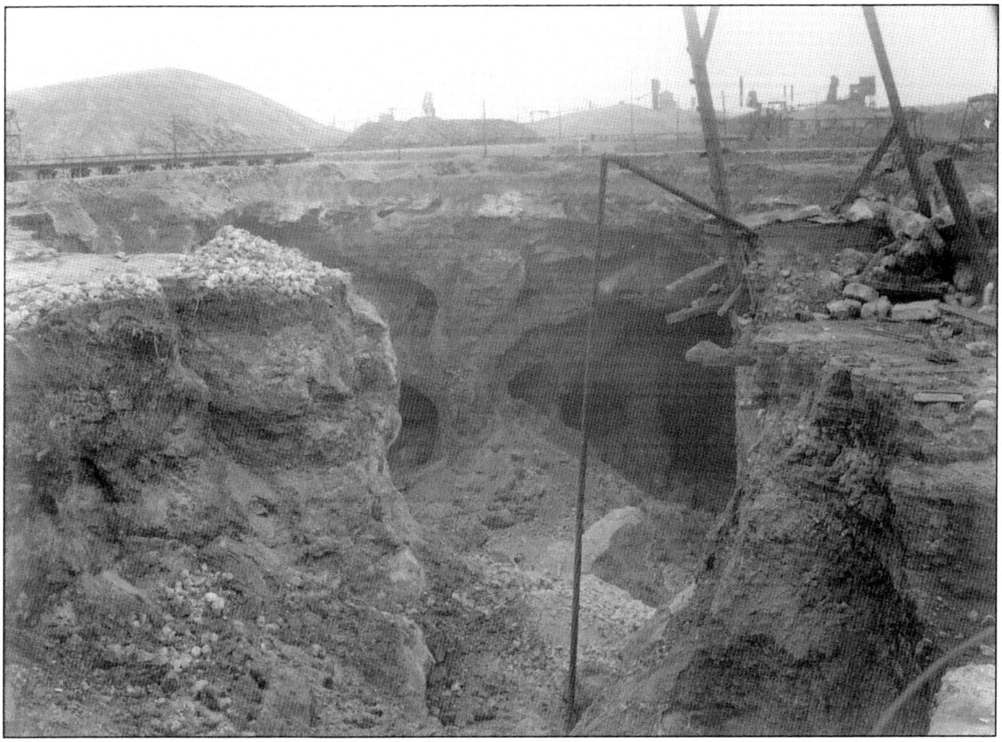

**Bradford–Kansas City Mine, 1910.** The fear of cave-ins and accidents was something that miners knew all too well. Mining was a dangerous business, and a cave-in not only endangered the lives of miners, but it also had the potential to cause large losses of property. (Both, courtesy of Missouri Digital Archive.)

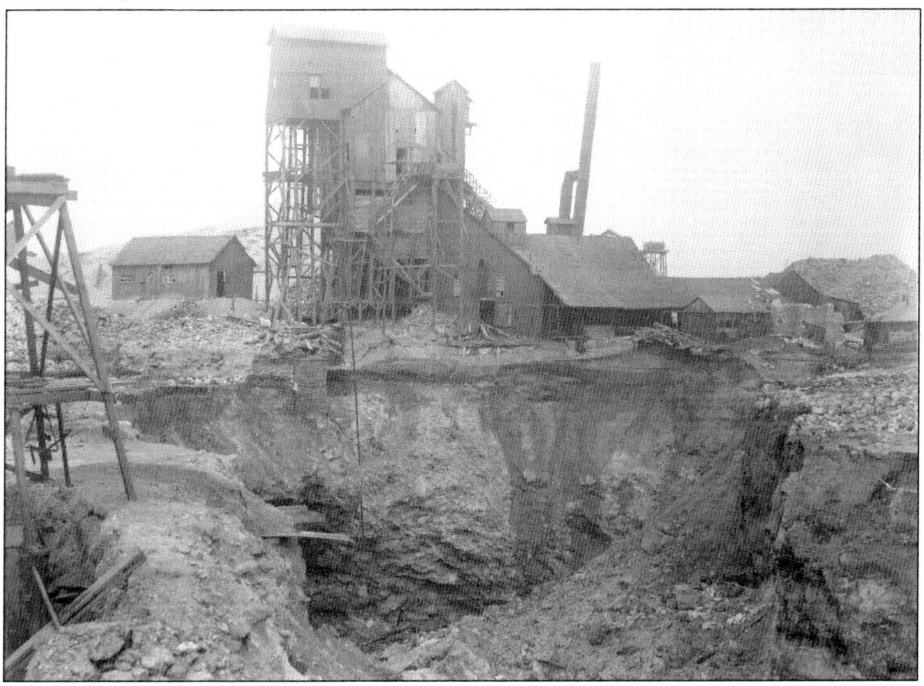

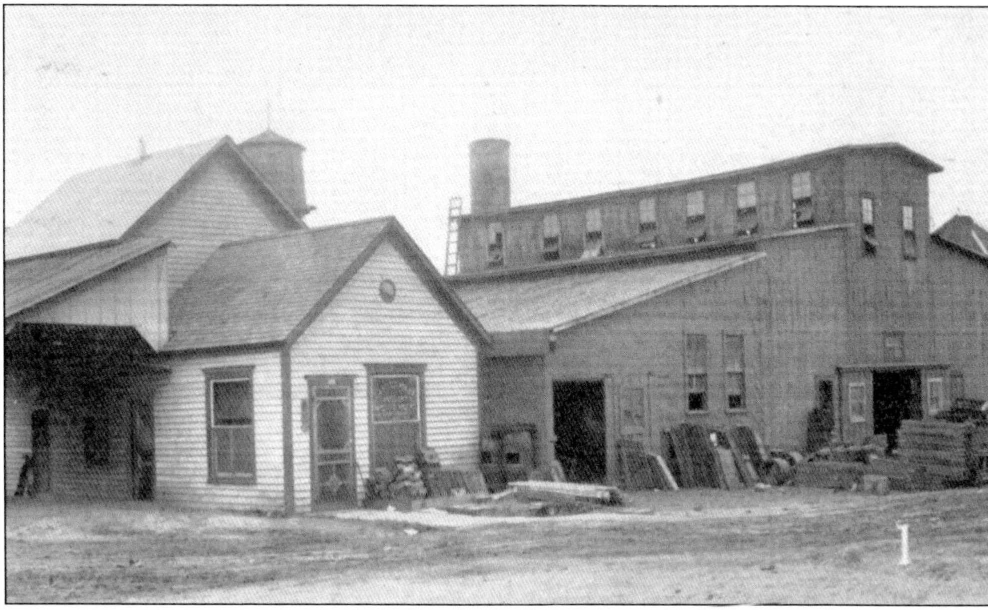

**Webb City and Carterville Foundry, 1907.** The foundry was established in 1881. It is still doing business at the same location on Route 66. (Courtesy of Webb Corporation.)

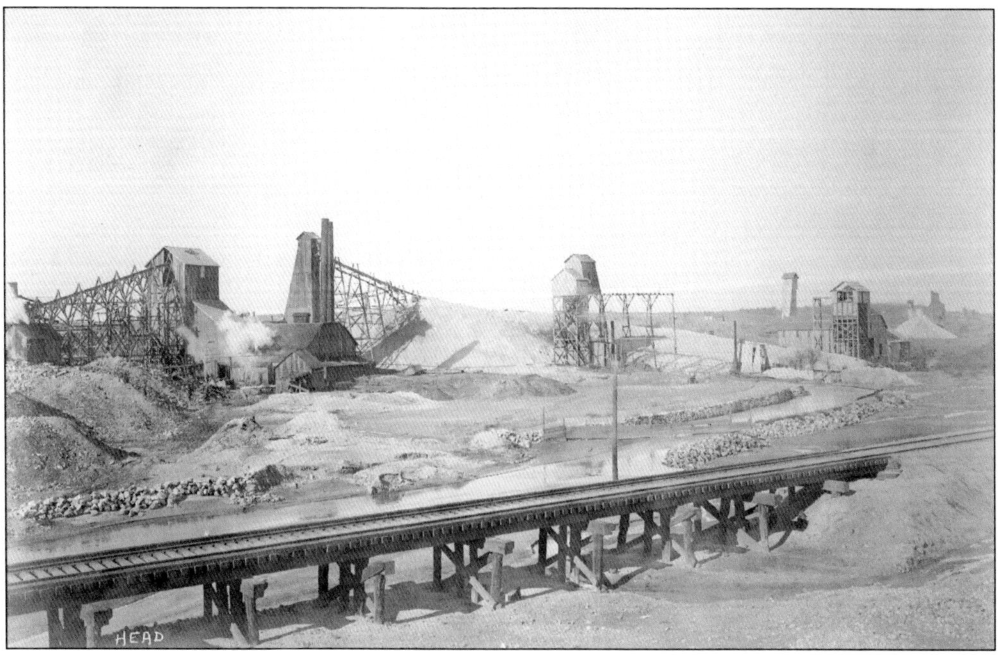


**Bradford–Kansas City and Dinger Mines, 1910.** Spurs from the railroad tracks connected the mining camps and mines. When the mine closed, the tracks were abandoned. (Courtesy of the Missouri Digital Archive.)

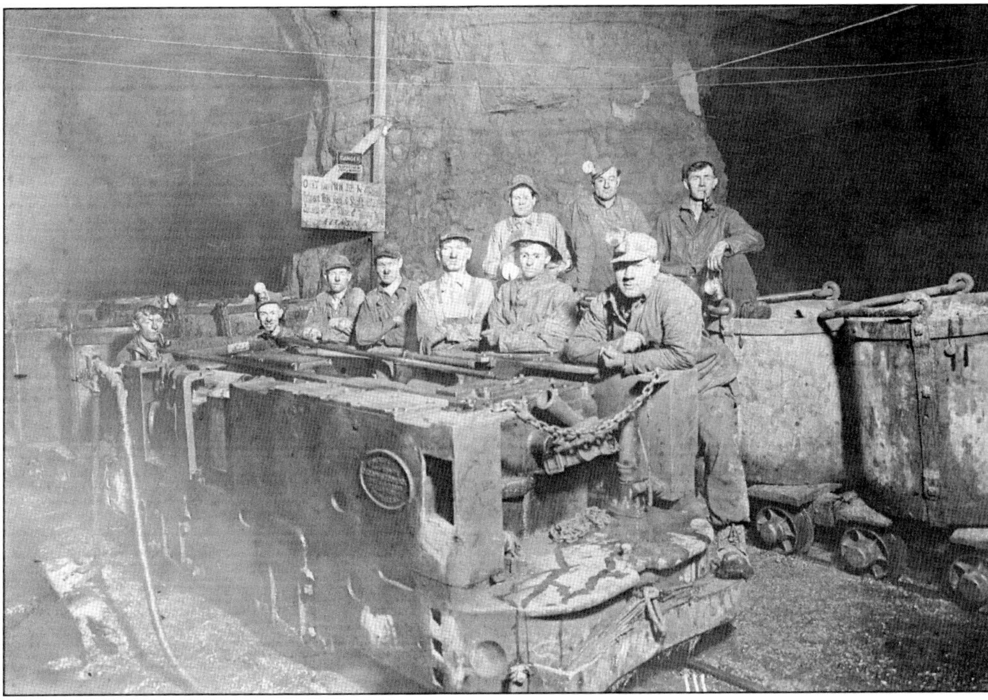

**American Zinc, Lead & Smelting Company Mine, 1908.** Small electric-powered locomotives, called "dinkies" or "electric mules," replaced the Missouri mules that had been used to pull ore carts. (Courtesy of Missouri Digital Archive.)

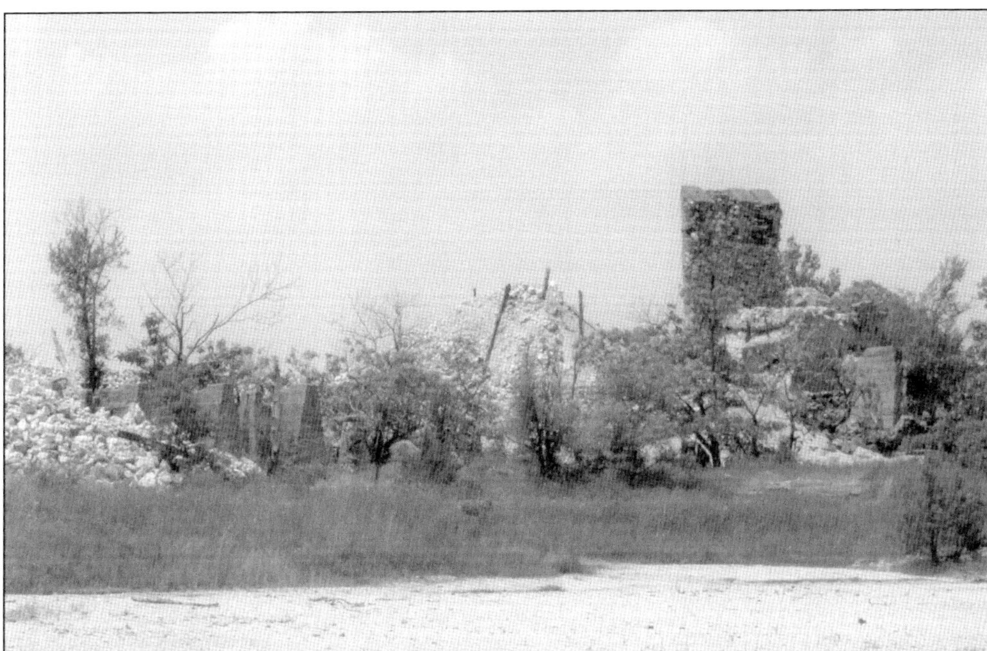

**Tailing Piles, 2004.** These tailing piles north of Webb City, on Madison Street, were an everyday sight until they were removed in an Environmental Protection Agency project.

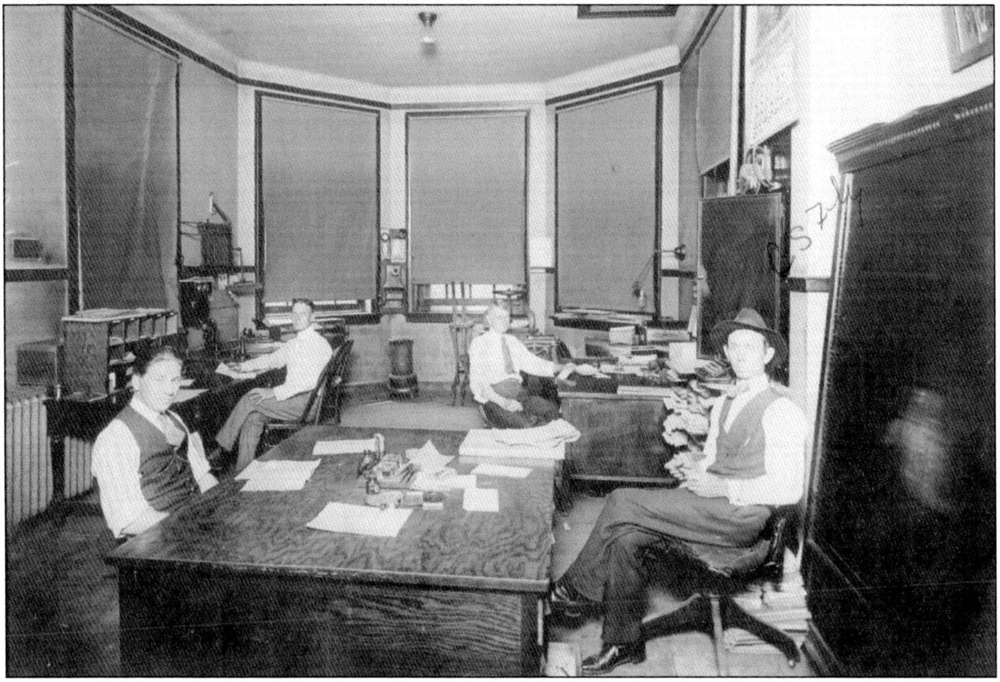

**Clarence S. Fly, June 1919.** Fly (far right) was pay clerk at the Independent Gravel Company in Webb City for 25 years. He served as councilman for the Third Ward and was elected mayor in April 1952. (Courtesy of George Twigger.)

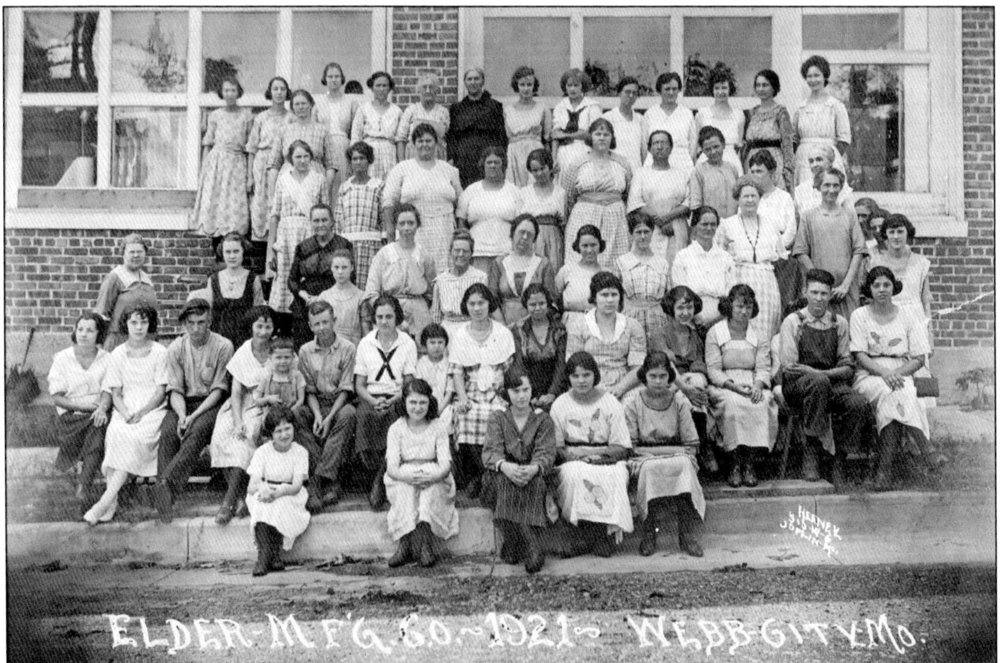


**Elder Manufacture, 1921.** As the mining boom was winding down, Webb City turned its attention to manufacturing. Elder provided employment—often called working at the "shirt factory"—to a large number of Webb City and area women.

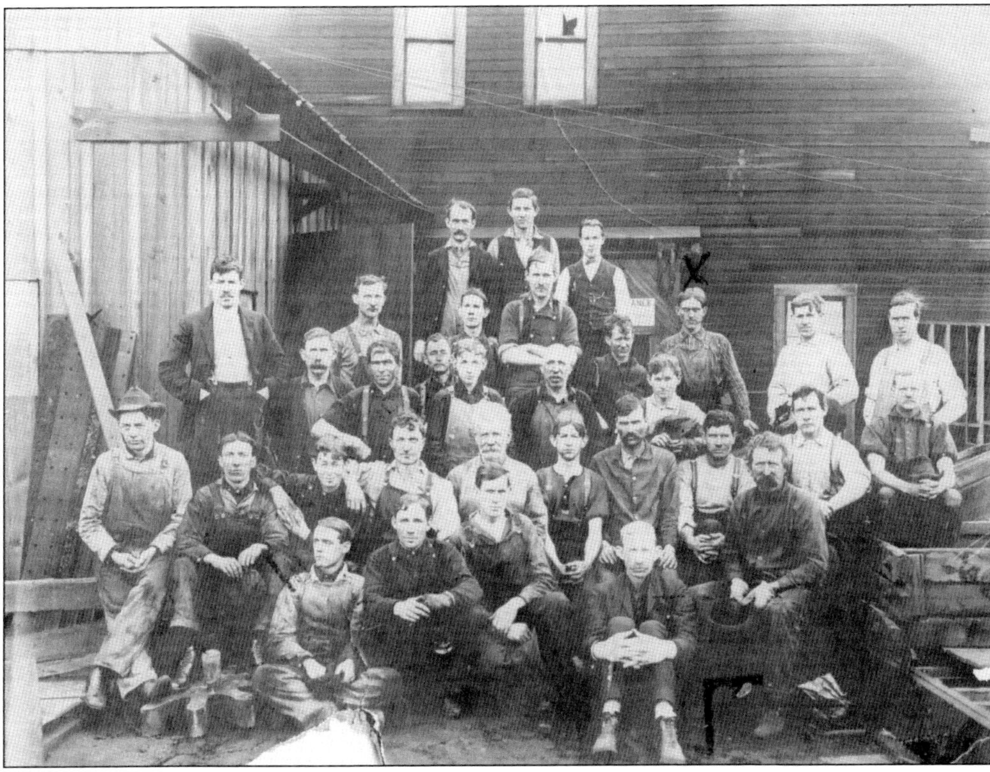

**WEBB CORPORATION EMPLOYEES, 1881.** This photograph was taken only six years after John Webb platted the city. Webb Corporation continues to do business in Webb City today at the same location. (Courtesy of the Webb Corporation.)

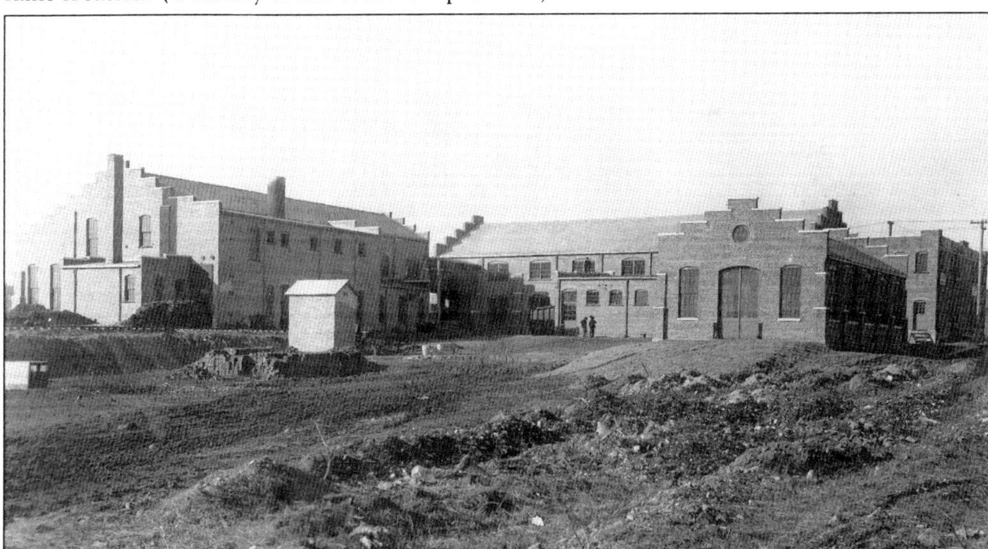

**WEBB CITY AND CARTERVILLE FOUNDRY & MACHINE WORKS.** Shown here are the company's office building, sheet-metal works, and machine shop. The firm manufactures sheet-metal products. (Courtesy of the Webb Corporation.)

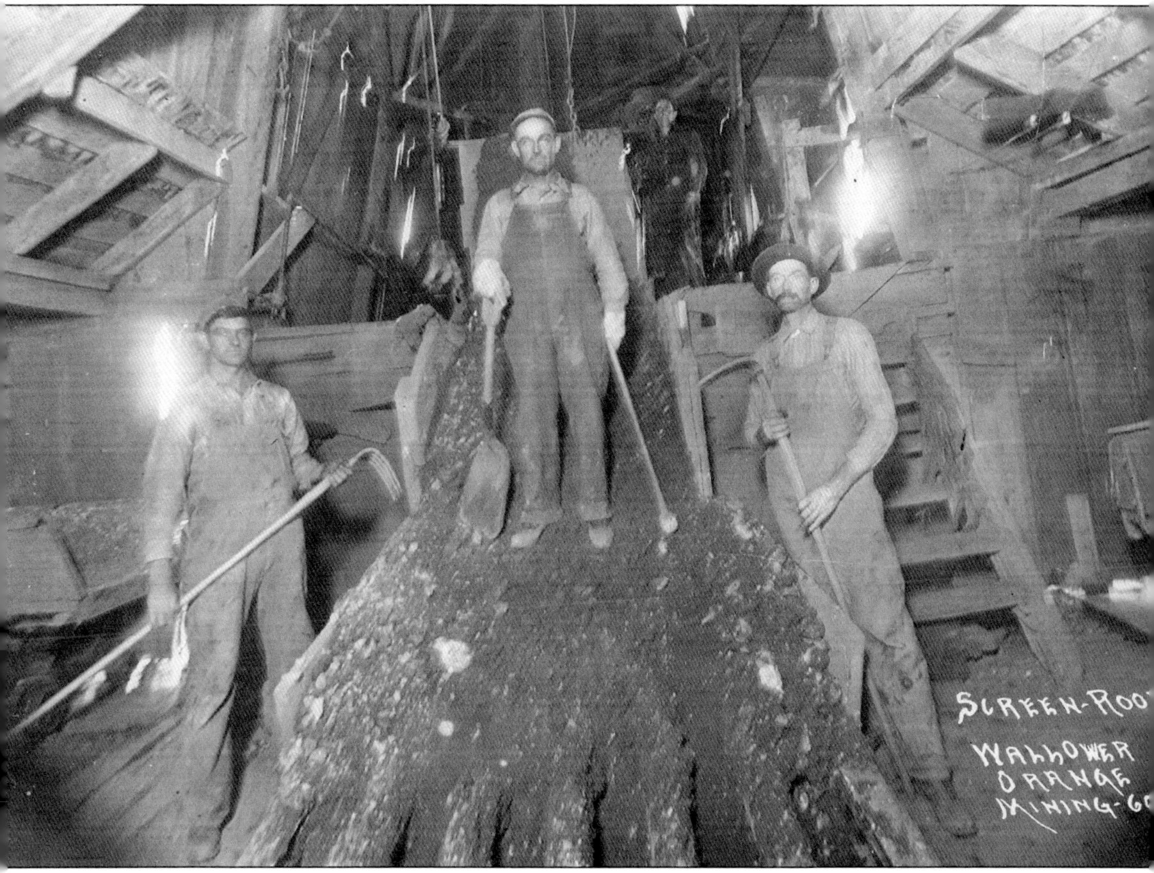


**SCREEN ROOM AT THE ORANGE MINE, 1919.** This is one of the mines that Frank Wallower developed. The men are raking rock and dirt through a grate called "Grizzly." Large rocks are removed, crashed with sledgehammers, and then returned to the screen room. Miners doing this job received many injuries to their eyes and lower legs from pieces of flying flint rock. The Orange Mine was located between Webb City and Carterville. (Courtesy of the Missouri Digital Archive.)

**FRANK CARMANY WALLOWER.** A mining pioneer for the Tri-State Mining District, Wallower was also general manager of the Daylight Mine, located between Webb City and Carterville. He was the developer of the Bird-dog, Disbrow, and Orange Mines. Later, he became a trustee at Jane Chinn Hospital. (Courtesy of the Missouri Digital Archives.)

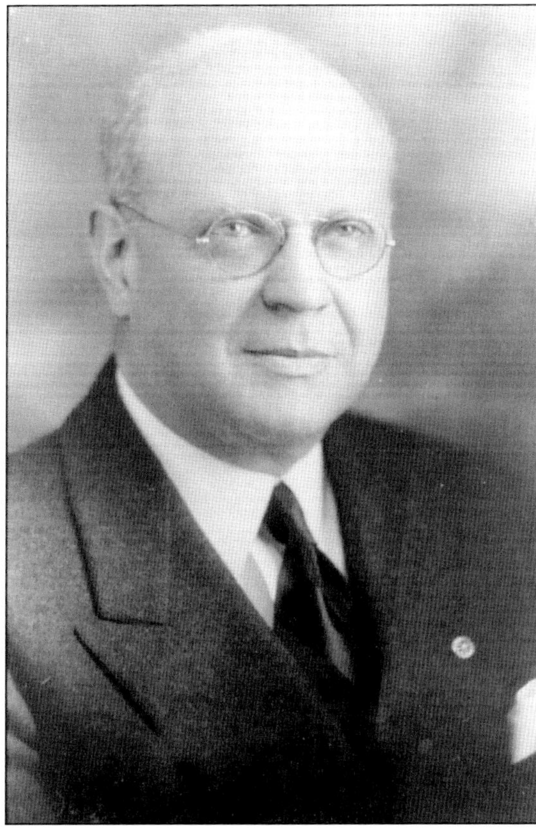

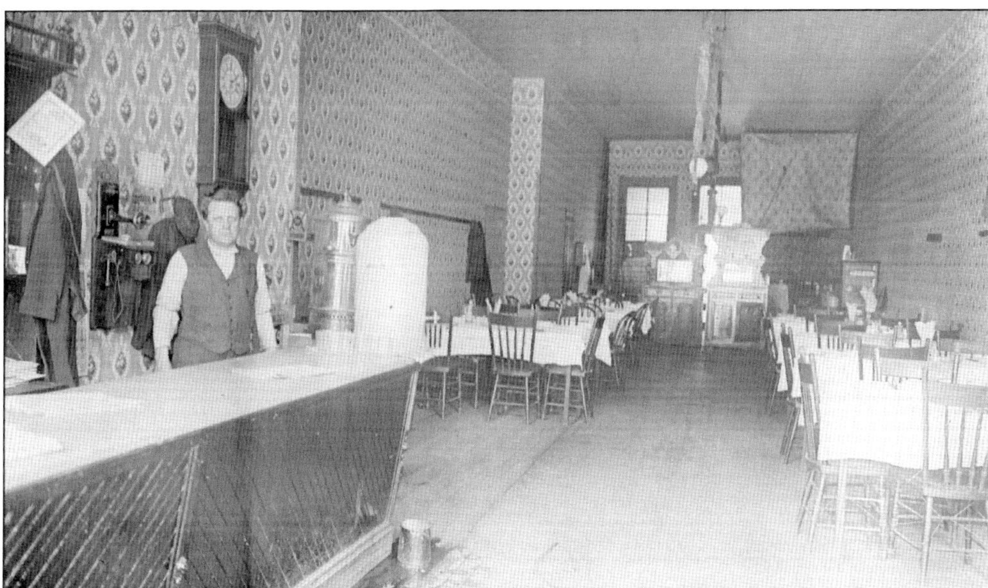

**WEBB CITY RESTAURANT.** The only thing known about this restaurant is that it was in Webb City. When old photographs cannot be identified, much history can be lost. (Courtesy of William H. King Jr.)

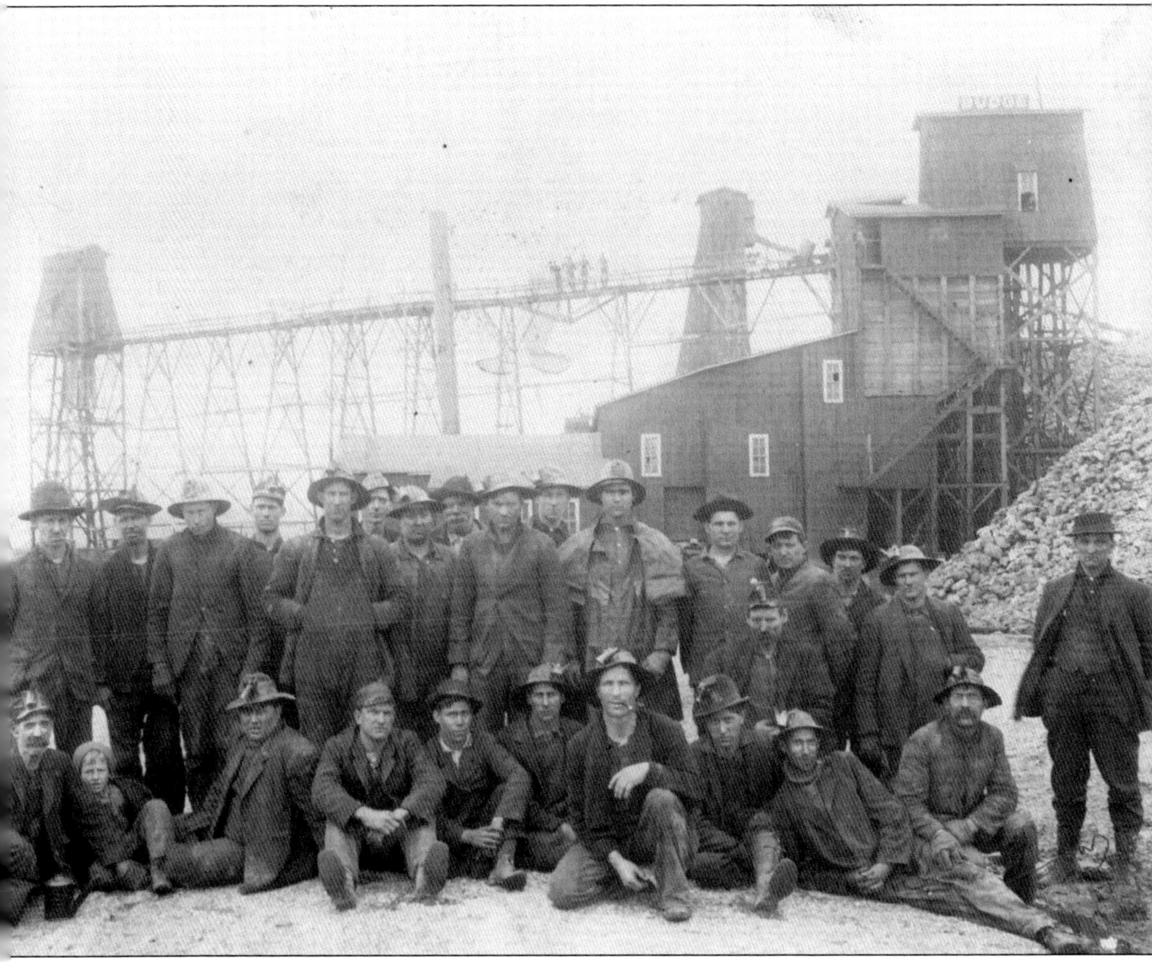

**BUDGE MINE, 1902.** This mine was owned by the Joplin, Kentucky, Granby Land Company. The identities of these miners are not known. (Courtesy of the Missouri Digital Archive.)

**Oklahoma Tire & Supply Company, 1960.** This company was located in the Parker Building, erected in 1889 on Main Street. (Courtesy of William H. King Jr.)

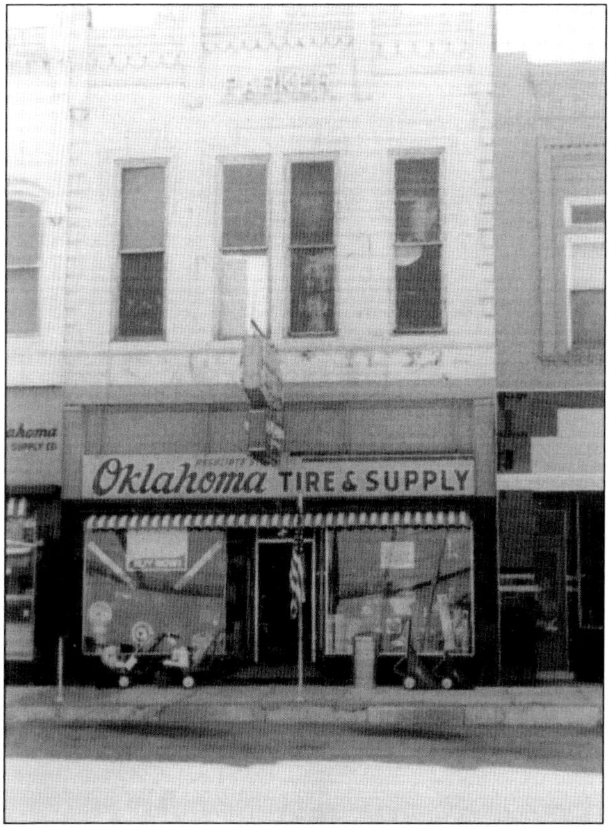


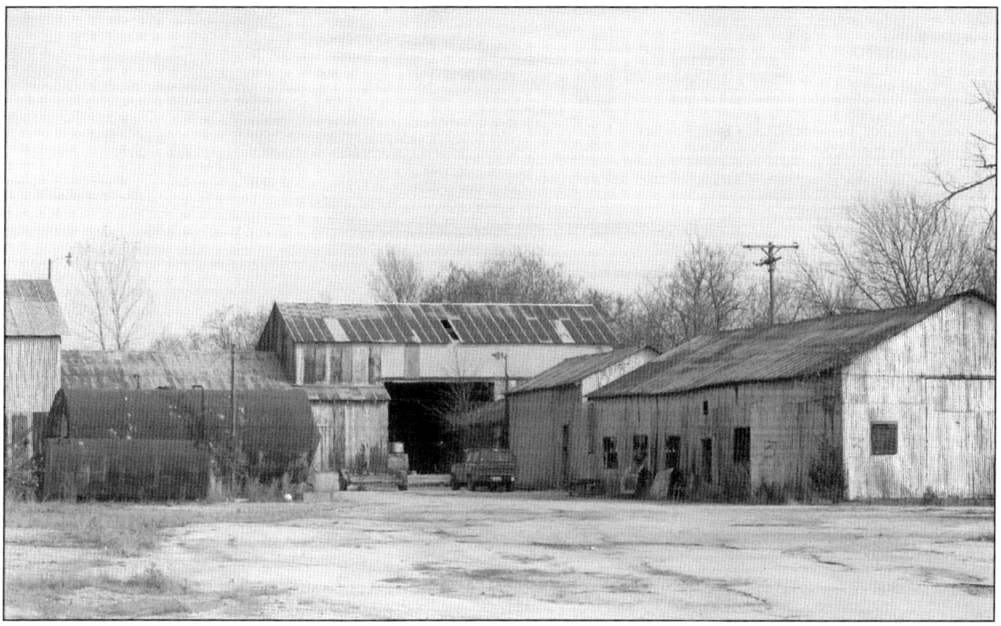

**Independent Gravel Company, 2005.** The company launched its business in October 1906. This photograph was taken during its last days before all of the equipment was sold at auction. (Courtesy of the Bob King Collection.)

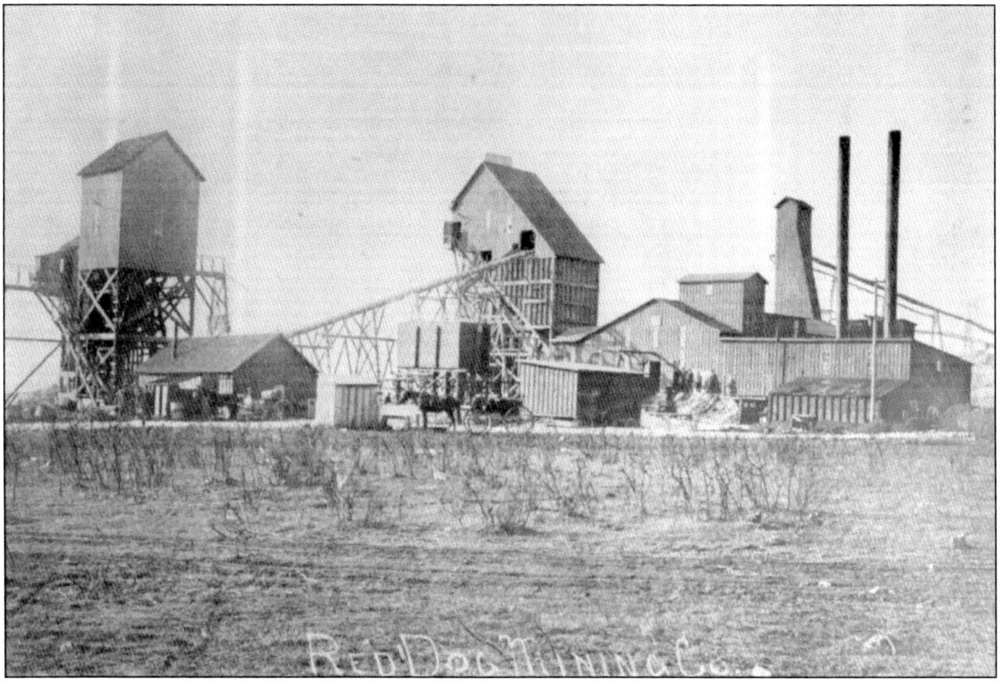


**Red Dog Mine, 1907.** This mine was owned by Chapman and Lennon. It produced $10,000 a month in profits.

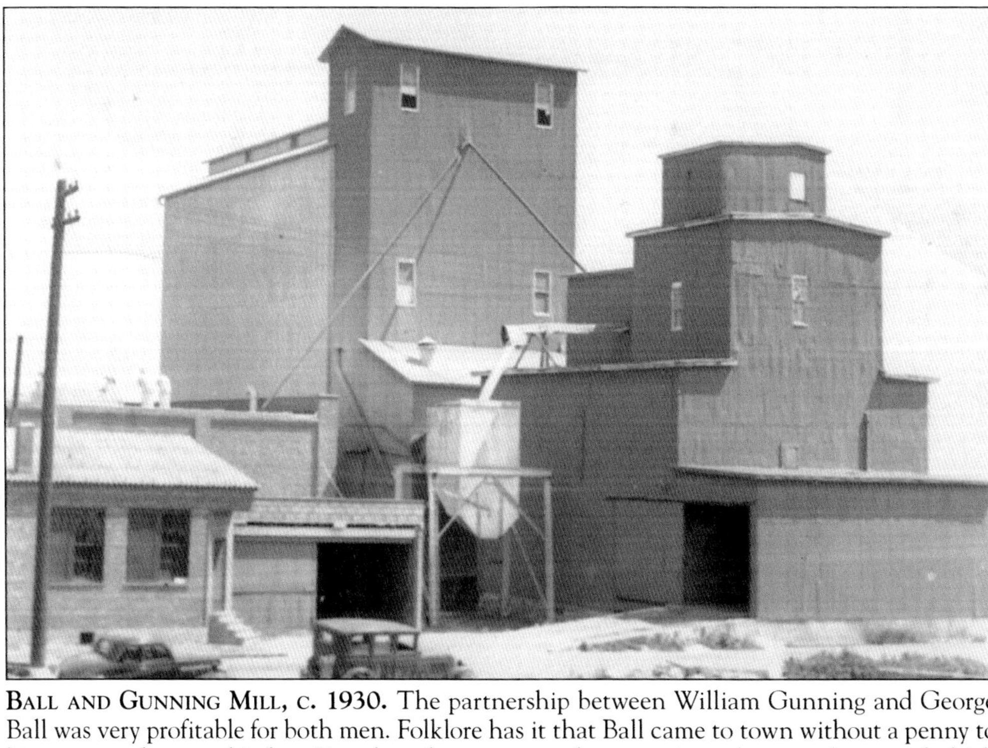

**Ball and Gunning Mill, c. 1930.** The partnership between William Gunning and George Ball was very profitable for both men. Folklore has it that Ball came to town without a penny to his name or shoes on his feet. Together, the men owned many mines, the most famous of which was the Oronogo Circle.

# *Five*

# Transportation

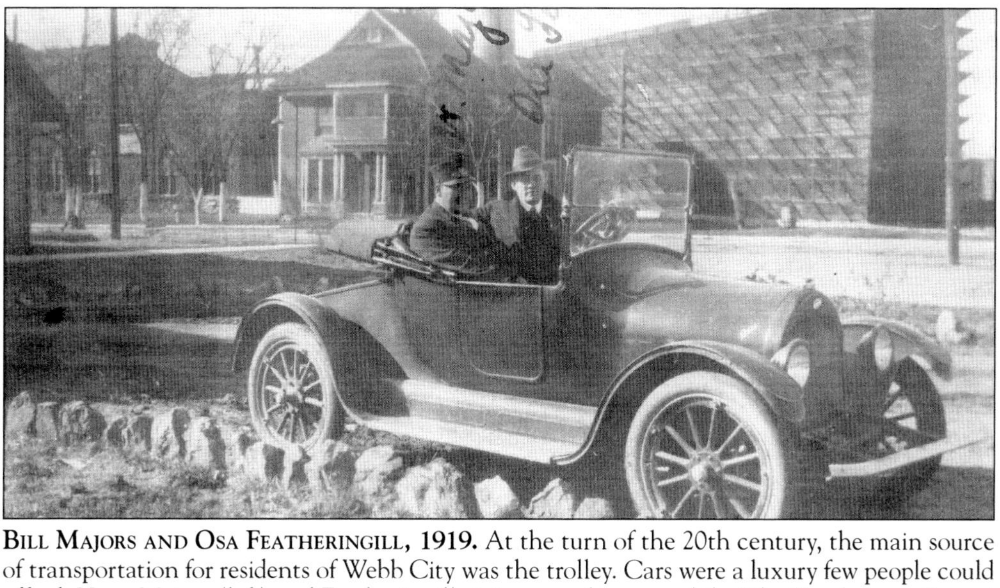

**Bill Majors and Osa Featheringill, 1919.** At the turn of the 20th century, the main source of transportation for residents of Webb City was the trolley. Cars were a luxury few people could afford. Here, Majors (left) and Featheringill sit in an early automobile. The Southwest Missouri Electric Railway Company was based in Webb City. The line connected most area towns. (Courtesy of the Bob King Collection.)

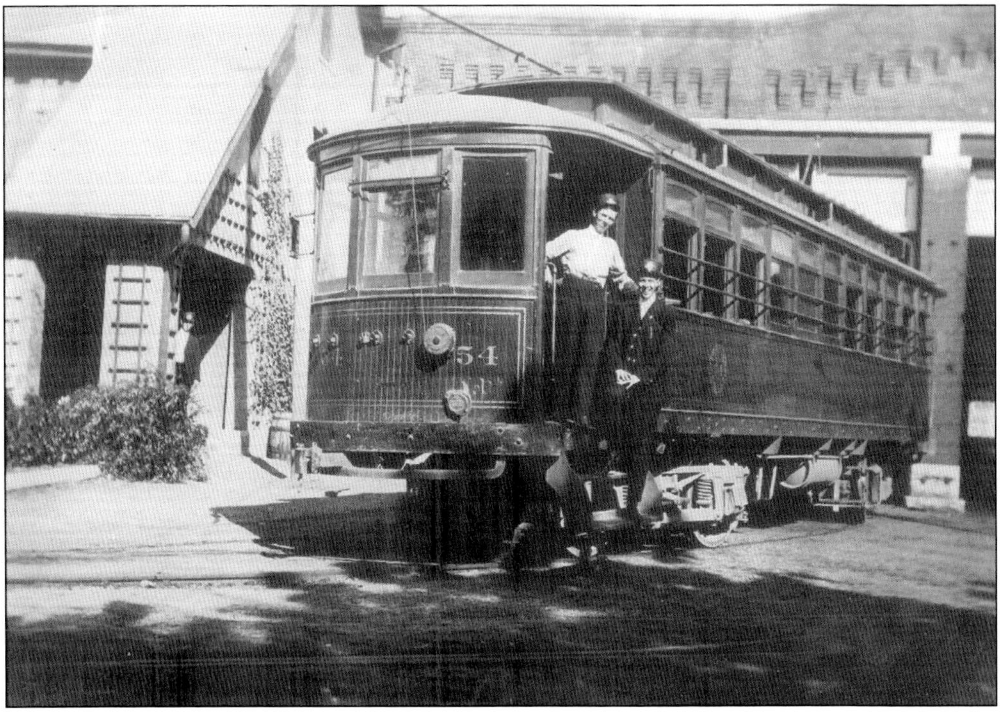

**SOUTHWEST MISSOURI STREETCAR NO. 54, 1915.** June Sibert (left) and Arthur Holcomb of the Southwest Missouri Electric Railway Company pose outside the carbarn. (Courtesy of the Bob King Collection.)

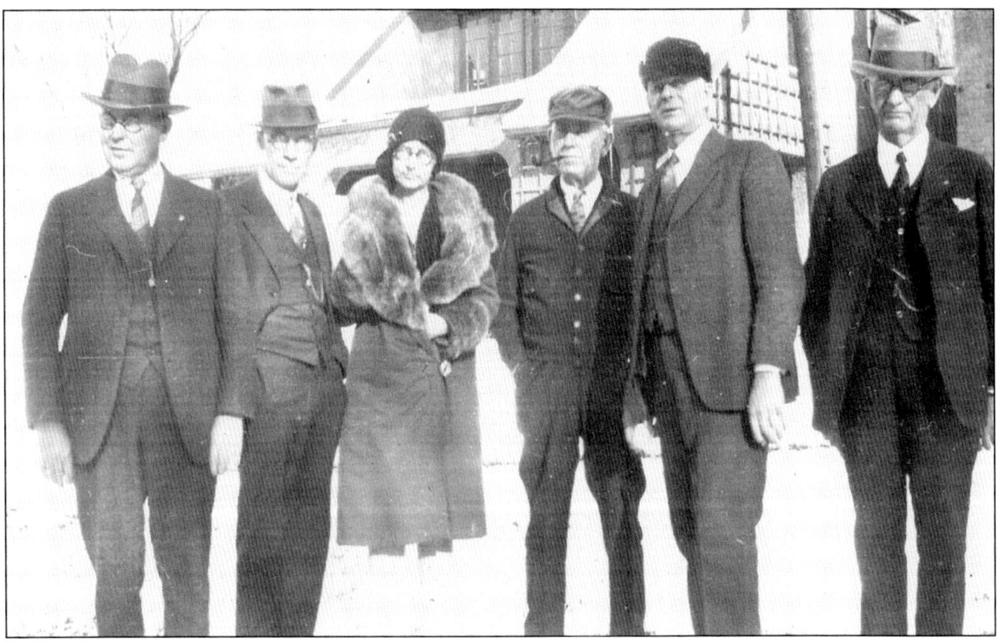

**OFFICE STAFF, 1920.** Employees of the Southwest Missouri Electric Railway pose for a photograph. They are, from left to right, Tom Harbaugh, Herbert Brock, Lura Grandstaff, W.E. McMechan, W.H. "Bill" Gray, and E.J. Pratt. (Courtesy of the Bob King Collection.)

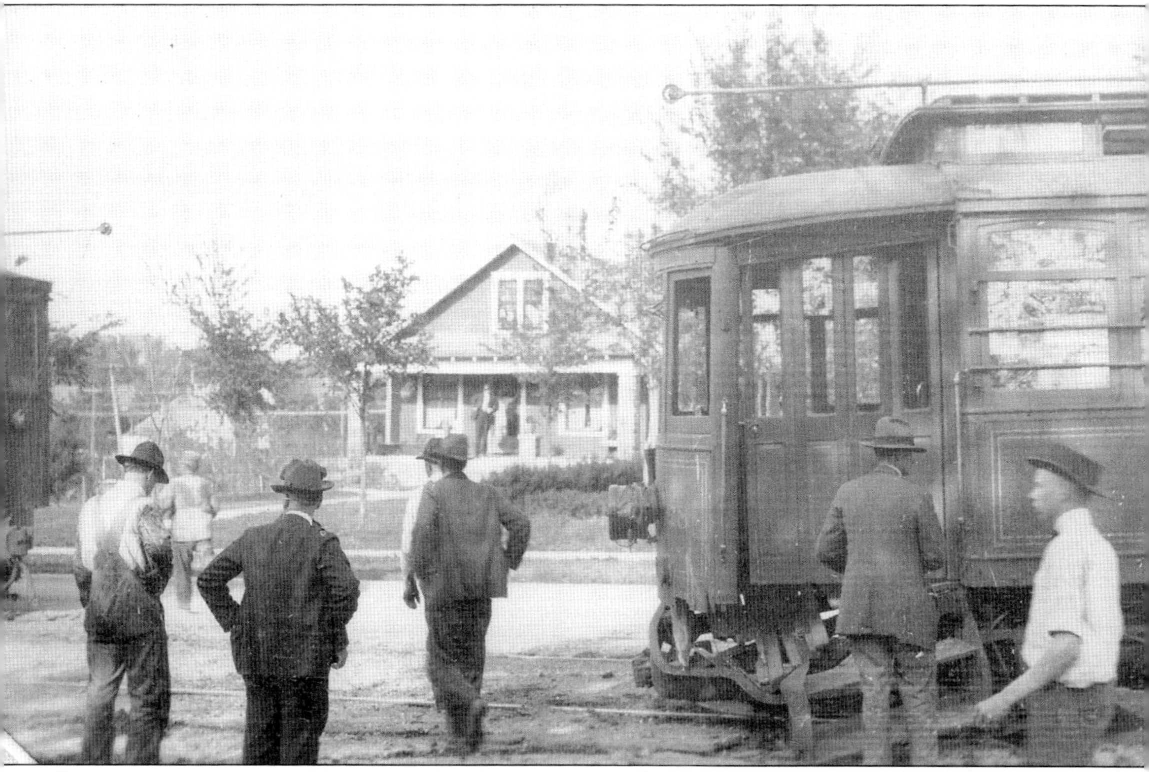

**Streetcar Derailment, May 1920.** Accidents sometimes happened, as here at Fourth and Madison Streets. Car No. 28 jumped the track when it hit a dog. (Courtesy of the Bob King Collection.)

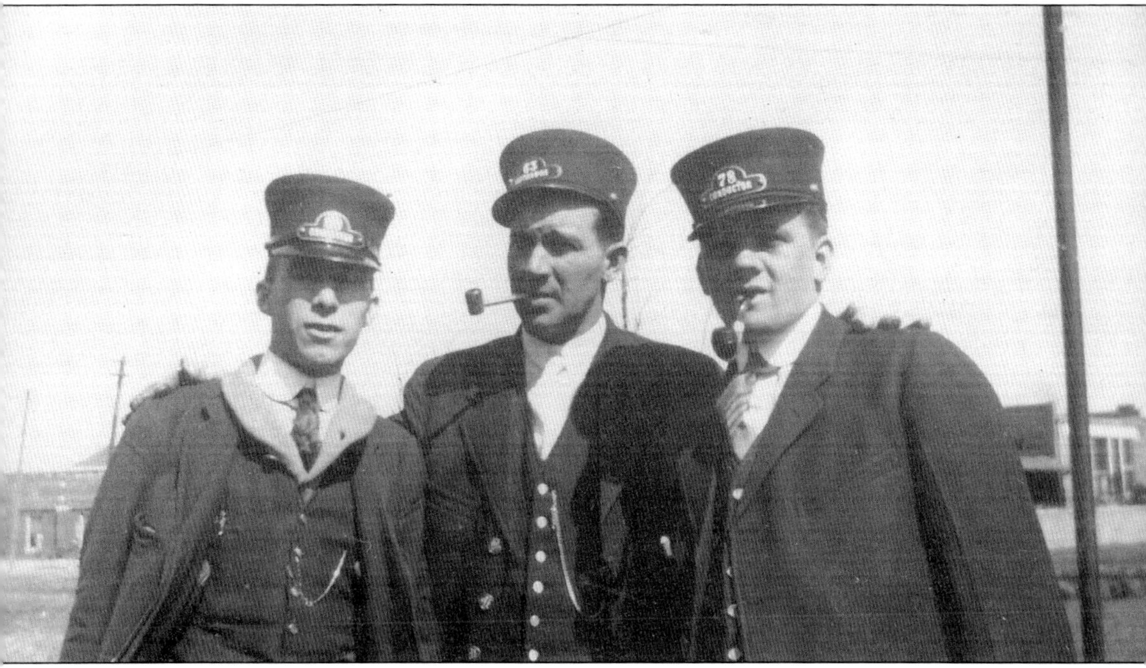

**Streetcar Conductors, 1919.** From left to right are Harry Palmer, Van Young, and Osa Featheringill. They are standing across the street from the Southwest Missouri Electric Railway employees' clubhouse. (Courtesy of the Bob King Collection.)

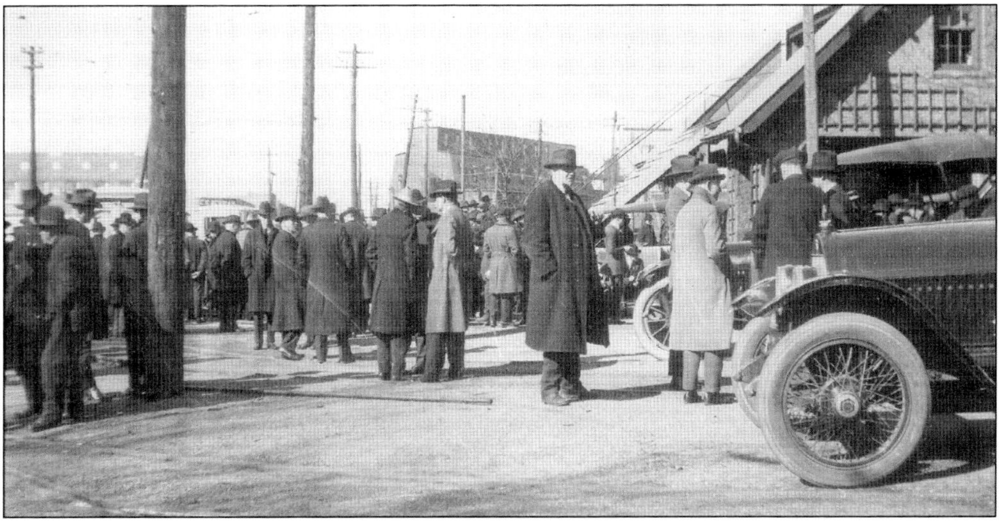

**Funeral of Alfred Harrison Rogers, March 1920.** Rogers started the first trolley in Webb City with a mule-drawn streetcar. It later became Southwest Missouri Electric Railway. (Courtesy of the Bob King Collection.)

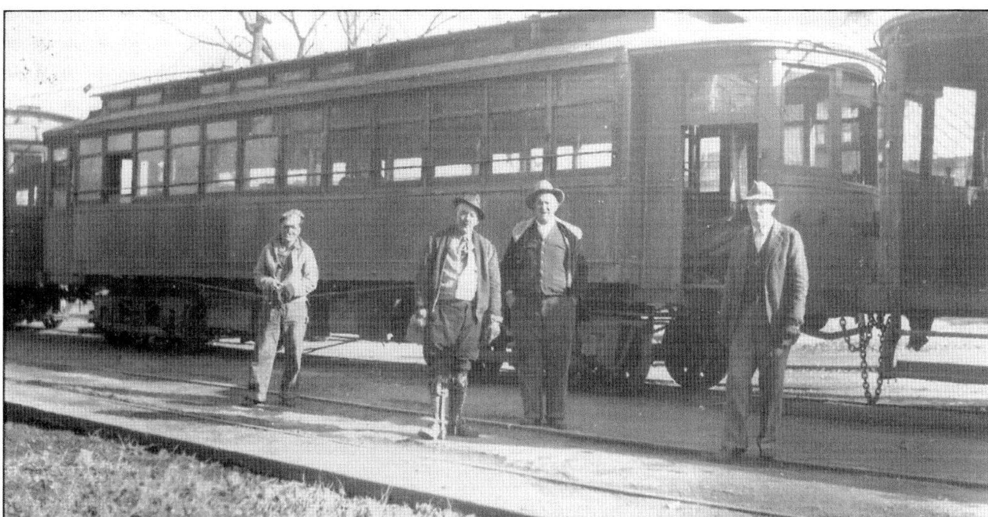

**Troubleshooters, Southwest Missouri Railway, 1919.** Shown here are, from left to right, Frank Green, Claude Frye, George Mayfield, and Fred Herron. Frye, a lineman, is wearing spikes. (Courtesy of the Bob King Collection.)

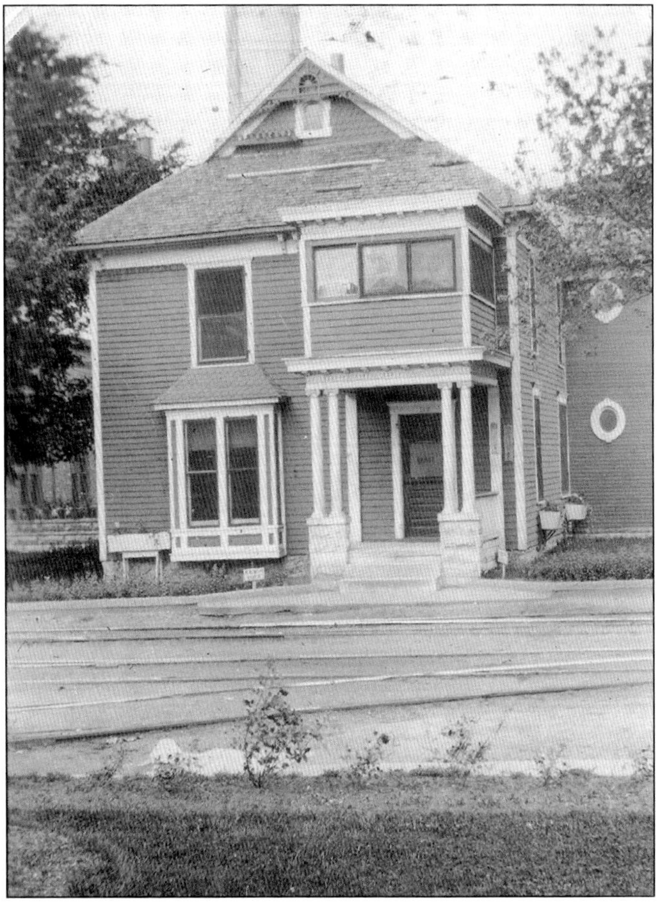

**Railway Company Office, 1919.** This is the Southwest Missouri Electric Railway Company's Webb City office. It stood one block off of Route 66 on Madison Street, next to the powerhouse. (Courtesy of the Bob King Collection.)

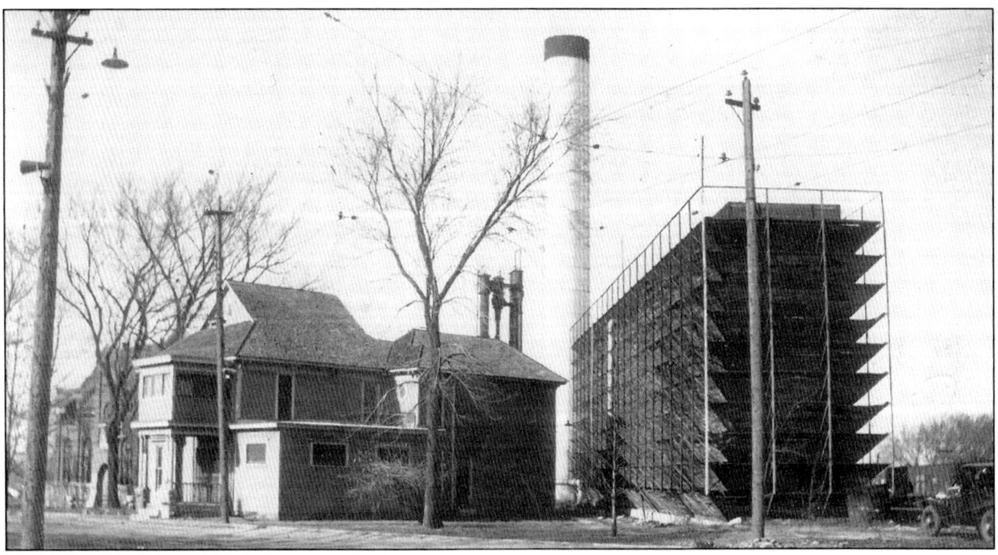

**Condenser and Smokestack, 1919.** The condenser is the cooling system for the Southwest Missouri Electric Railway powerhouse. The company office is also shown in this photograph. (Courtesy of the Bob King Collection.)

**June Sibert and Van Young, 1915.** Sibert (left) and Young, employees of the streetcar company, are seen here out of their conductor uniforms. (Courtesy of the Bob King Collection.)

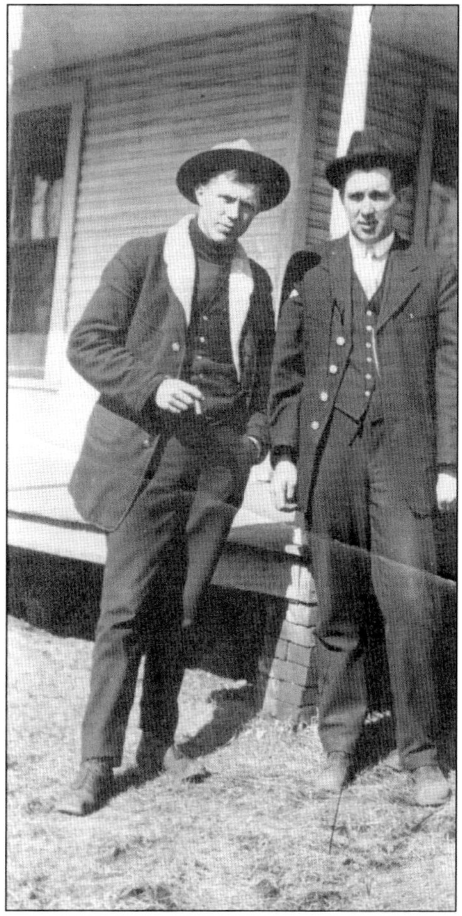

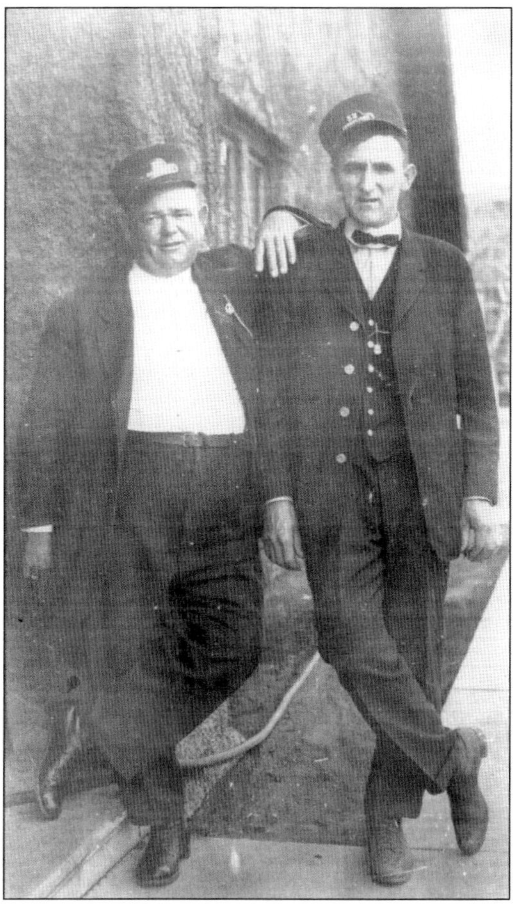

**Tom Cowan and Archie McDoughgall, 1915.** Cowan (left), the motorman, drove the streetcar. McDoughgall, the conductor, collected the fares and looked after the passengers. (Courtesy of the Bob King Collection.)

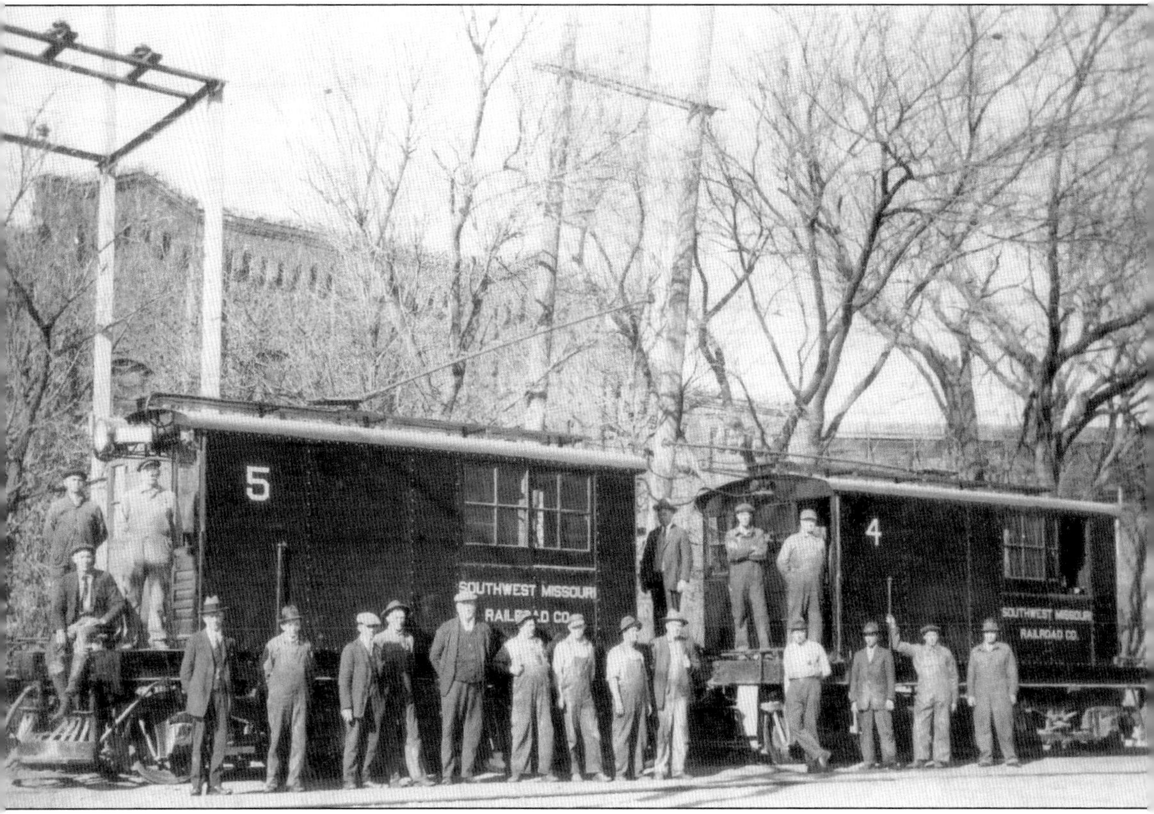


**Railway Employees and Two Locomotives.** Employees of the Southwest Missouri Electric Railway Company gather for a photograph. Shown here are, from left to right, (on locomotive No. 4) John Hill, Bill Webb, and Loren Fullerton; (in front of locomotive No. 4) Bill Pelt, John Herd, Drew Walker, and Mike Herrin; (on locomotive No. 5) R.F. Fair, Fred Herrin, and L.W. Porter; (in front of locomotive No. 5) E.J. Pratt, Bob Huey, Fred Hulett, Tom Riggs, Sam Downey, H. Sparks, Bert Carpenter, George Smith, and "Pappy" Carmicheal. (Courtesy of the Bob King Collection.)

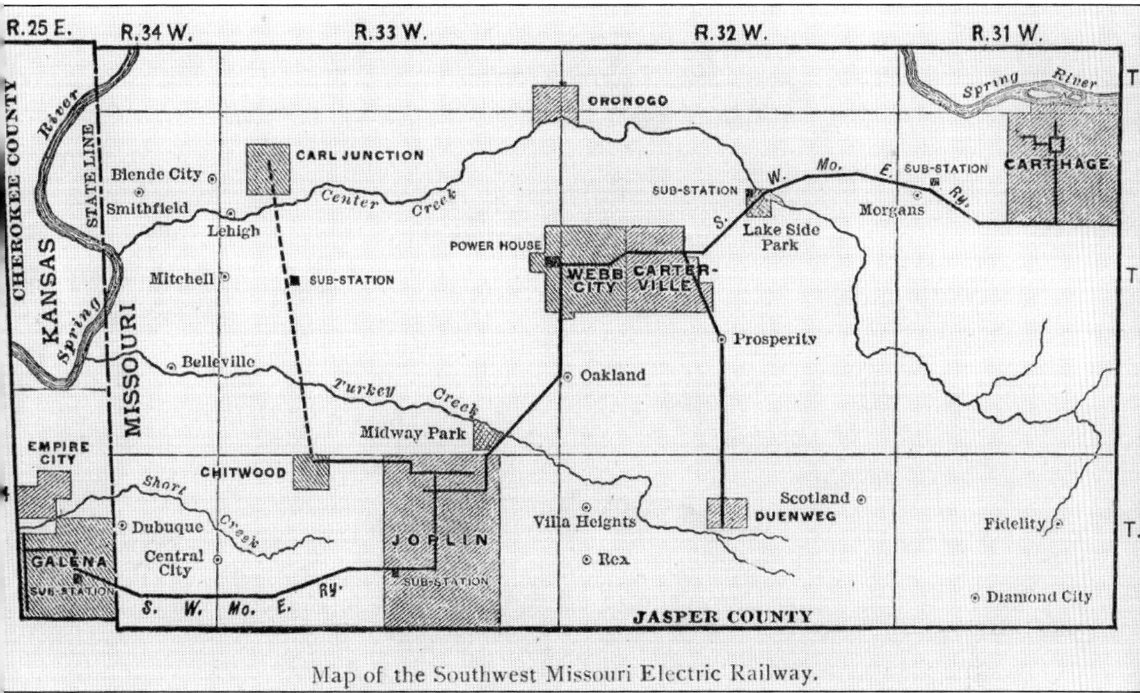


**SOUTHWEST MISSOURI ELECTRIC RAILWAY COMPANY ROUTE.** The trolley company served Galena, Kansas, then crossed the Missouri state line into Joplin. It stopped at mining camps Chitwood and Oakland before reaching home base in Webb City. After Carterville, the route split, turning south to Duenweg and northeast to Carthage. (Courtesy of Missouri Digital Archive.)

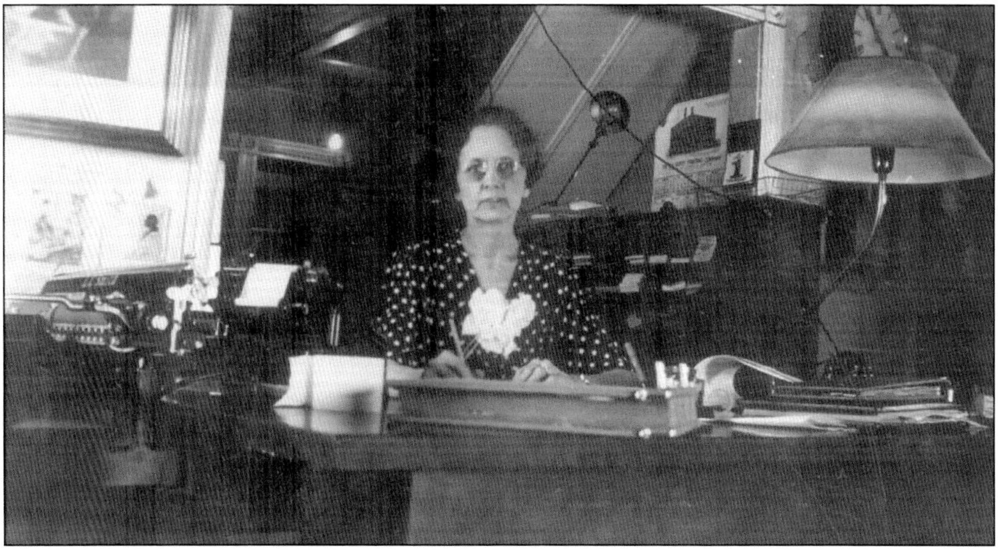

**LURA GRANDSTAFF, 1924.** Grandstaff worked at the Webb City office of the Southwest Missouri Electric Railway Company from 1922 until 1937. She then moved to the Joplin office in 1937, staying there until 1939. (Courtesy of the Bob King Collection.)

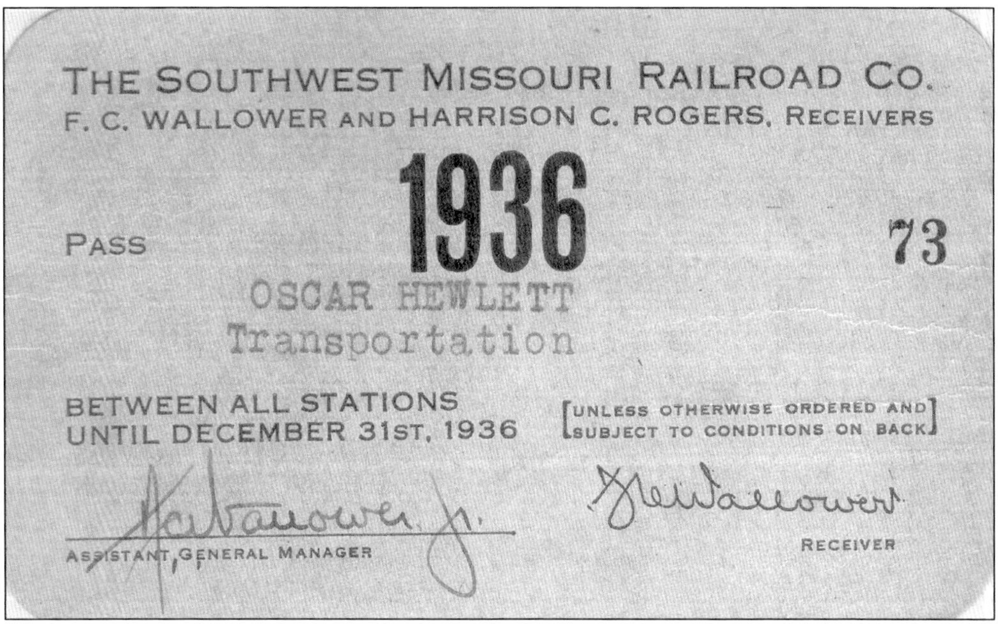
THE SOUTHWEST MISSOURI RAILROAD CO.
F. C. WALLOWER AND HARRISON C. ROGERS, RECEIVERS
1936
PASS
73
OSCAR HEWLETT
Transportation
BETWEEN ALL STATIONS
UNTIL DECEMBER 31ST, 1936
[UNLESS OTHERWISE ORDERED AND SUBJECT TO CONDITIONS ON BACK]
ASSISTANT GENERAL MANAGER
RECEIVER

**STREETCAR PASS CARD, 1936.** The Southwest Missouri Electric Railway Company issued passes. This one is signed by the assistant general manager. (Courtesy of the Bob King Collection.)

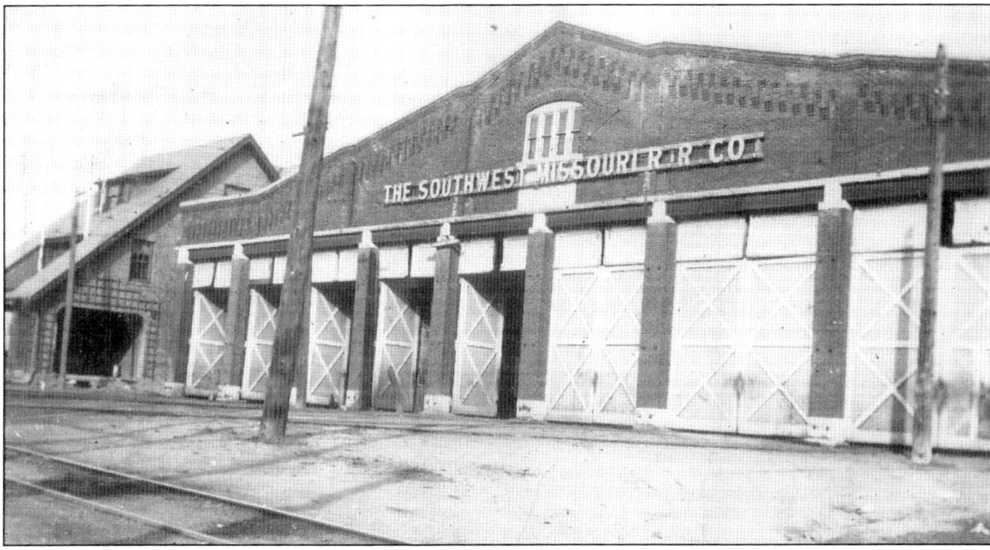


**CARBARN, 1919.** The Southwest Missouri Electric Railway Company's carbarn was where streetcars were built, repairs were made, and cars were stored when not in use. The carbarn was next to the employees' clubhouse on Route 66. (Courtesy of the Bob King Collection.)

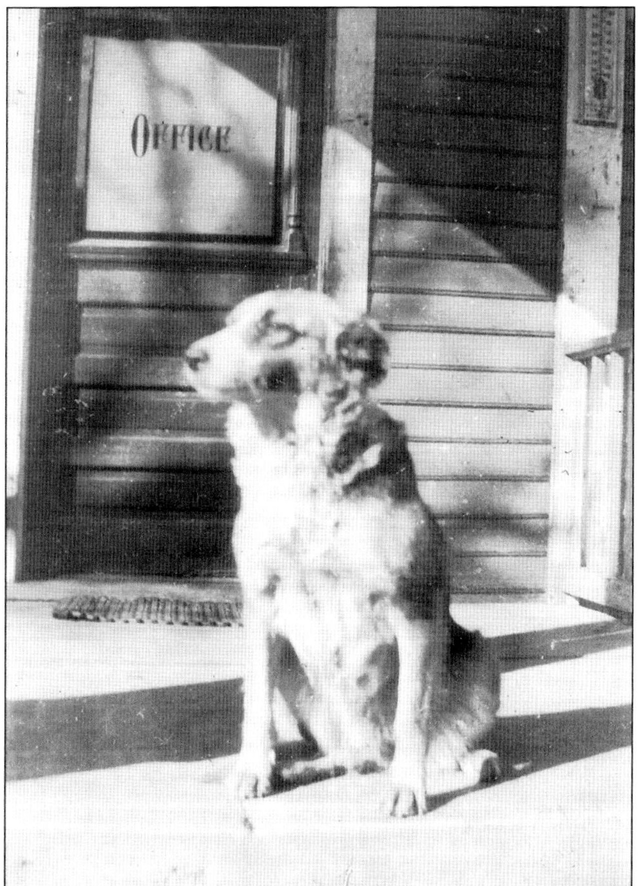


**QUEEN, CARBARN AND CLUBHOUSE MASCOT, 1919.** It is rare to come across an old photograph featuring only a dog. In this case, knowing the dog's name, Queen, and her role in Webb City's streetcar history make this an extraordinary find. She was a friendly face for employees resting between shifts. (Courtesy of the Bob King Collection.)

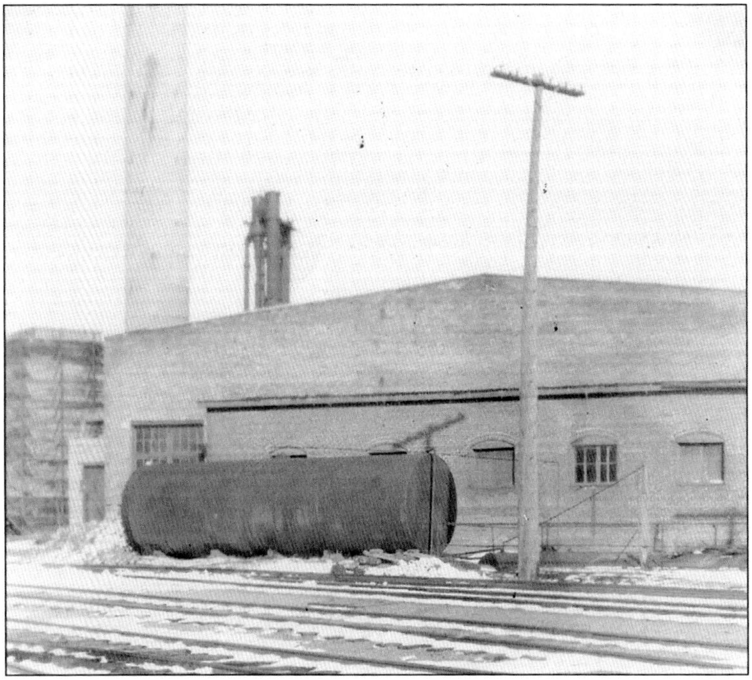

**Rear of Powerhouse, 1920.** The powerhouse sits on Route 66. Over the years, the building has undergone many changes. Today, it is a skating rink. (Courtesy of the Bob King Collection.)

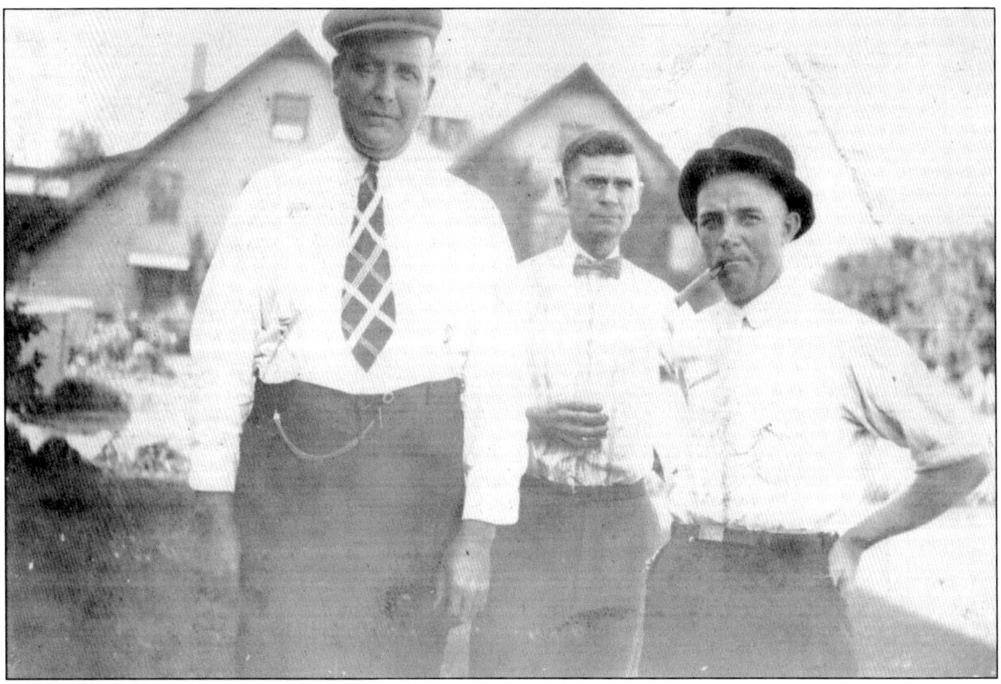

**Southwest Missouri Electric Railway Workers, 1920.** Seen here are Sam "Big Sam" Downey (left), Jim Adams (center), and B.R. Morgan. The men are standing on the north side of the employees' clubhouse. (Courtesy of the Bob King Collection.)

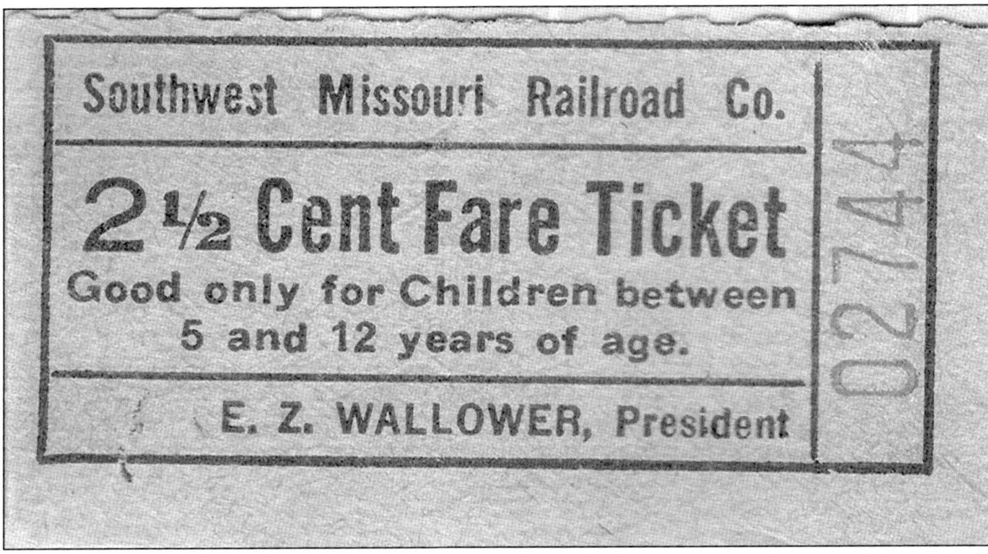


**STREETCAR TICKET.** The fare price of 2.5¢ was good for children between the ages of 5 and 12 on the Southwest Missouri Electric Streetcar Railway. (Courtesy of the Bob King Collection.)

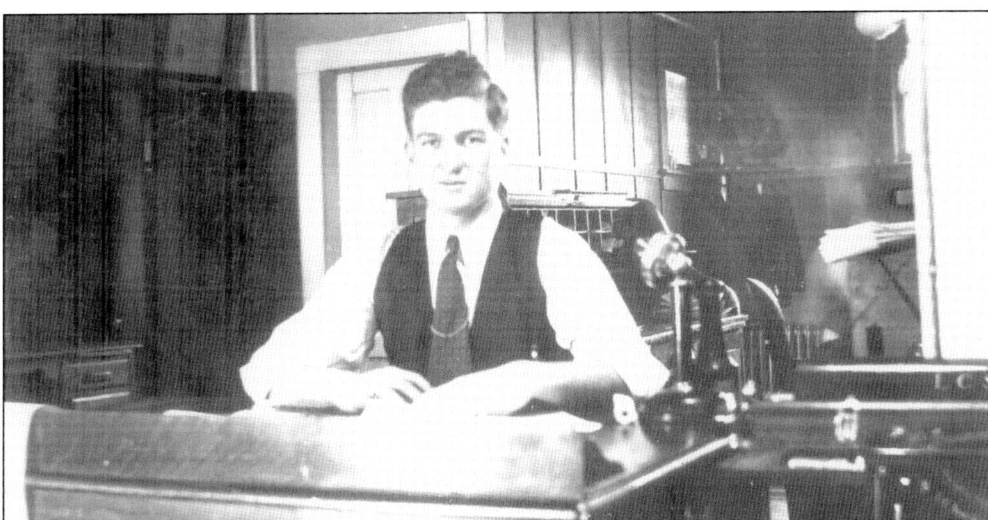

**GEORGE LAMB, 1920.** Lamb worked at Southwest Missouri Electric Railways' Webb City office. The company also had an office in Joplin. (Courtesy of the Bob King Collection.)

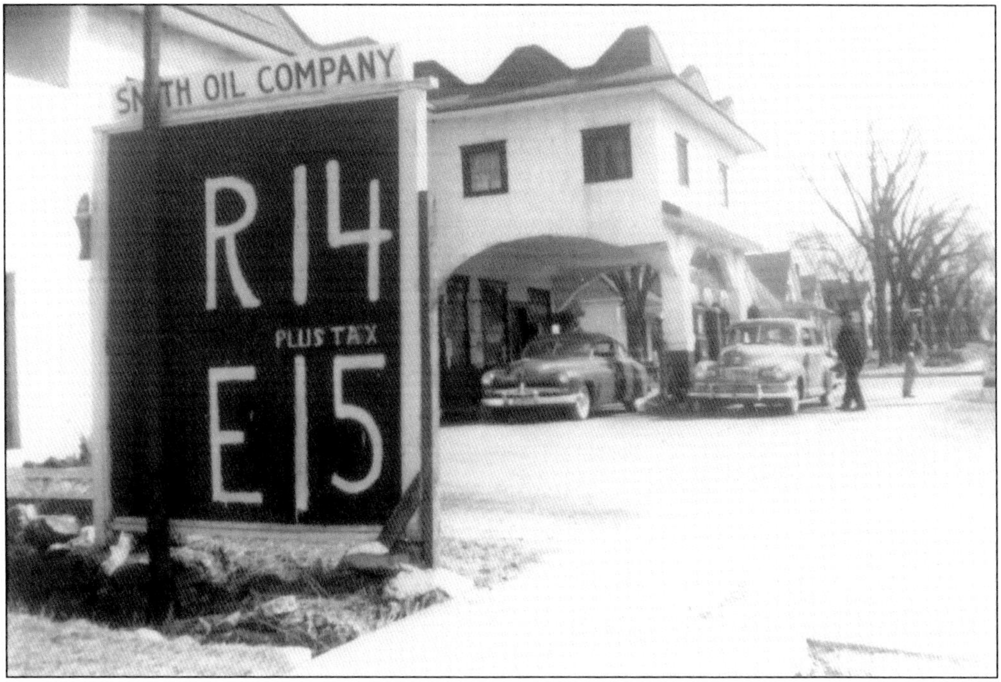


**Gas Station, c. 1940.** It seems unbelievable that one could buy gas for 14¢ a gallon. Today, this station on Broadway has been converted into apartments. (Courtesy of the Webb City Route 66 Visitors Center.)

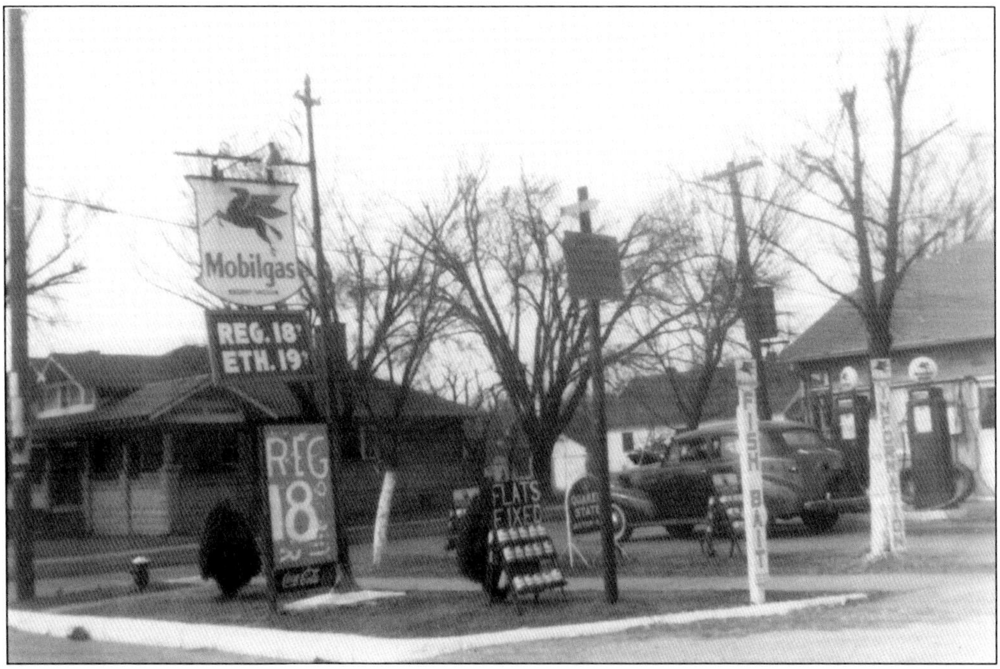


**Gas, 18¢ a Gallon, c. 1930.** This photograph of a Webb City gas station offers a look back in history. Gasoline really was that cheap at one time. (Courtesy of the Webb City Route 66 Visitors Center.)

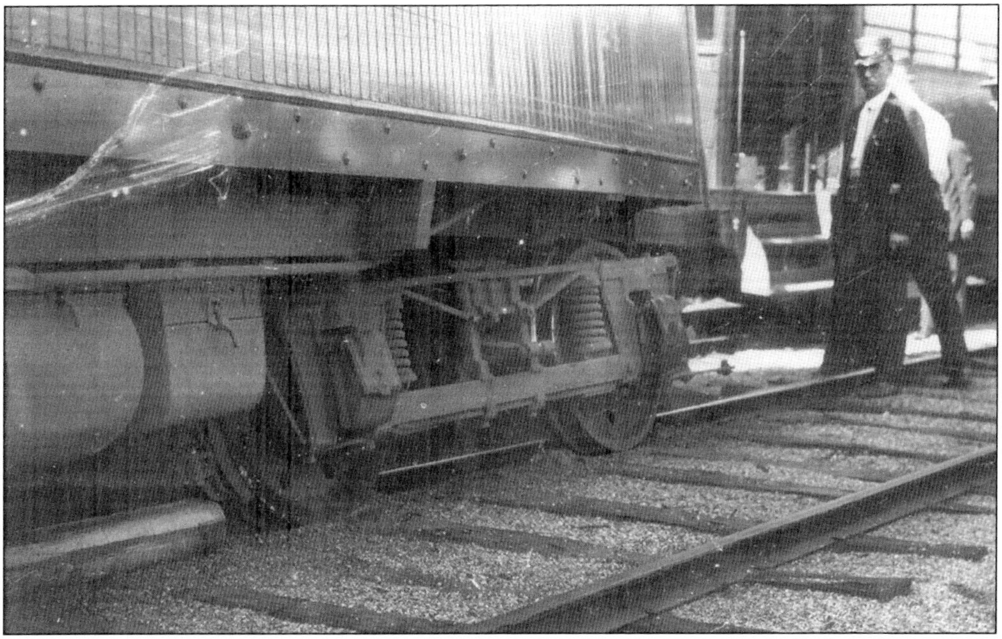

**Derailed Streetcar, 1920.** This derailment occurred when car No. 24 broke a flange on a 1,000-foot curve. Streetcar accidents, though uncommon, did happen. (Courtesy of the Bob King Collection.)

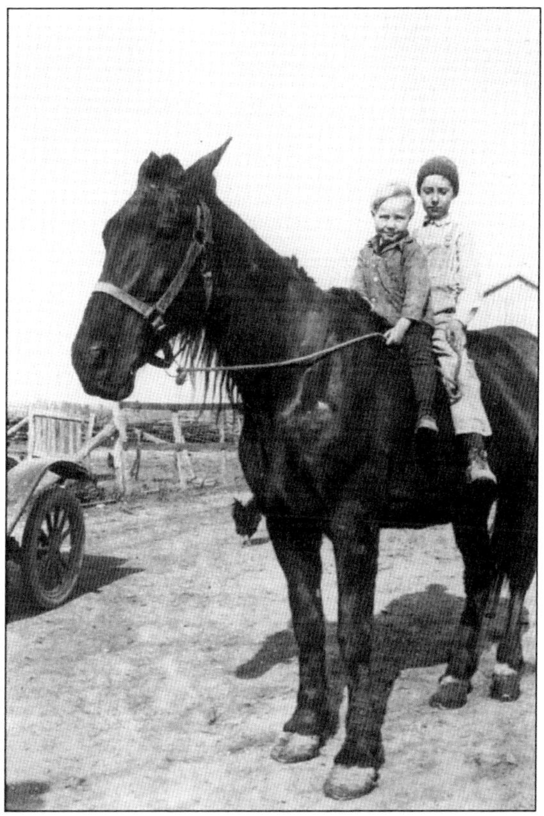

**Horse and Riders.** Before there were trains, trolleys, or automobiles, there were horses. (Courtesy Of William H. King Jr.)

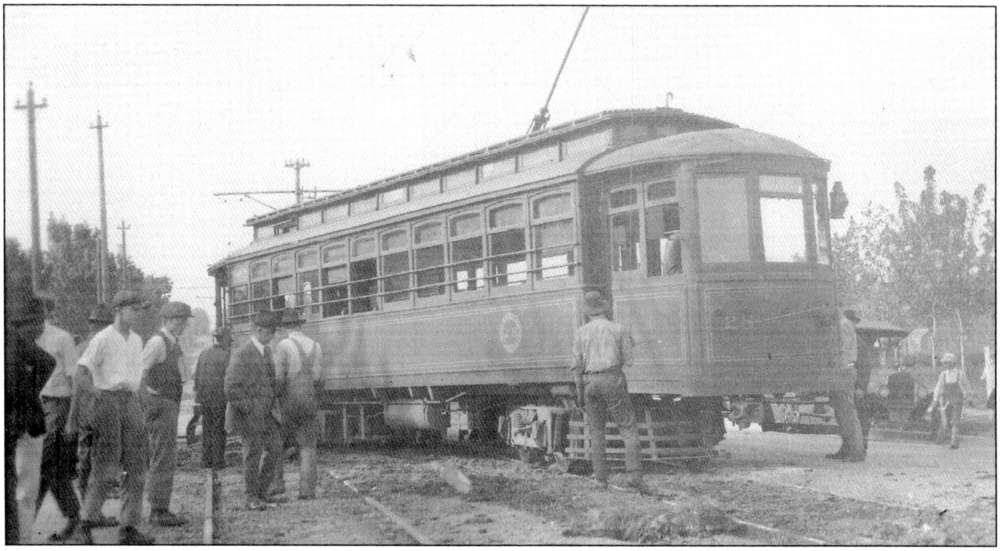

**Derailed by a Dog, May 1920.** The derailment, on Fourth and Madison Streets, occurred when car No. 28 hit a dog and jumped the tracks. Damage was limited to a pole. (Courtesy of the Bob King Collection.)

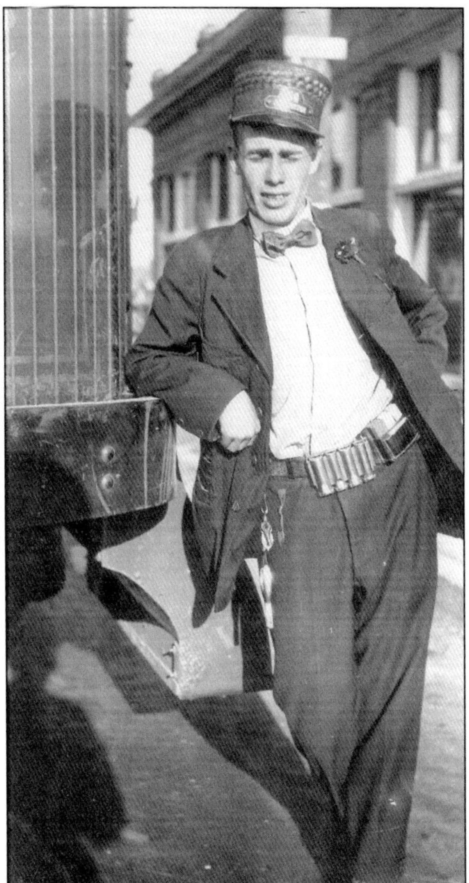

**Streetcar Conductor, 1919.** Standing beside his streetcar is conductor Tommy Hafford. He is an employee of the Southwest Missouri Electric Railway. (Courtesy of the Bob King Collection.)

**Running for the Trolley, 1919.** Osa Featheringill appears to be in a hurry to get to the streetcar. Each streetcar had a motorman to drive the car and a conductor to collect the money and see to the riders. Badges above the bill of their hats signified if they were a motorman or a conductor. (Courtesy of the Bob King Collection.)

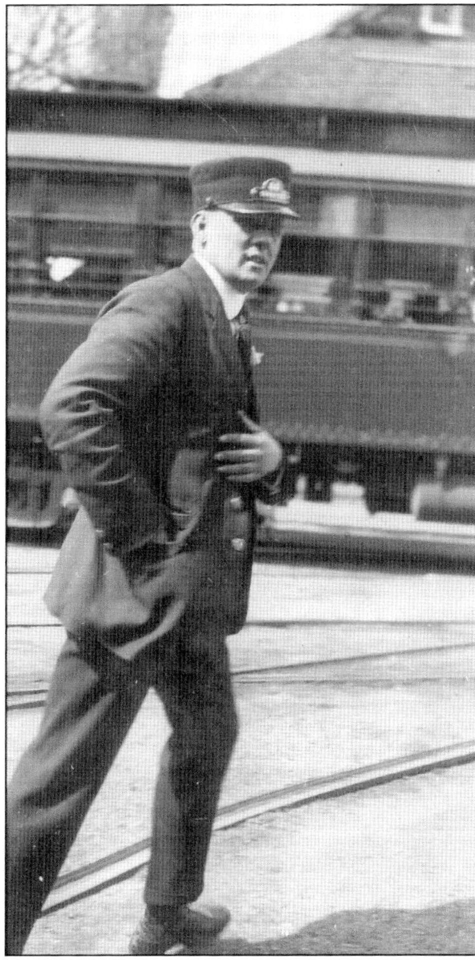

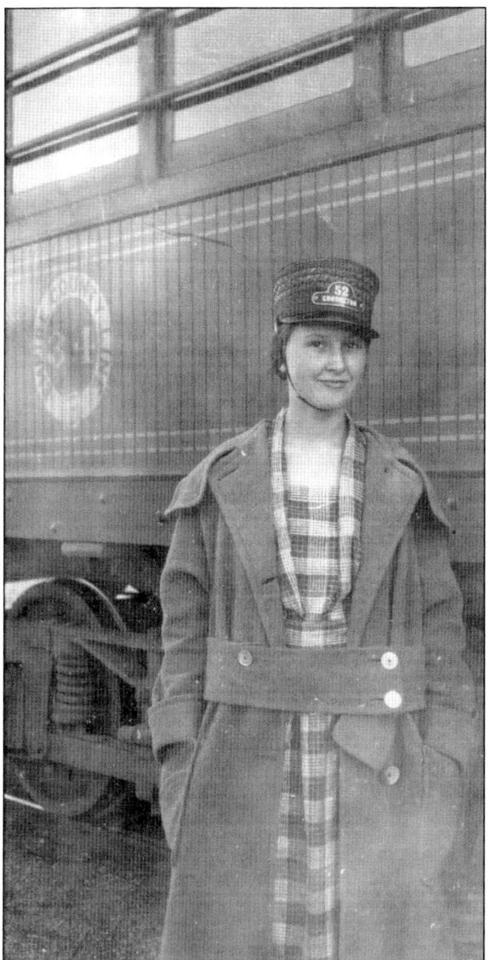


**No Conductor, 1919.** The job of streetcar conductor would not have been considered a proper one for young ladies. It is presumed that the hat does not belong to this woman, Lola Mae Hess. She was the daughter of Homer Hess, an employee of Southwest Missouri Elector Railway. (Courtesy of the Bob King Collection.)

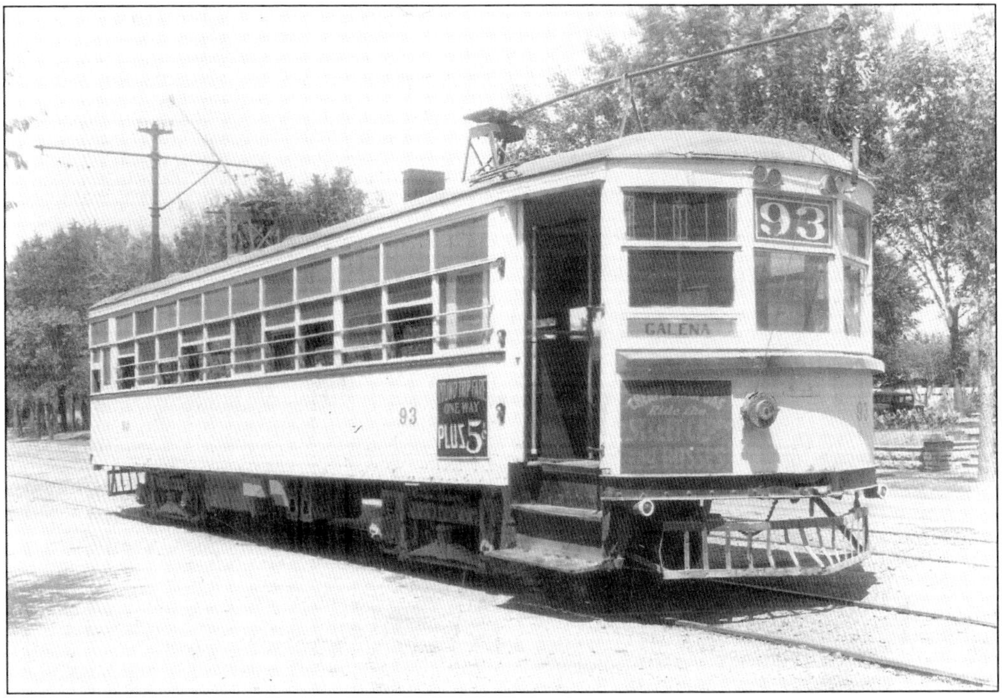


**Streetcar No. 93, 1938.** This car was built in the Webb City shop for the Southwest Missouri Electric Railway one year before all routes were closed. The car has a more modern look than most of the other cars owned by the company. (Courtesy of the Bob King Collection.)

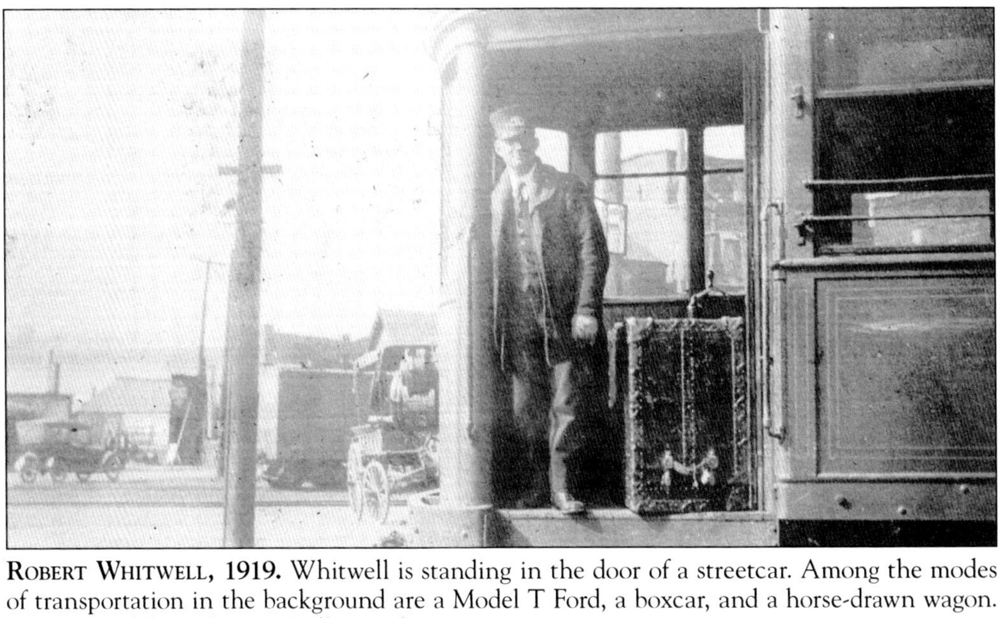

**Robert Whitwell, 1919.** Whitwell is standing in the door of a streetcar. Among the modes of transportation in the background are a Model T Ford, a boxcar, and a horse-drawn wagon. (Courtesy of the Bob King Collection.)

# *Six*

# Route 66

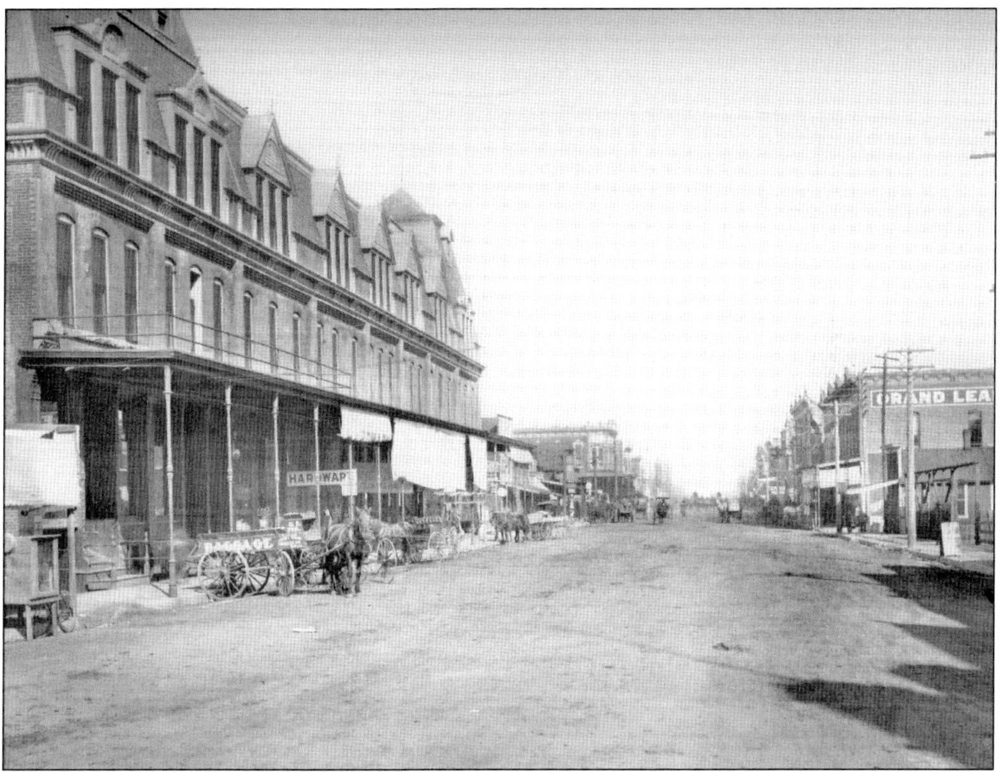

**Allen Street (or Main Street), 1900.** On the far left in this north-facing photograph is the Newland Hotel, located at 22 South Main Street. The hotel was built by James O'Neill and named for his son Robert Newland O'Neill. The luxury hotel had 100 rooms. It was believed to have been fireproof until it burned down. (Courtesy of Missouri Digital Archive.)

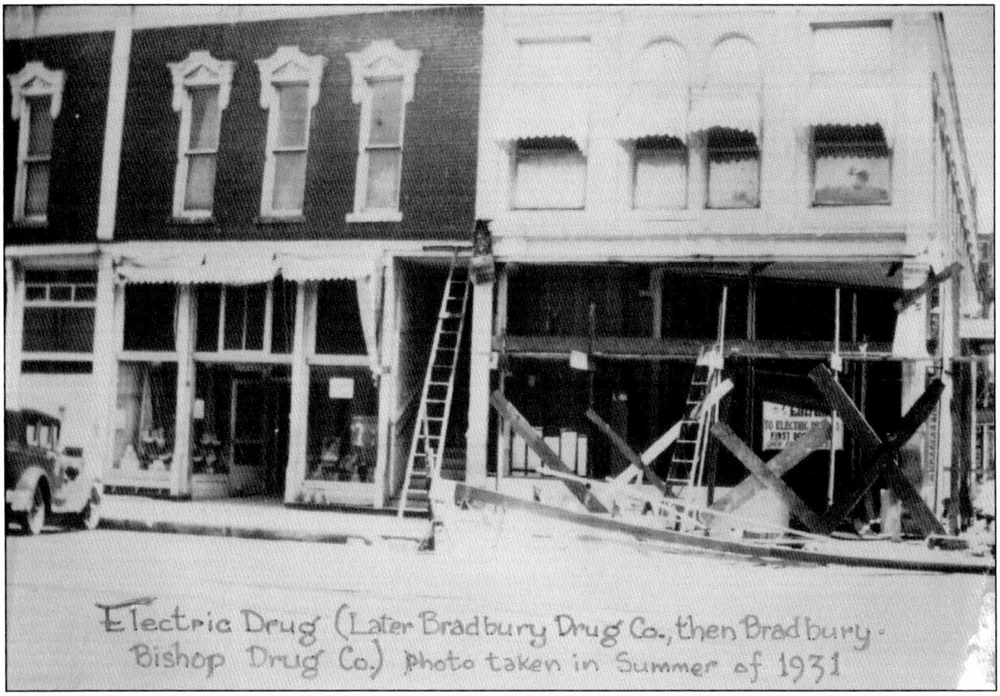


**ELECTRIC DRUG, 1931.** This drugstore, at 201 North Main Street, later became Bradbury Drug Company and then Bradbury Bishop Drug Company. The drugstore is now a vintage icon on Missouri Route 66. (Courtesy of Bradbury Bishop Deli and Route 66 Diner.)

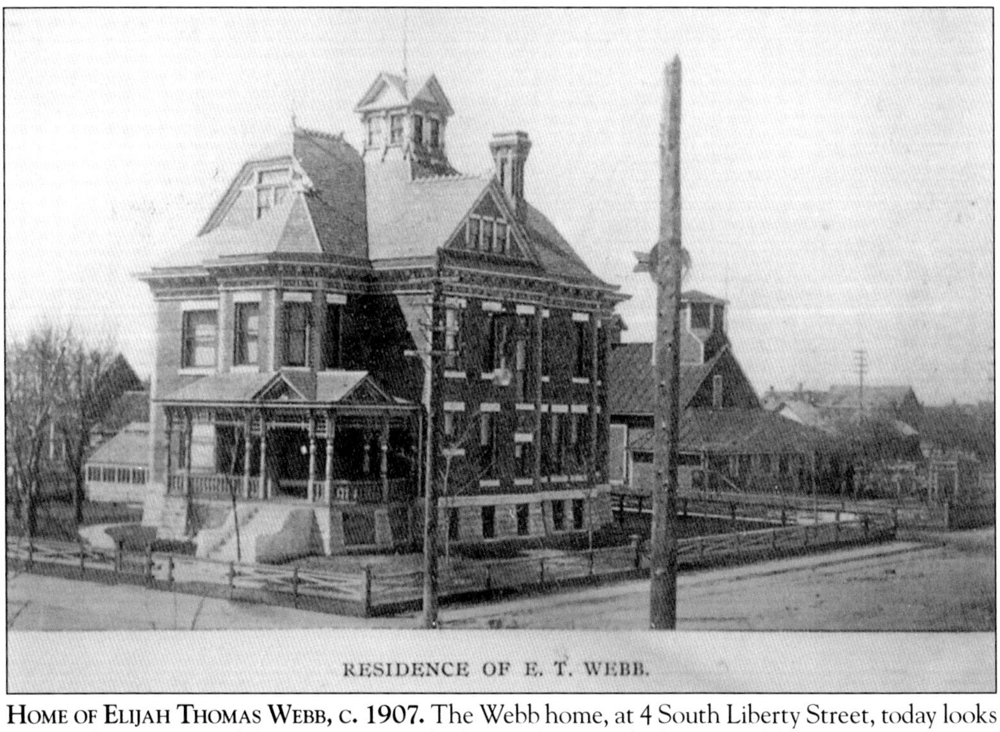


**HOME OF ELIJAH THOMAS WEBB, C. 1907.** The Webb home, at 4 South Liberty Street, today looks almost the same as it did 100 years ago. Elijah was the son of John C. Webb.

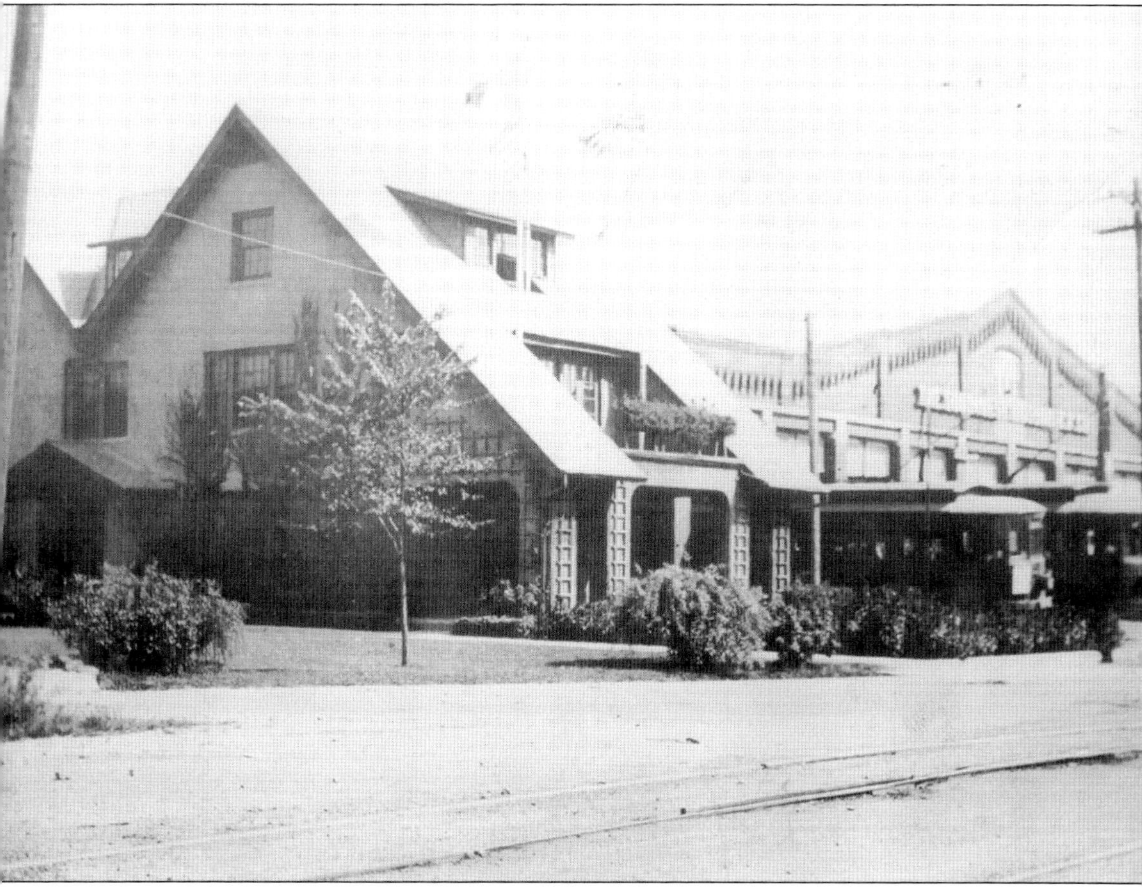

**RAILWAY COMPANY CLUBHOUSE, 1919.** Built in 1910, the Southwest Missouri Electric Railway employees' clubhouse, at 115 North Madison Street, has survived over the years. For the most part, it appears much the same. It has served the community in many different ways, including housing the Jasper County Health Department. Today, it is owned by the Webb City Historical Society. (Courtesy of the Bob King Collection.)

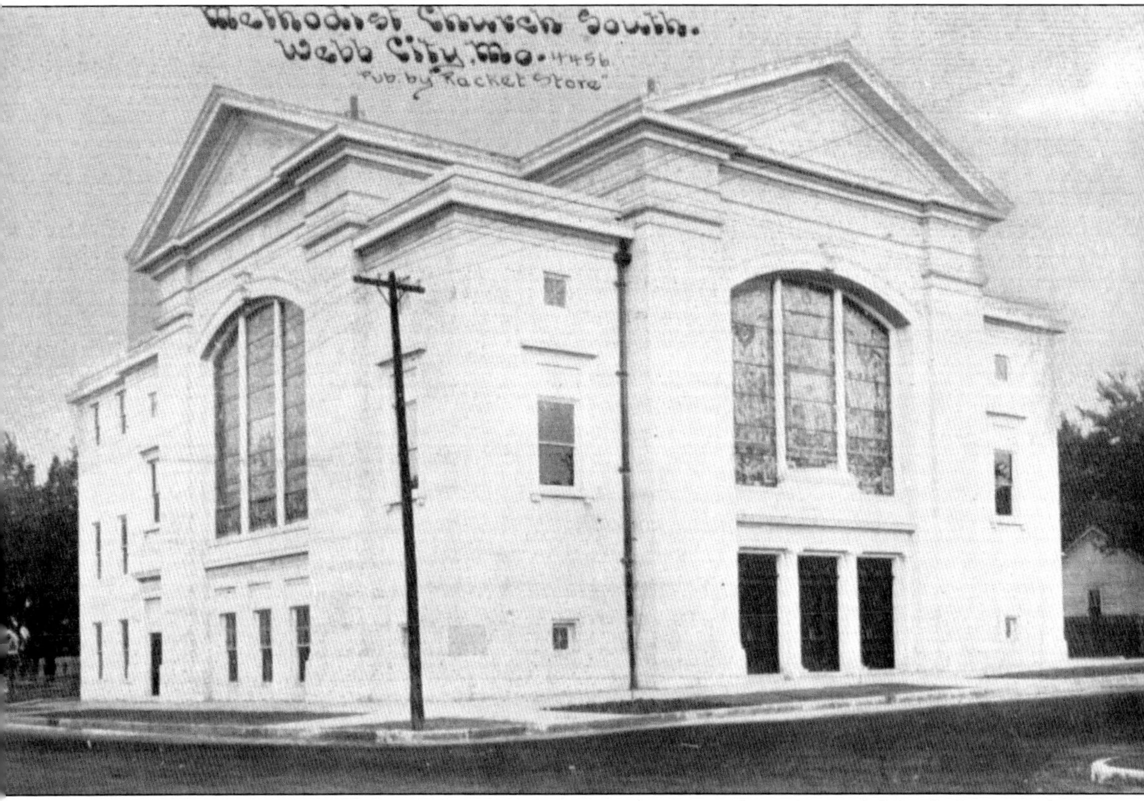


**CENTRAL METHODIST EPISCOPAL CHURCH, 1913.** There are three beautiful lead-glass windows adorning this spectacular church. The church is located at 5 South Pennsylvania Street (Route 66) at the intersection with Daugherty Street. (Courtesy of Missouri Digital Archive.)

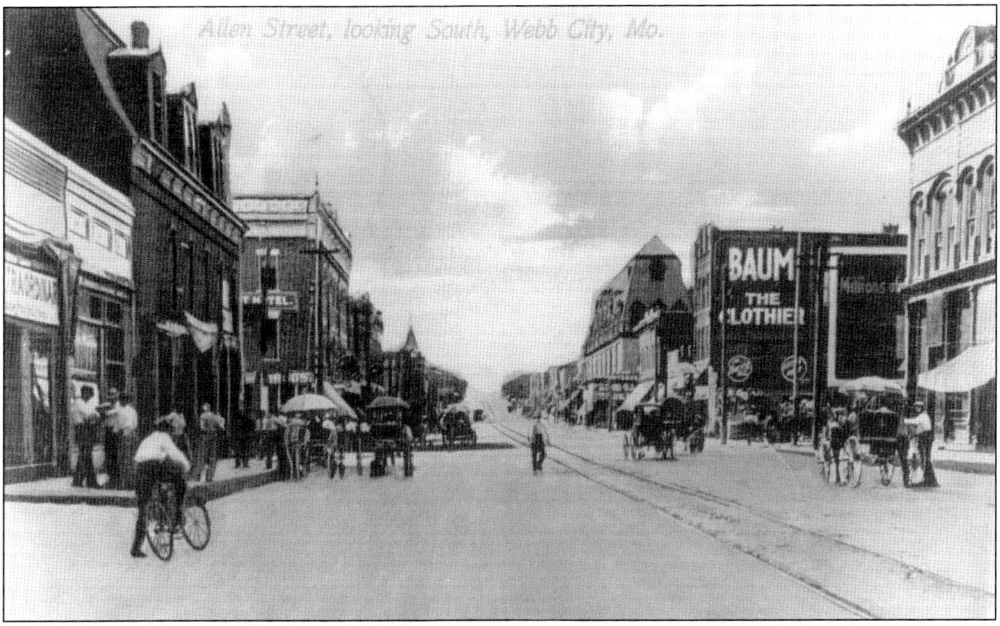


**Allen (Main) Street.** This photograph of Webb City looks south, where Route 66 crossed Main Street in 1926. Route 66 followed Daugherty Street east and then turned south on Madison Street. (Courtesy of Cooper's 66 Eatery.)

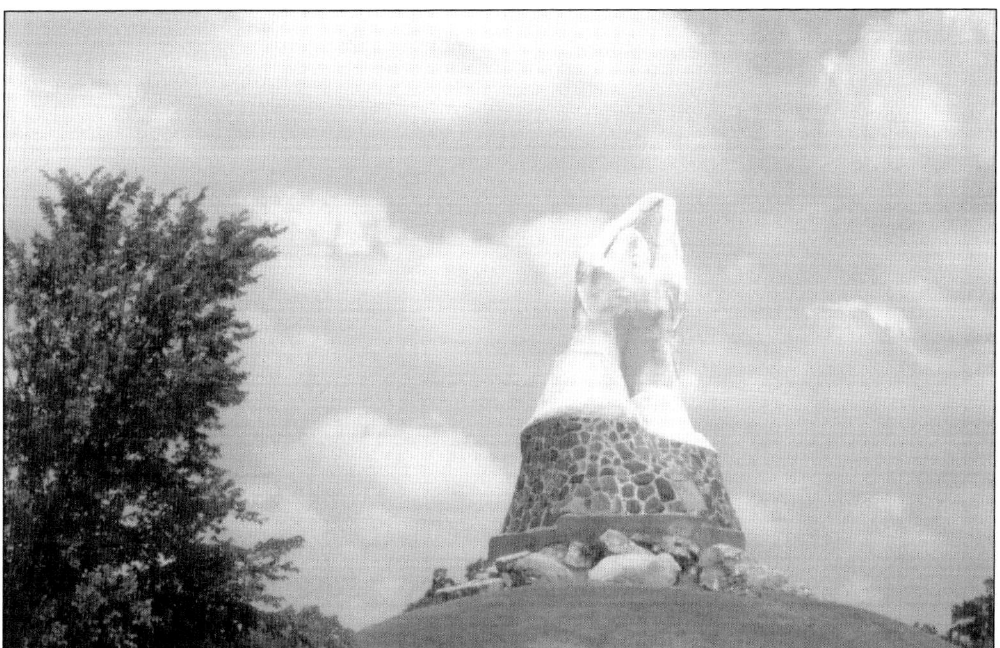

**Praying Hands, 2004.** The *Praying Hands* statue was the creation of artist Jack Dawson. It is 32 feet tall and stands atop a 40-foot-tall man-made hill in King Jack Park. The dedication was held in 1976 during Webb City's centennial.

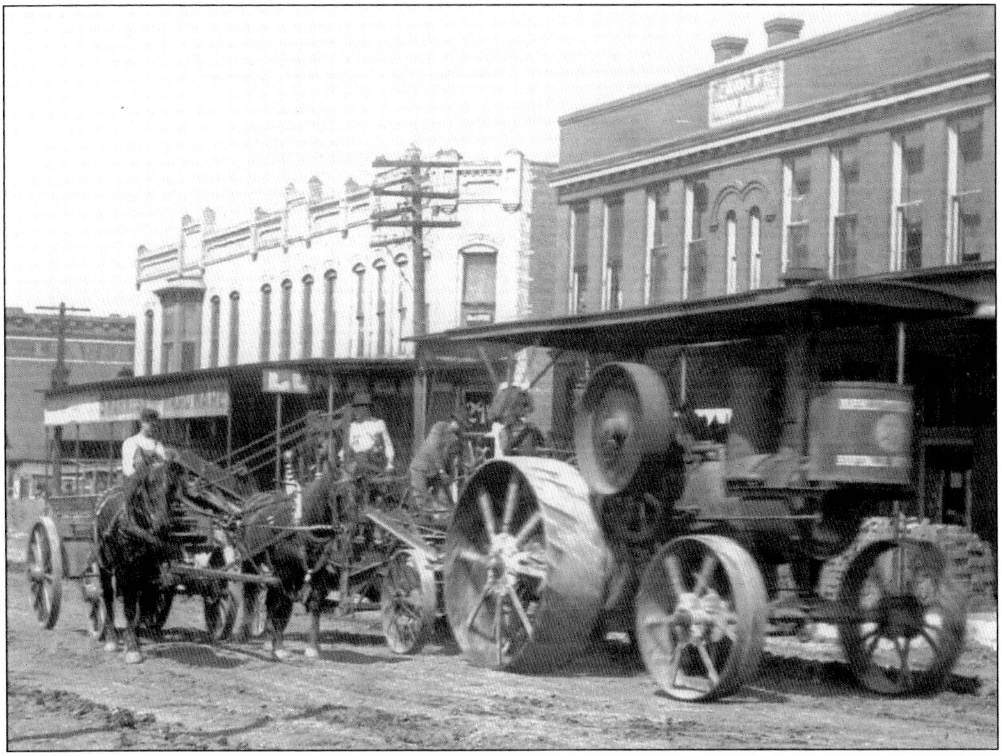

**Steam-Traction Engines.** As Webb City grew, so did the need for public services, including paved streets. In the above photograph, at right, a pile of bricks waits to be put to use in paving the street. The machinery in these photographs cannot be identified with complete confidence, but it is believed to be a Harrison Jumbo steam-traction engine, built in Belleville, Illinois. The company was established in 1848. (Both, courtesy of Webb City Public Works.)

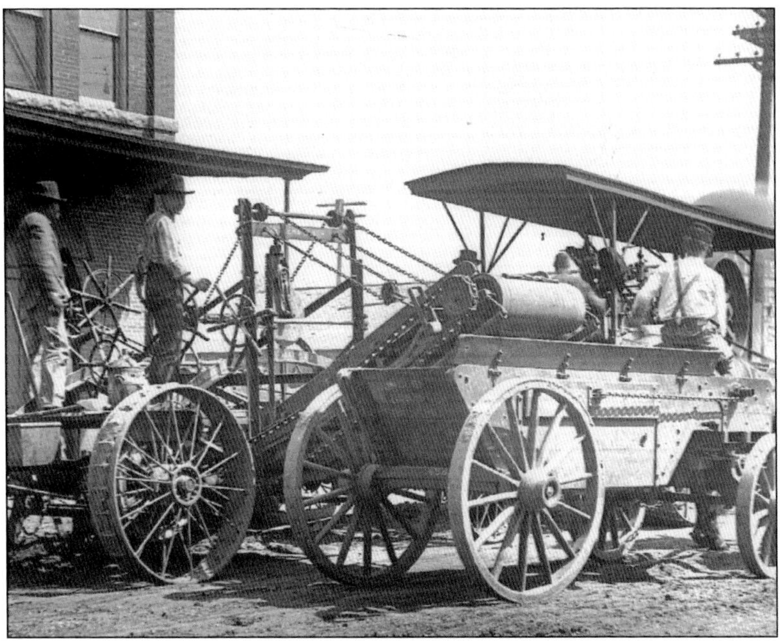

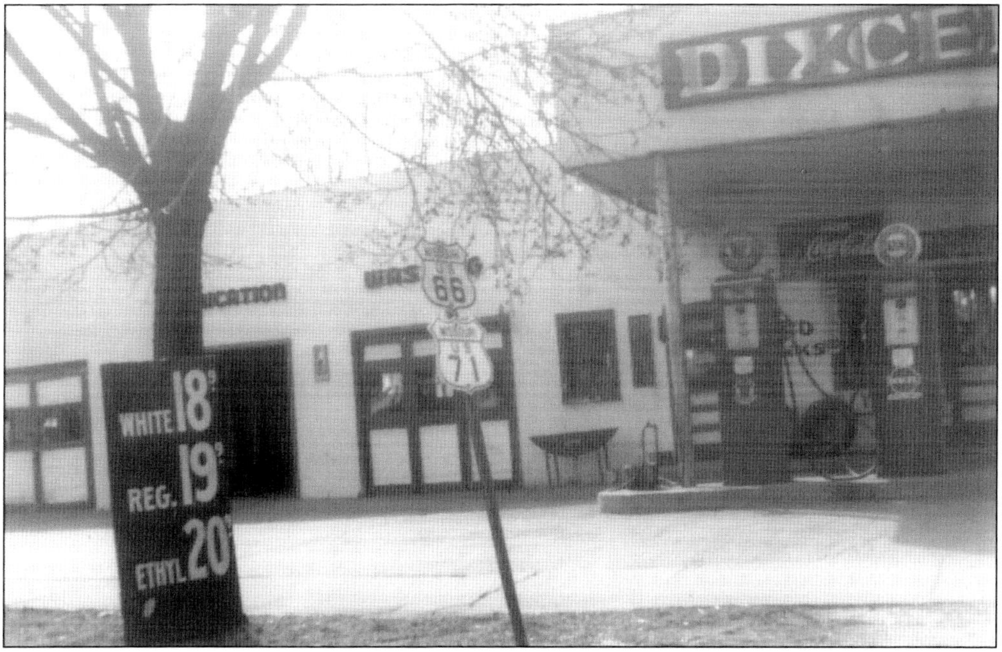


**Gas Station, Route 66.** This photograph indicates that Route 66 going east-west overlapped with Route 71 going north-south in Webb City. Both highways were built in 1926. (Courtesy of the Webb City Route 66 Visitors Center.)

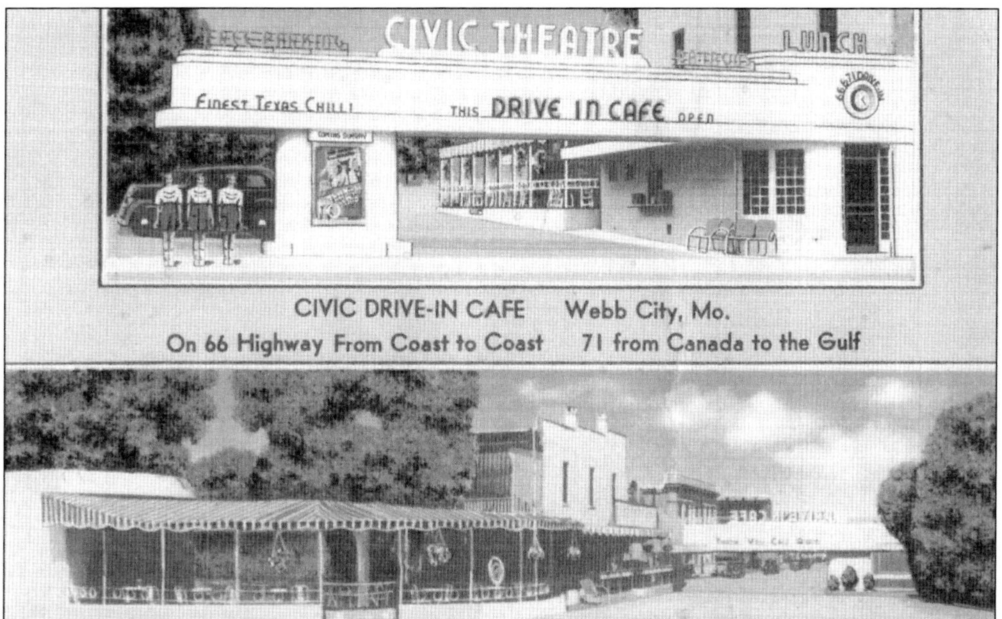


**Civic Theatre.** This theater and drive-in café were popular spots for travelers on Route 66. Carhops served hamburgers and chili on window trays. (Courtesy of the Webb City Route 66 Visitors Center.)

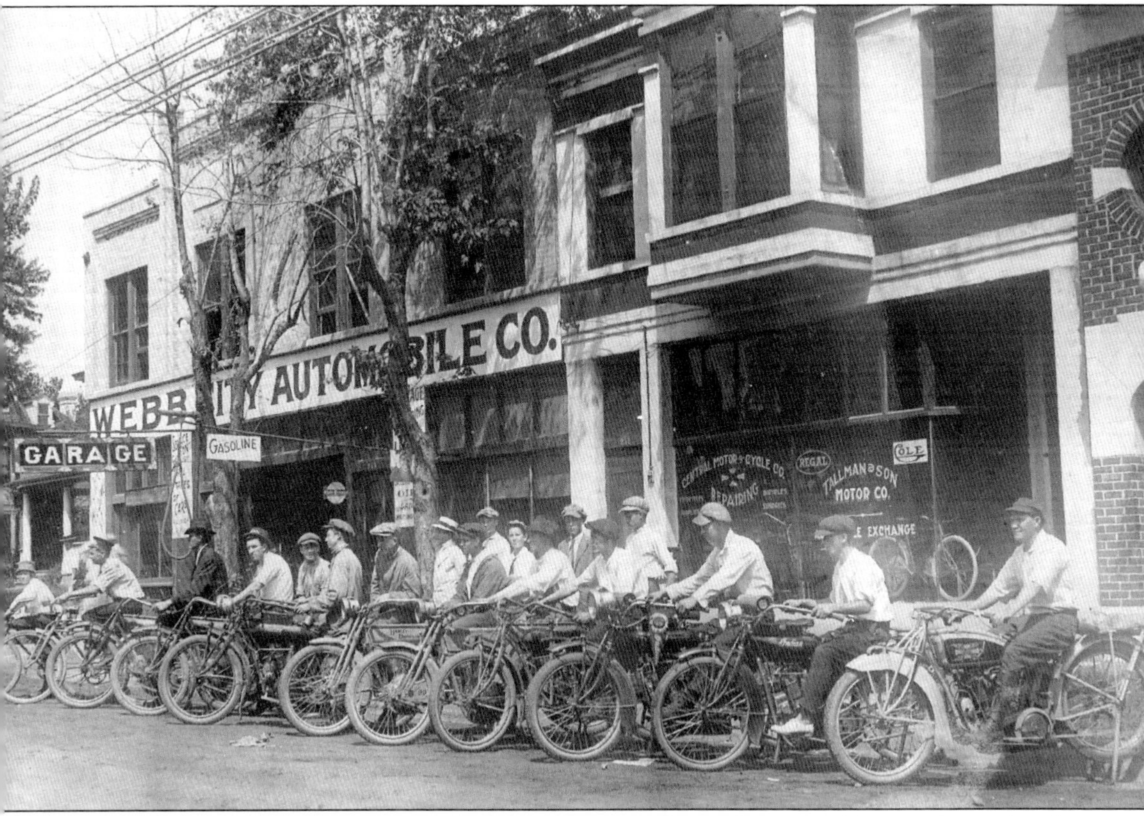


**Motorcycles in Front of the Central Motor and Cycle Company.** Motorcycles are lined up in front of the store. The vehicles have emblems of Harley Davidson and Indian. Indian Motorcycle was America's first motorcycle company. Established in 1901, the company has gone in and out of business over the years. (Courtesy of the Webb City Route 66 Visitors Center.)

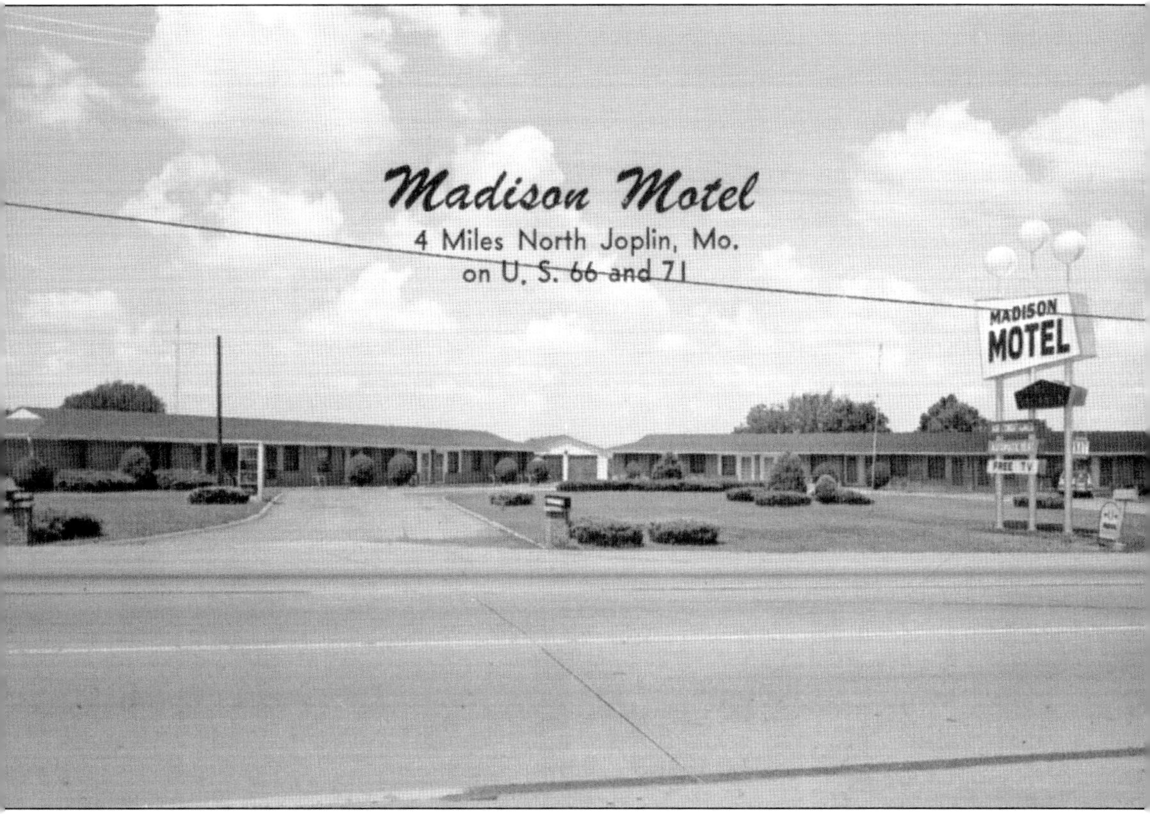


**MADISON MOTEL, ROUTE 66.** The motel shown in this postcard was demolished to build a strip mall in the late 1990s. The postcard identifies the motel as being four miles north of Joplin, although it was within Webb City's city limits.

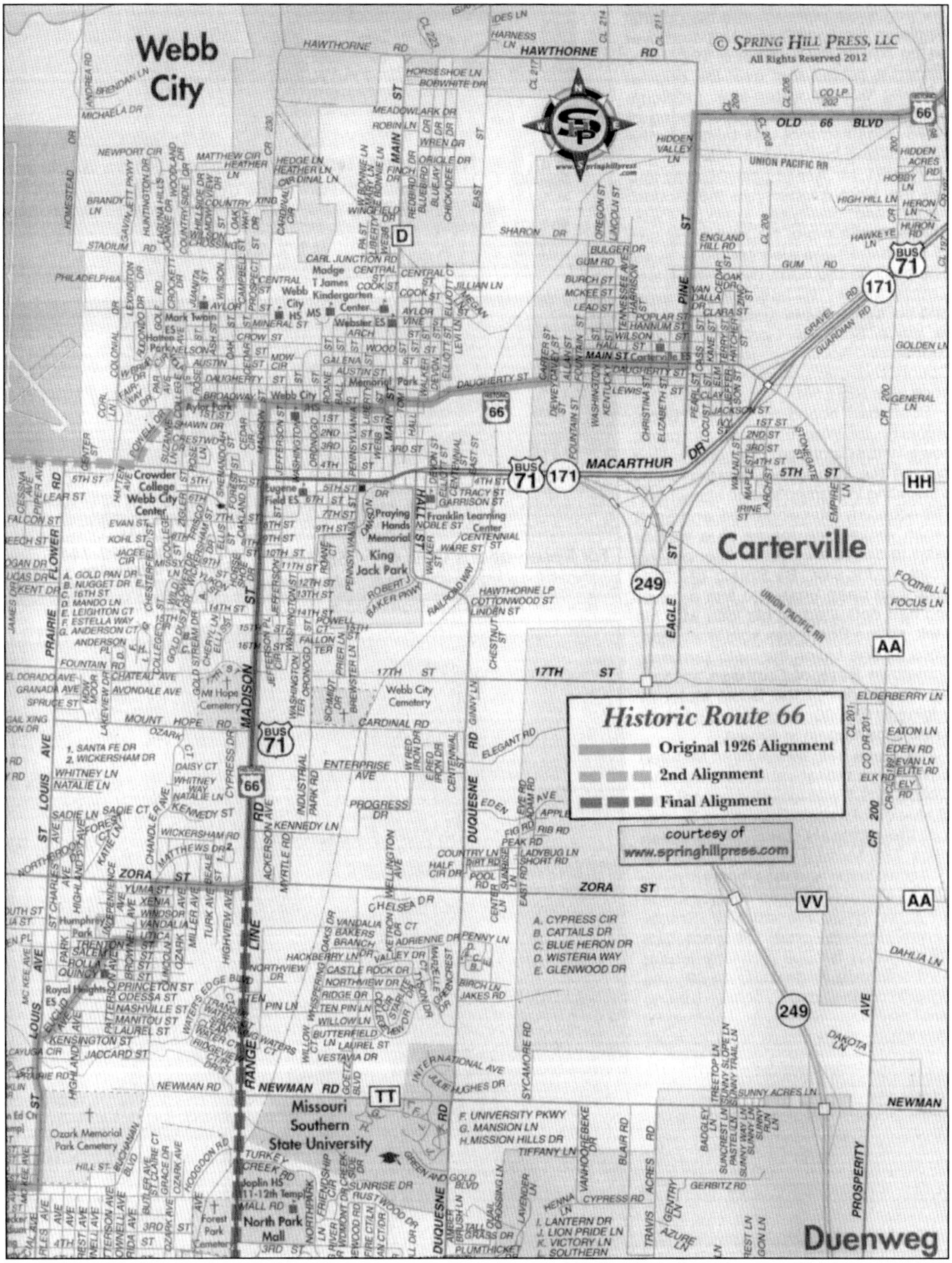


**Route 66 in Webb City.** The original 1926 route is marked with a solid gray line. This map shows how Route 66 followed existing streets through town. (Courtesy of the Webb City Route 66 Visitors Center.)

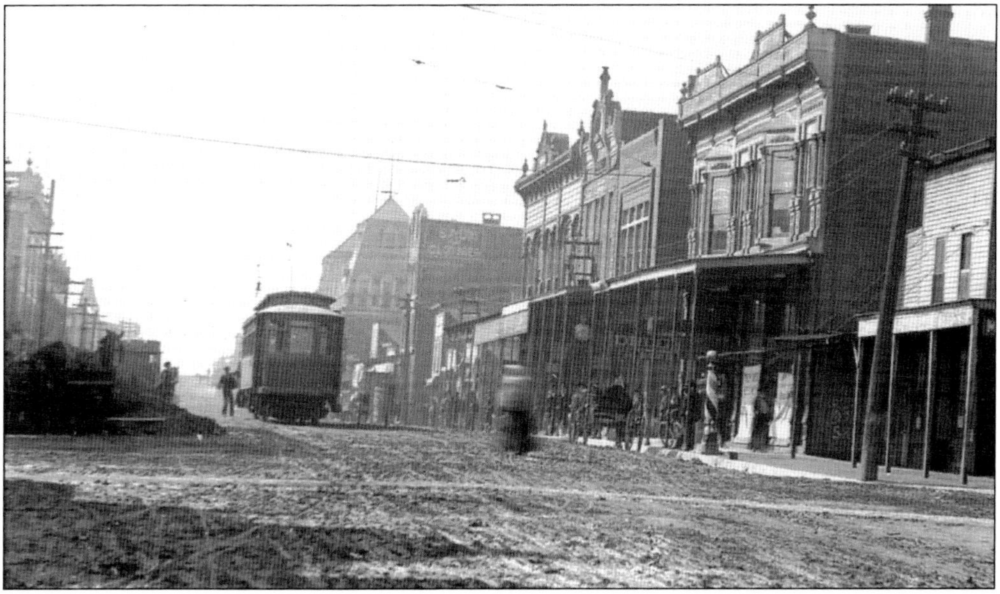

**MAIN STREET, C. 1890.** This photograph of Main Street in Webb City looks south toward the Newland Hotel. The trolley must be horse-drawn, because there is no rail evident. (Courtesy of Webb City Public Works.)

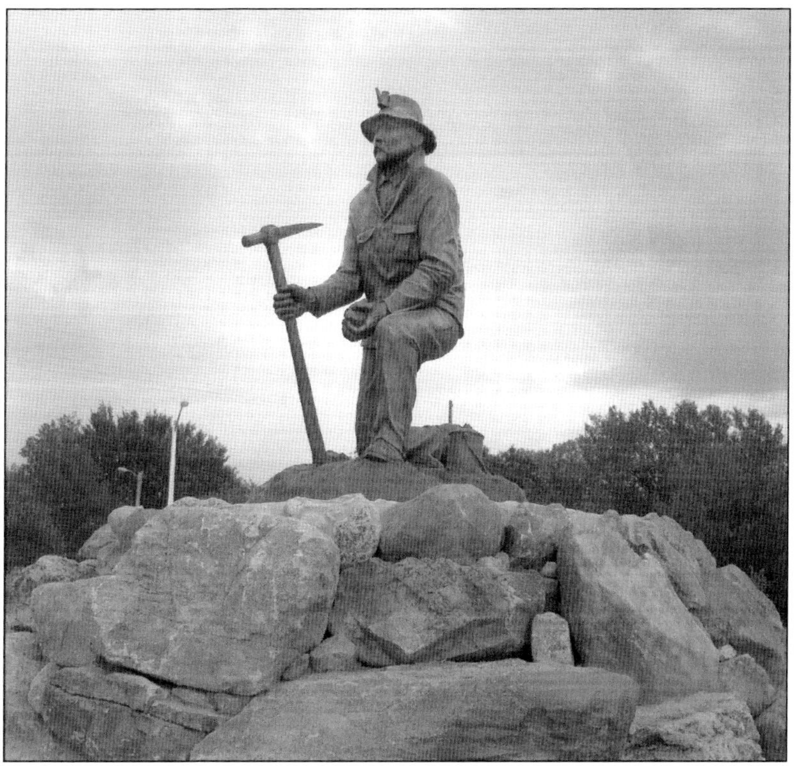

***THE KNEELING MINER*, 2009.** Located in King Jack Park on Route 66, *The Kneeling Miner* was created by Webb City artist Jack Dawson. The statue stands 10 feet tall and was dedicated to hard-rock miners at a Mining Days celebration in 2006.

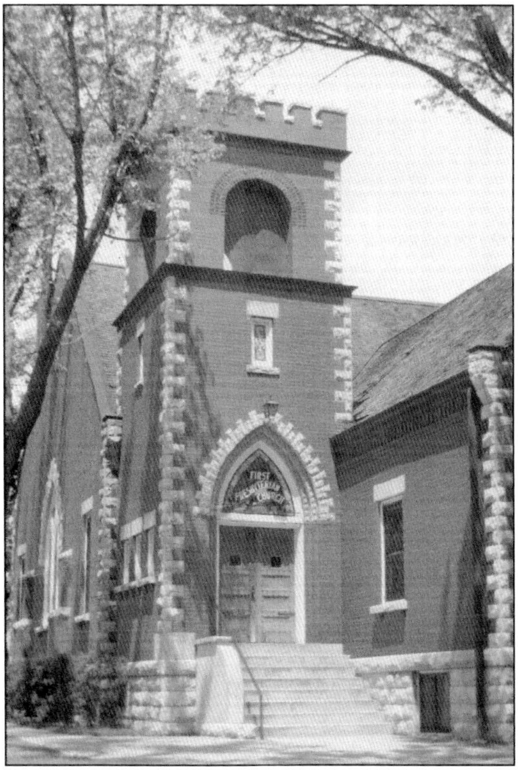


**PRESBYTERIAN CHURCH.** This beautiful red-brick church stands directly on Route 66 at 511 West Broadway. The church, seen here on a postcard, was established in March 1877, one year after the city was founded.

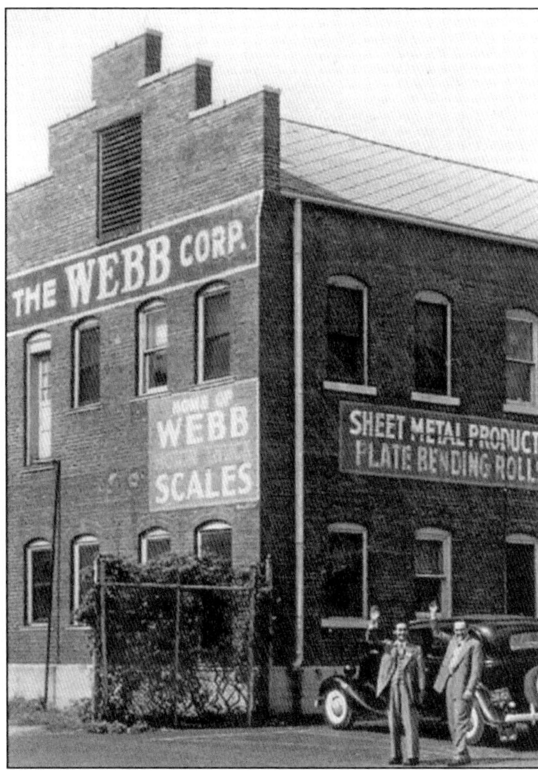


**WEBB CORPORATION, C. 1940.** The company is one of the oldest businesses in Webb City. Over the years, it has gone by different names. Manufacturing sheet-metal products is its main endeavor. Today, it still does business at the Route 66 location. (Courtesy of the Webb Corporation.)

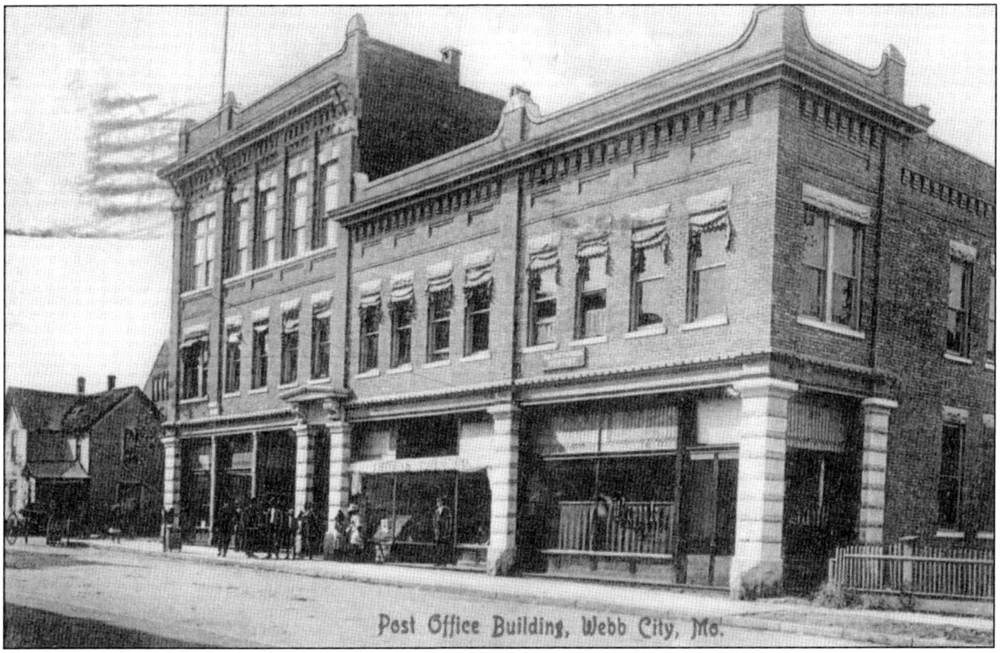


**WEBB CITY POST OFFICE, 1905.** Route 66 crosses Main Street, runs for a short distant on Webb Street in front of the old post office, and then turns east on Daugherty Street. The post office seen on this postcard, at 106 Webb Street, operated until 1916, when the present post office opened.

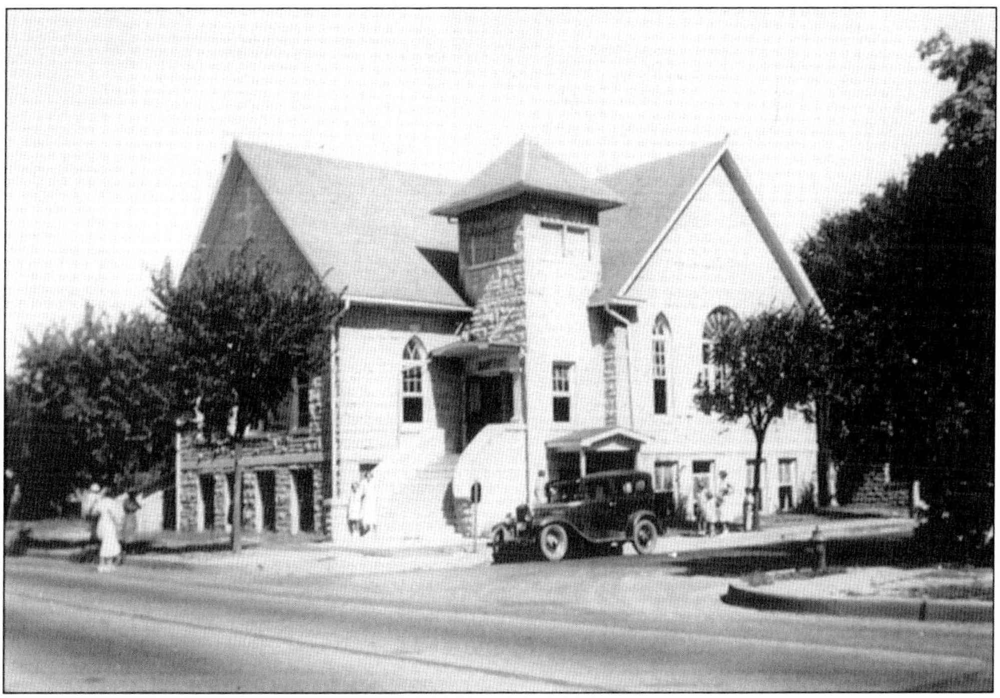

**FIRST BAPTIST CHURCH OF WEBB CITY, 1940.** This church was established in 1883 at the corner of Roane and Broadway Streets. A new, larger church was built on the same site 100 years later.

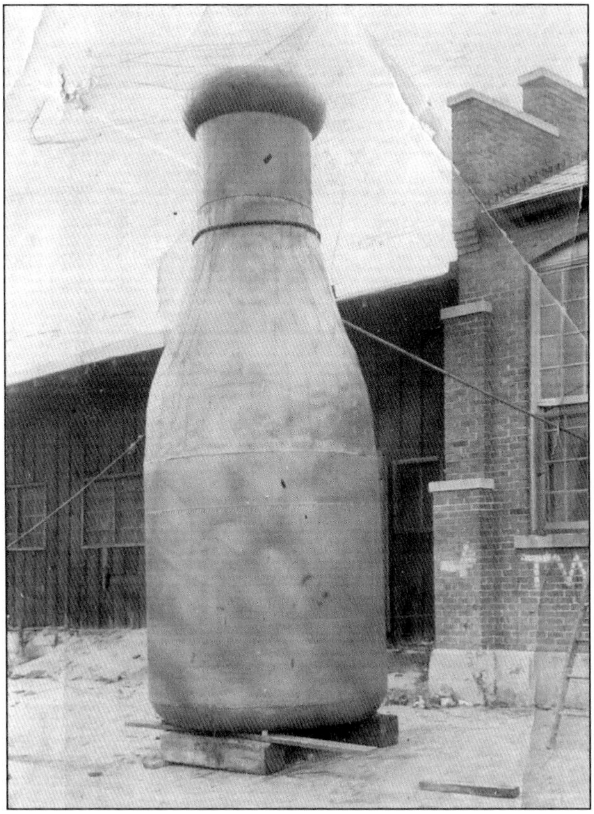

**GIANT STEEL MILK BOTTLE.** This giant bottle was made from 83 pieces of steel and has a capacity of 12,000 gallons. It was made at the Webb City Foundry by Earl Barton and George Hickam. (Courtesy of the Webb Corporation.)

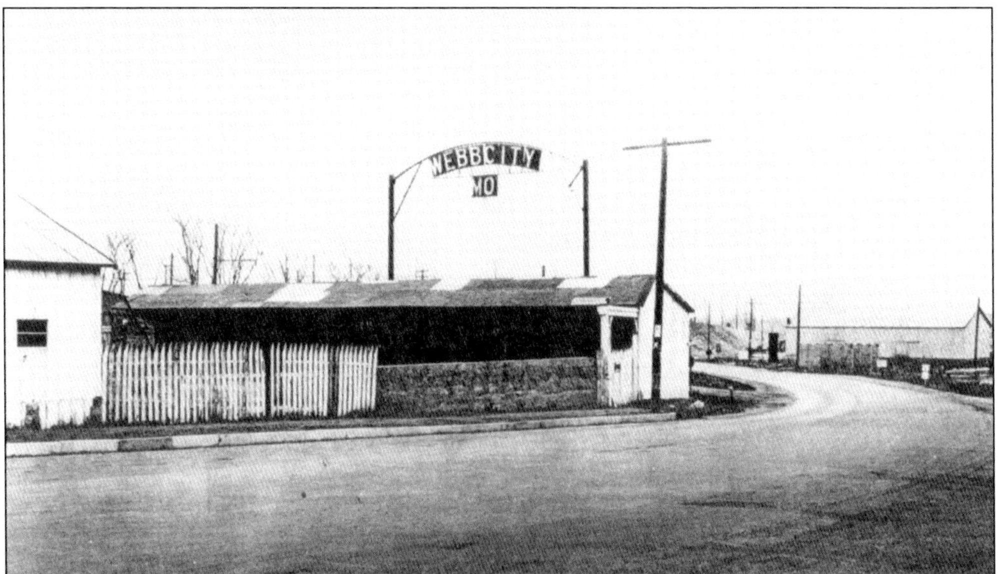


**WEBB CITY EAST SIDE SIGN, 1909.** Daugherty Street (Route 66) is seen in this photograph, looking east toward Carterville; the sign is actually one block north of this spot. Also shown here is Matthew Lumber Yard, across the street from Webb City and Carterville Foundry & Machine Works. (Courtesy of the Webb Corporation.)

# *Seven*

# The Outskirts

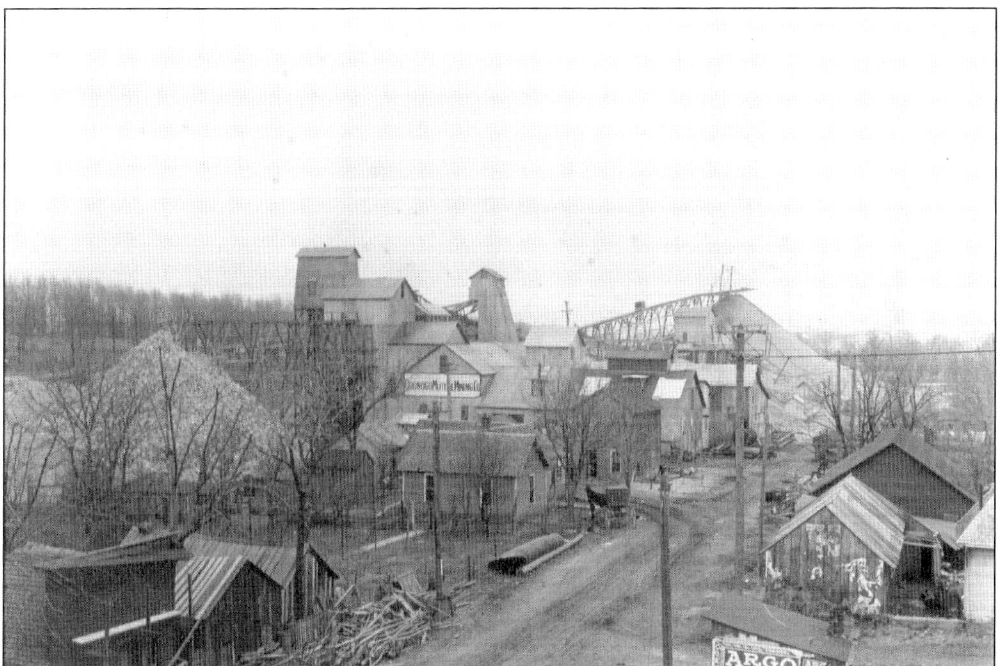


**Main Street in Oronogo, Missouri.** Folklore from the area states that the name Oronogo was made up by the miners. Their housing was portable, so if ore was not found, the miners would not relocate, meaning "ore-or-no-go," or Oronogo. This was a saying of miners when they used ore as a currency. (Courtesy of Missouri Digital Archive.)

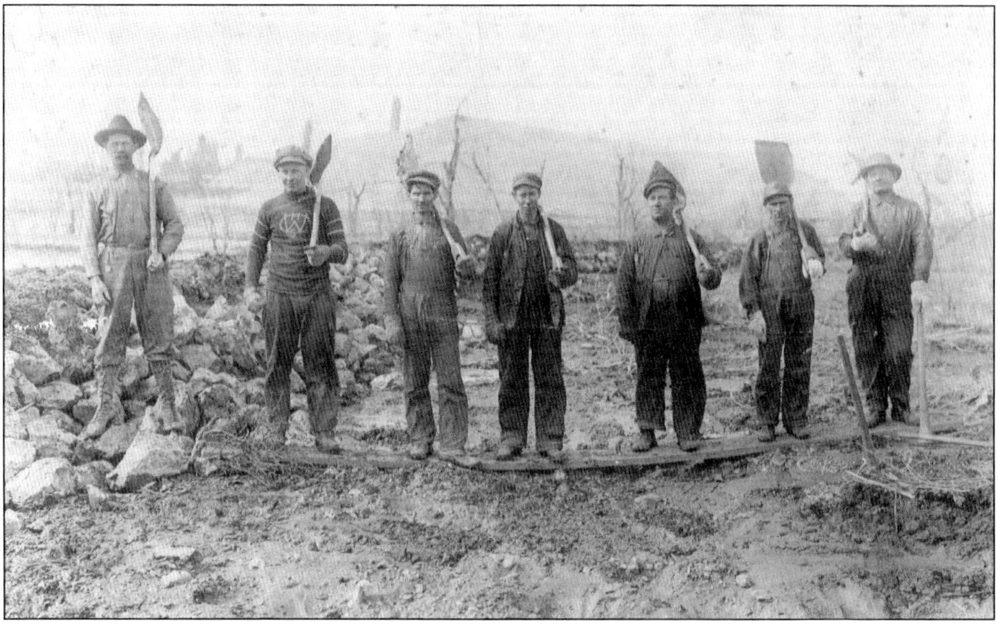

**DAVEY MINE NO. 3 PERSONNEL, CARTERVILLE, 1905.** Water reservoirs were necessary for the milling process. These workers are seen after repairing Mill Pond Dam. The worker on the far left is Dock Riggs. (Courtesy of Missouri Digital Archive.)

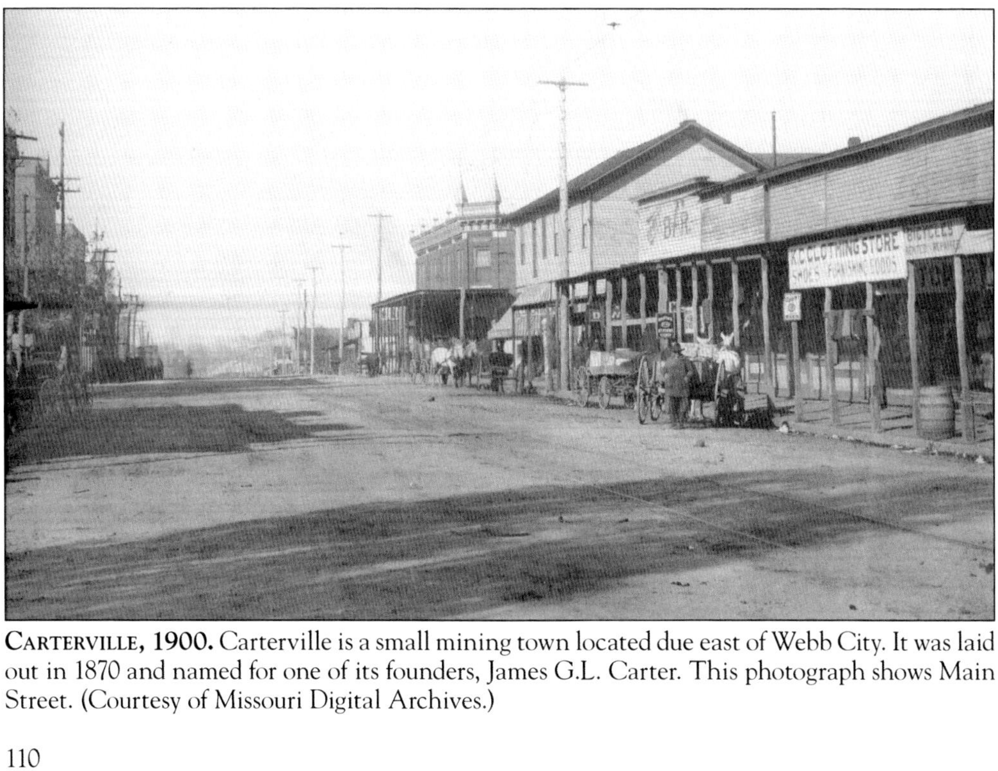


**CARTERVILLE, 1900.** Carterville is a small mining town located due east of Webb City. It was laid out in 1870 and named for one of its founders, James G.L. Carter. This photograph shows Main Street. (Courtesy of Missouri Digital Archives.)

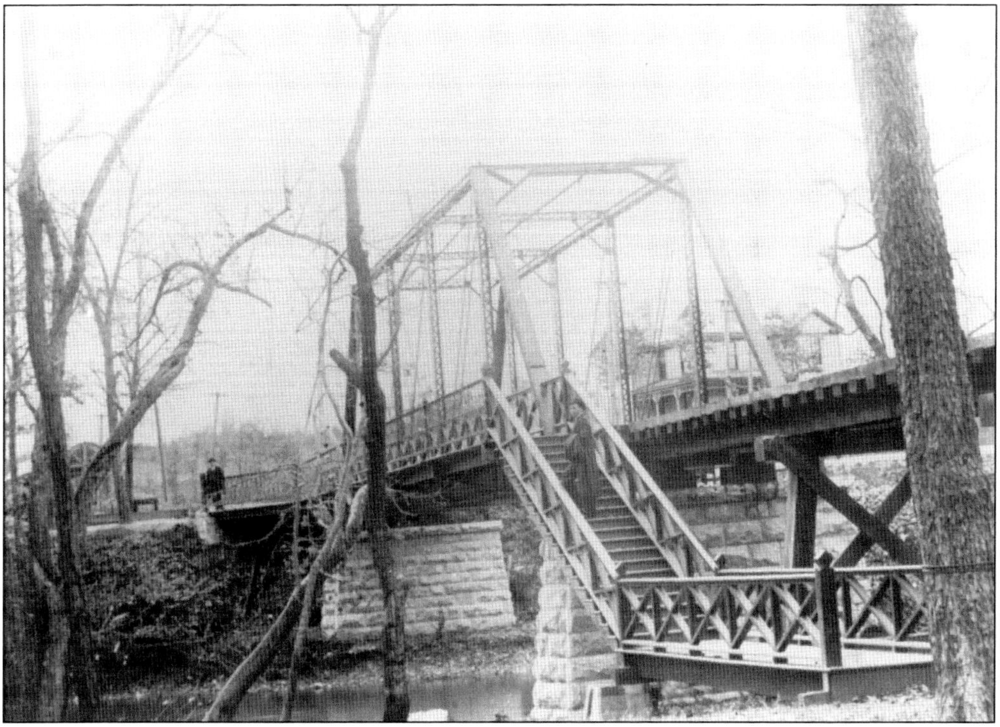

**Bridge at Lakeside Park, 1900.** Facilities at the park included a dance pavilion, movie theater, baseball field, and bathhouses. The park was owned and operated by Southwest Missouri Electric Railway Company. Lakeside Inn is visible in the background, behind the bridge. (Courtesy of Missouri Digital Archive.)

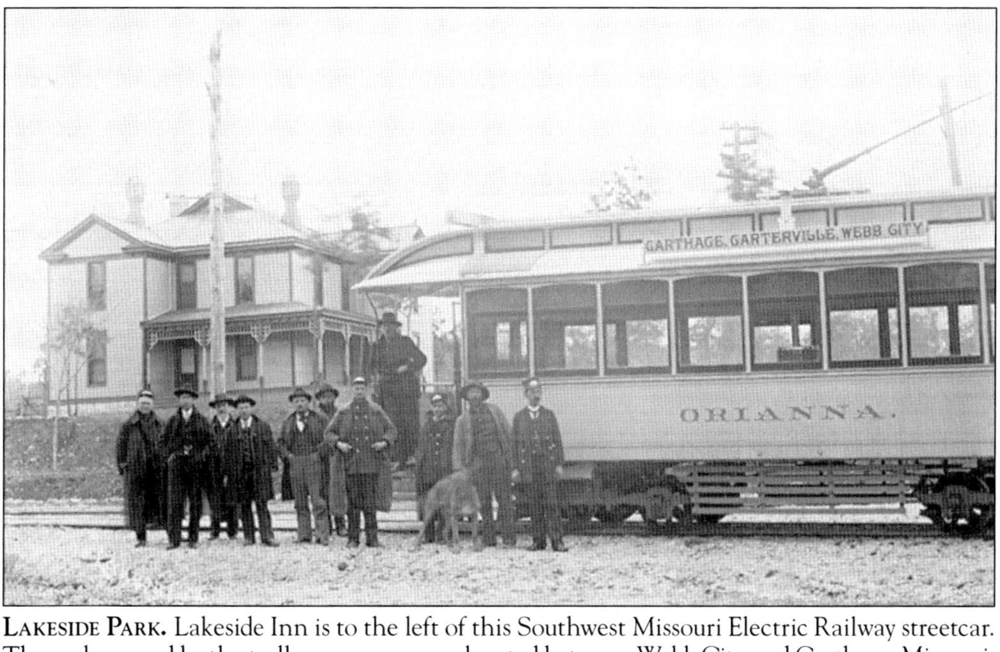


**Lakeside Park.** Lakeside Inn is to the left of this Southwest Missouri Electric Railway streetcar. The park, owned by the trolley company, was located between Webb City and Carthage, Missouri. (Courtesy of the Bob King Collection.)

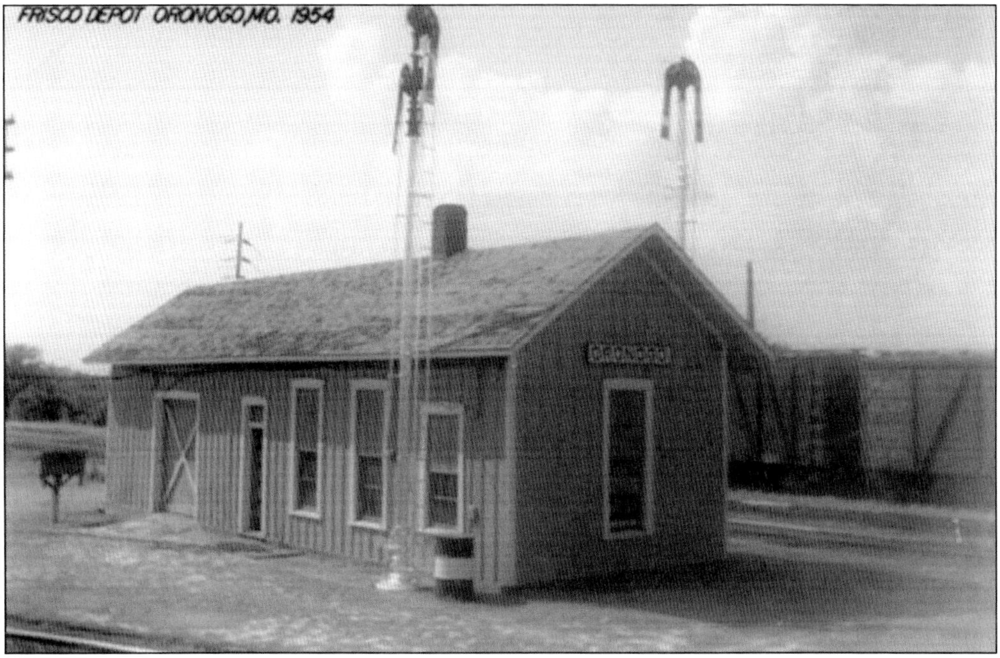


**FRISCO DEPOT, ORONOGO, 1954.** The Frisco Railroad was the first east-west line in the area, and Oronogo was its first depot. The rails on the far left served the traffic coming out of Joplin. The rails on the right served traffic going into Kansas. (Courtesy of Missouri Digital Archives.)

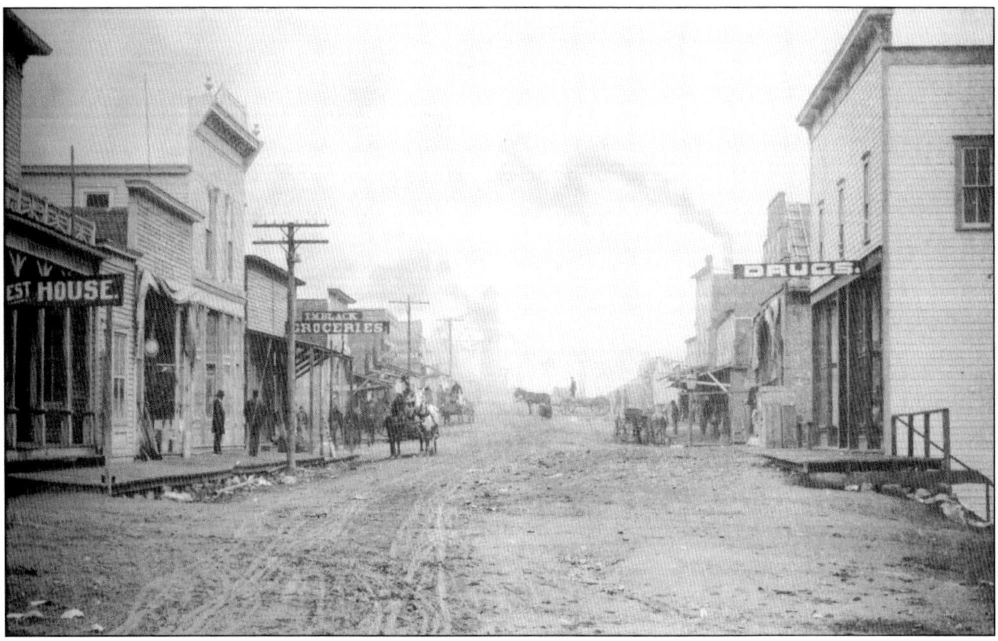


**MINERSVILLE, MISSOURI, 1900.** The city of Oronogo was platted in 1856 and named Minersville. It was renamed after additions were made to the town. The West House Hotel and T.M. Black Groceries identify this as Second Street. (Courtesy of Missouri Digital Archives.)

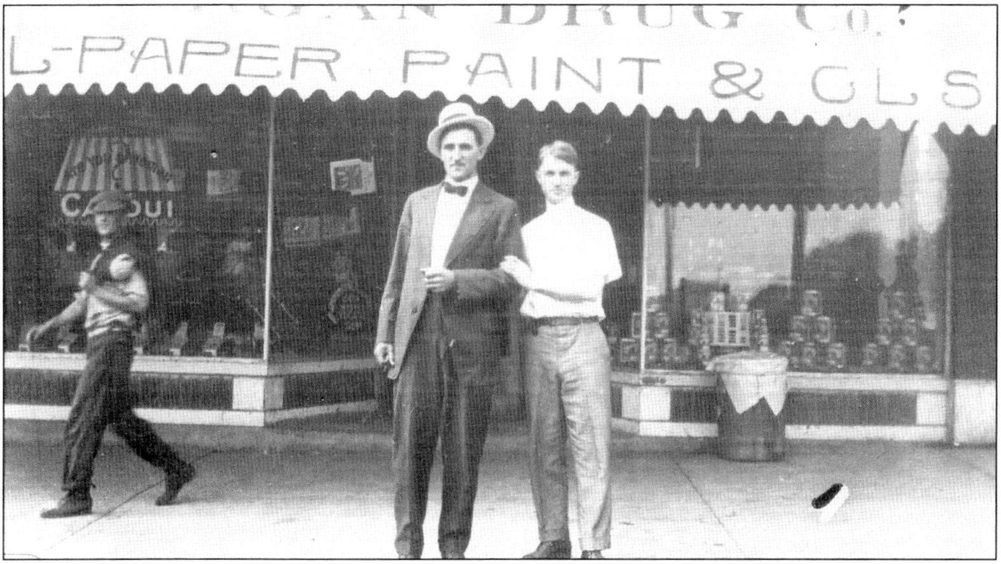


**Morgan Drug Store, Carterville, 1919.** Archie McDoughgall (left) and Jim Morgan, both employees of the Southwest Missouri Electric Railway, stand in front of the Morgan Drug Store. (Courtesy of the Bob King Collection.)

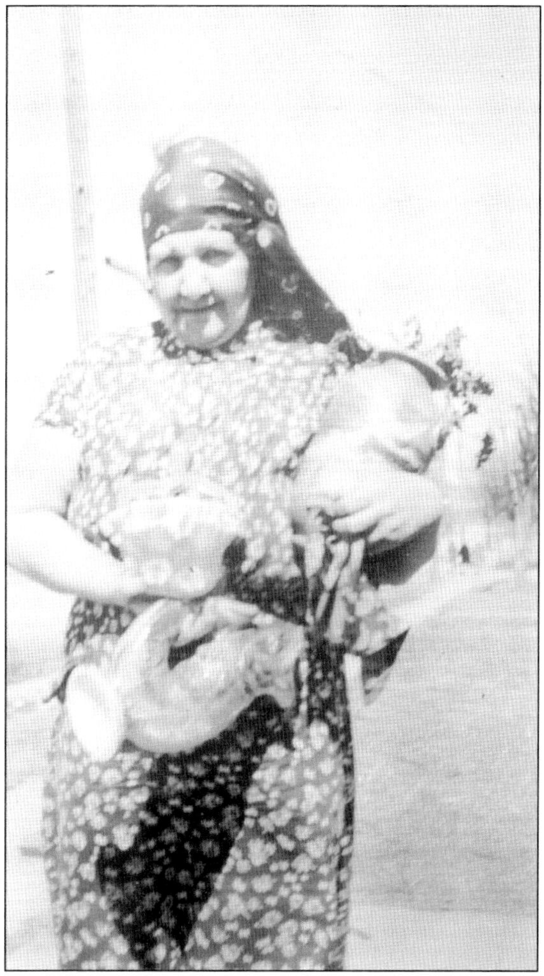

**Pearl May Bulger, Carterville, c. 1950.** Bulger was a Carterville businesswoman and store owner. Here, she is wearing a silk scarf tied around her head. This was very much the style of the day. (Courtesy of Mickey Bulger.)

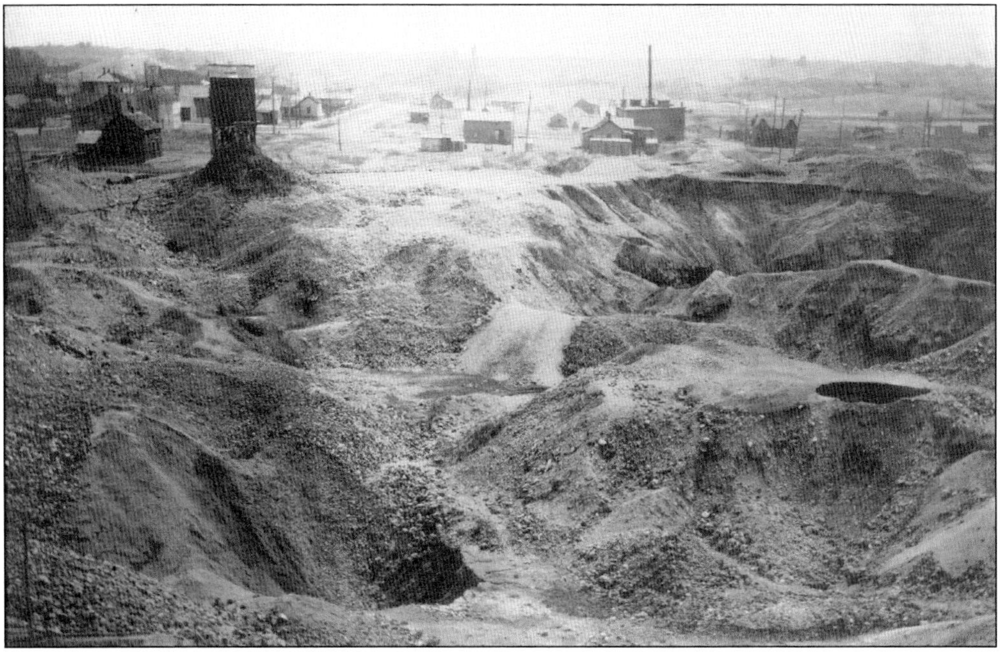

**Orange May Mine.** Even following the Environmental Protection Agency's cleanup, there are still large concrete ruins at this site, located between Webb City and Carterville. (Courtesy of the Missouri Digital Archive.)

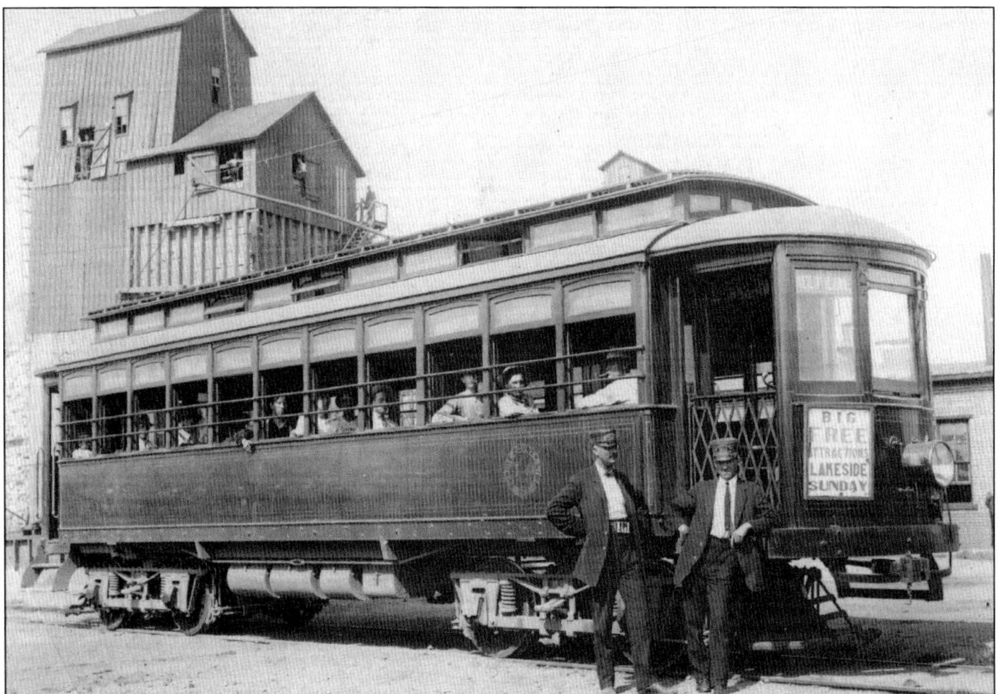


**Streetcar at Davy Mine No. 3, Carterville, 1905.** The trolley system connected the mines of the Tri-State Mine District. It crossed state lines, giving miners transportation to and from their jobs. (Courtesy of Missouri Digital Archives.)

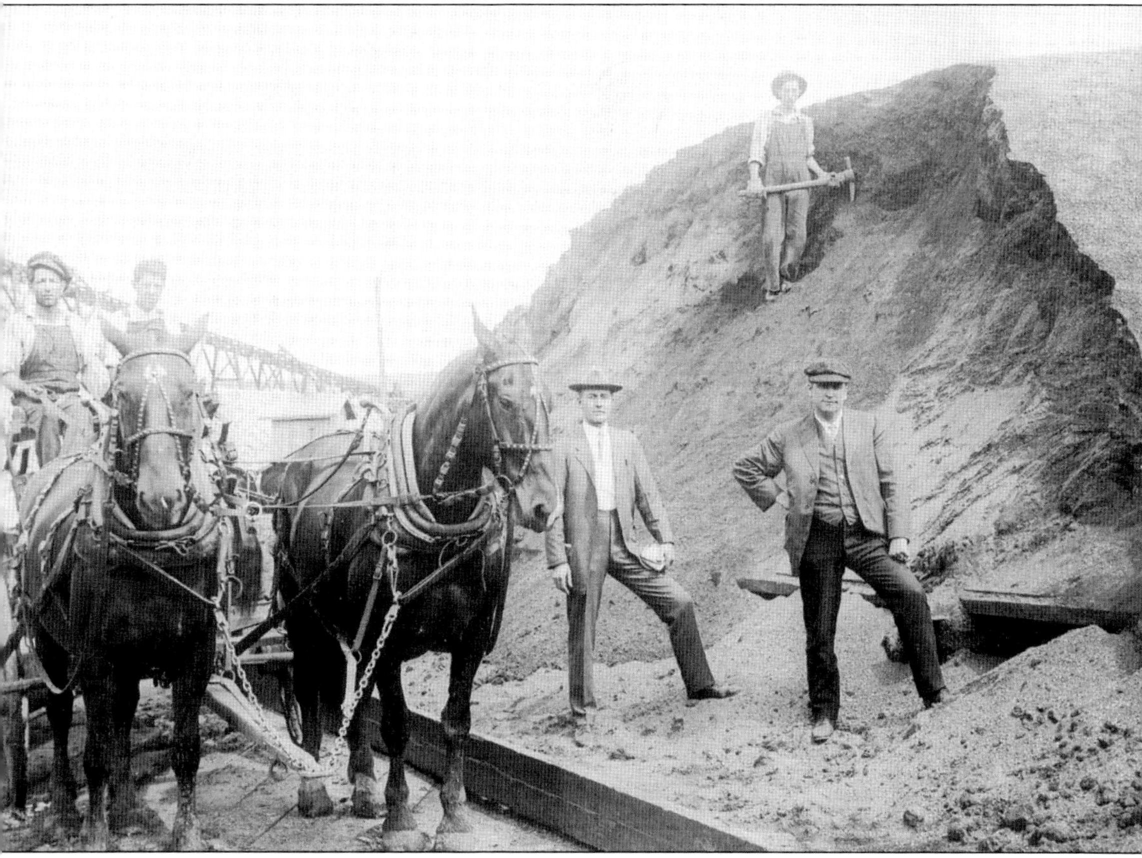

**Jack Wagon and Ore Pile, 1914.** The Davey Mine in Carterville, Missouri, was owned by American Zinc, Lead & Smelting Company. (Courtesy of the Missouri Digital Archive.)

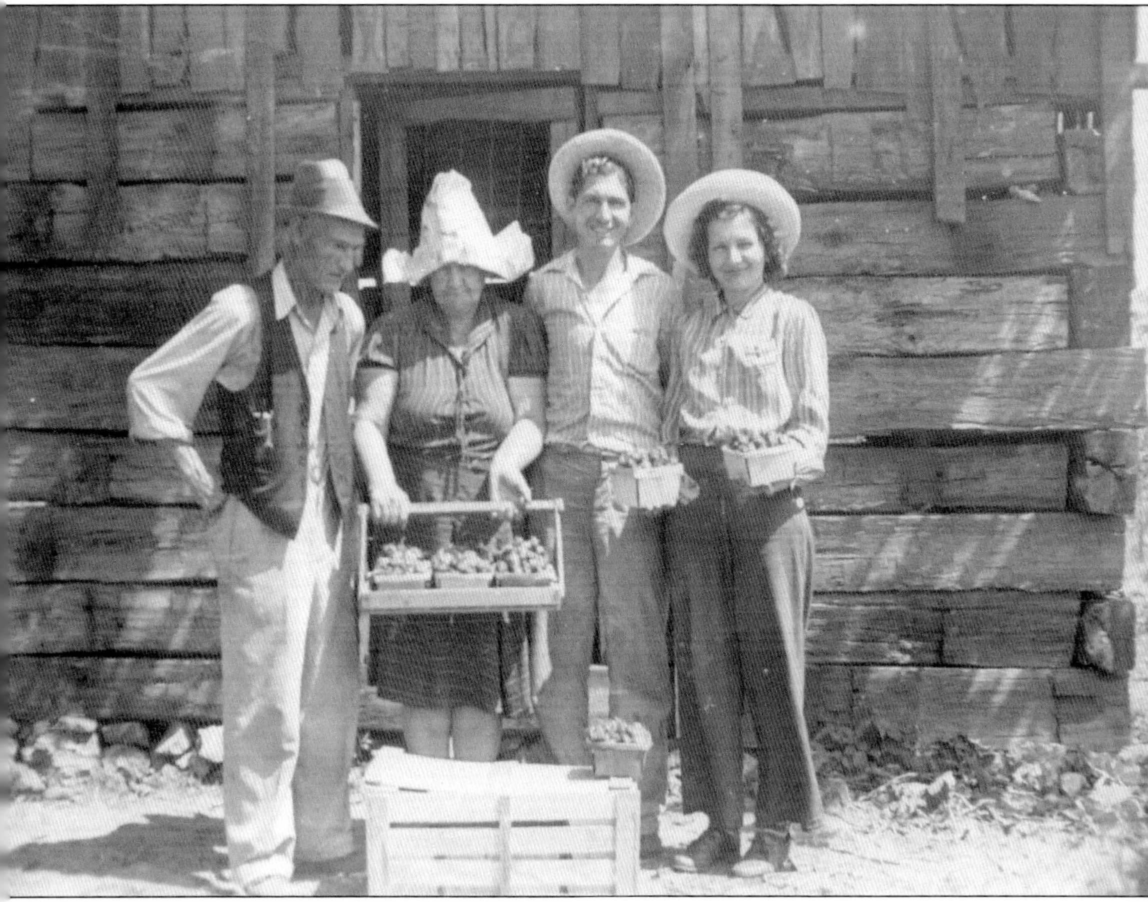

**BULGER FAMILY, C. 1950.** Posing here are, from left to right, Henry Clay Bulger and his wife, Pearl May Bulger, and Judd and Barbara Bulger. They are all wearing big hats to keep the sun off of them as they enjoy strawberry picking. (Courtesy of Mickey Bulger.)

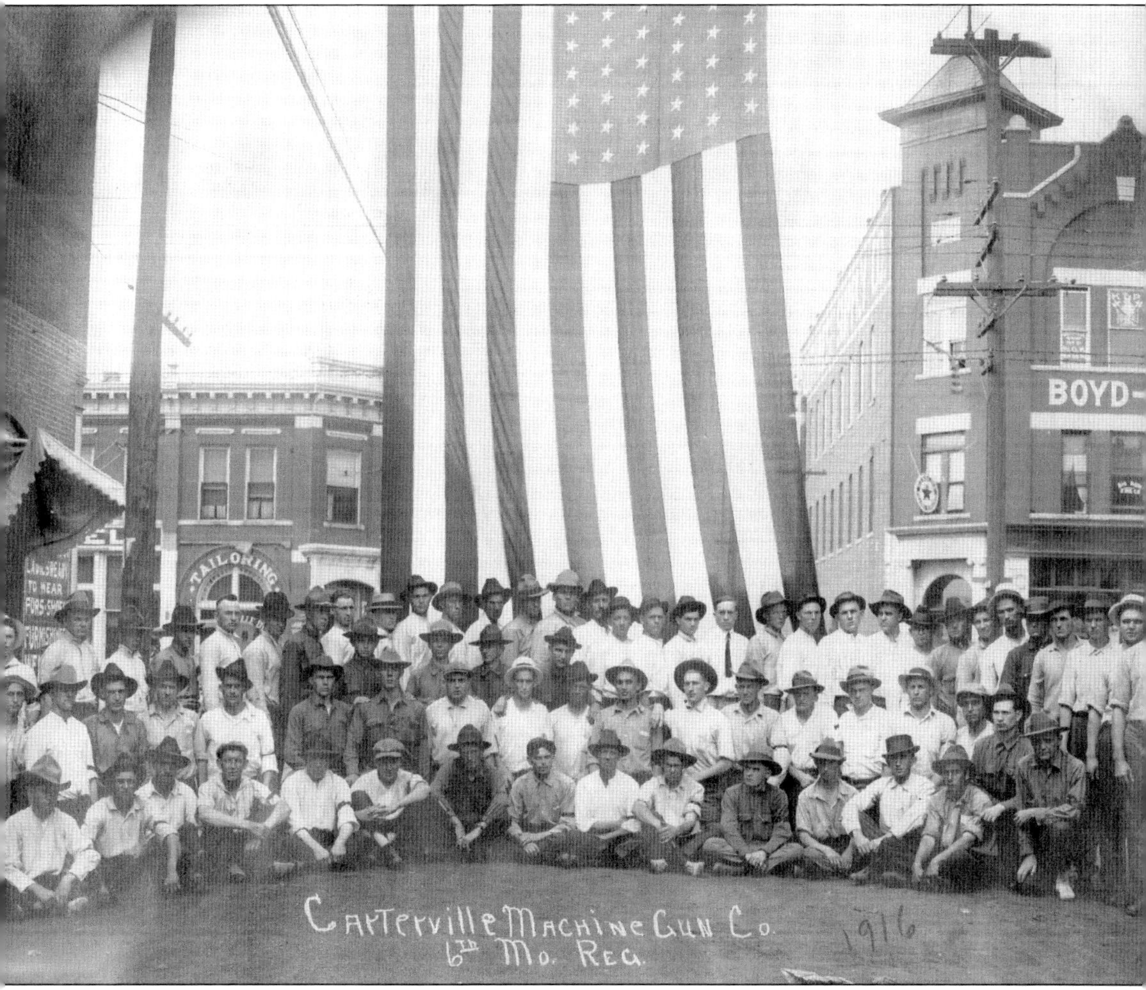


**CARTERVILLE MACHINE GUN COMPANY, CARTERVILLE, 1916.** The Machine Gun Corps was created in 1915. Prior to that time, each battalion had its own machine gun section with one officer and 12 men. The 6th Missouri Regiment served in France. Soldiers from World War I were given the nickname "Doughboys." (Courtesy of George Twigger.)

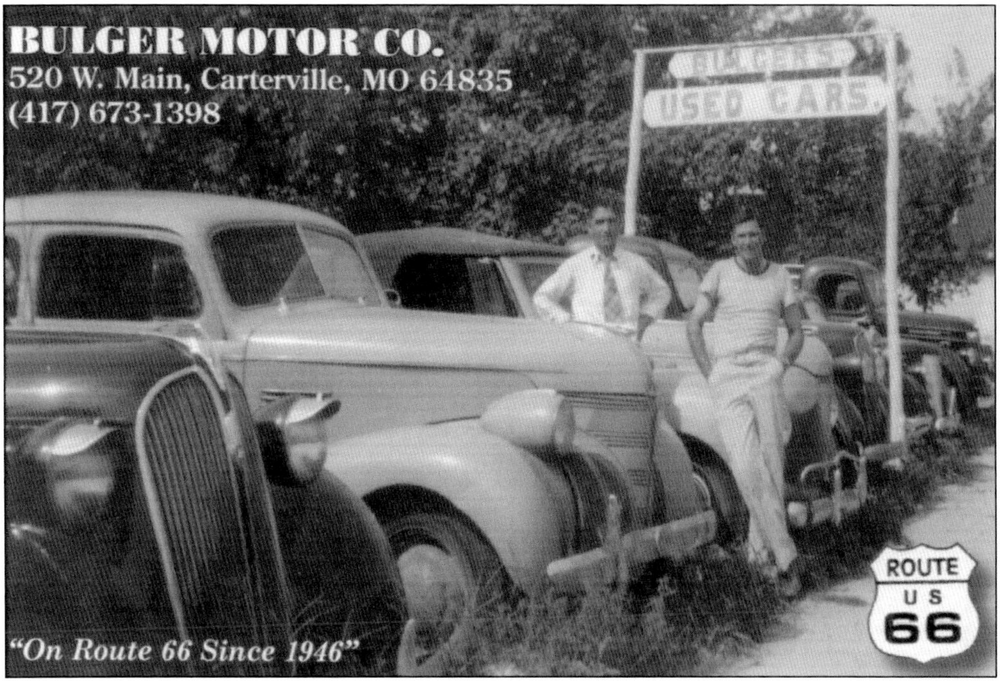


**Bulger Motor Company, Carterville, 1946.** The Bulgar family has been in the car business for generations. Their company is a familiar spot on Route 66. (Courtesy of Mickey Bulger.)

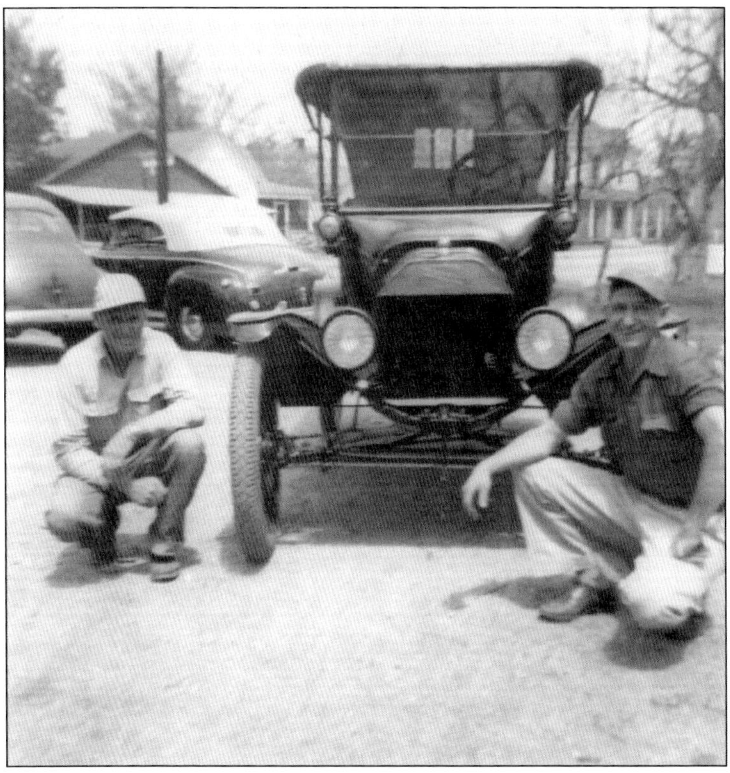

**1915 Ford Model T, c. 1940.** Kneeling in front of the car is Judd Bulger (left) and Camp Bulger. They were part of an early pioneer family of the Webb City and Carterville areas. (Courtesy of Mickey Bulger.)

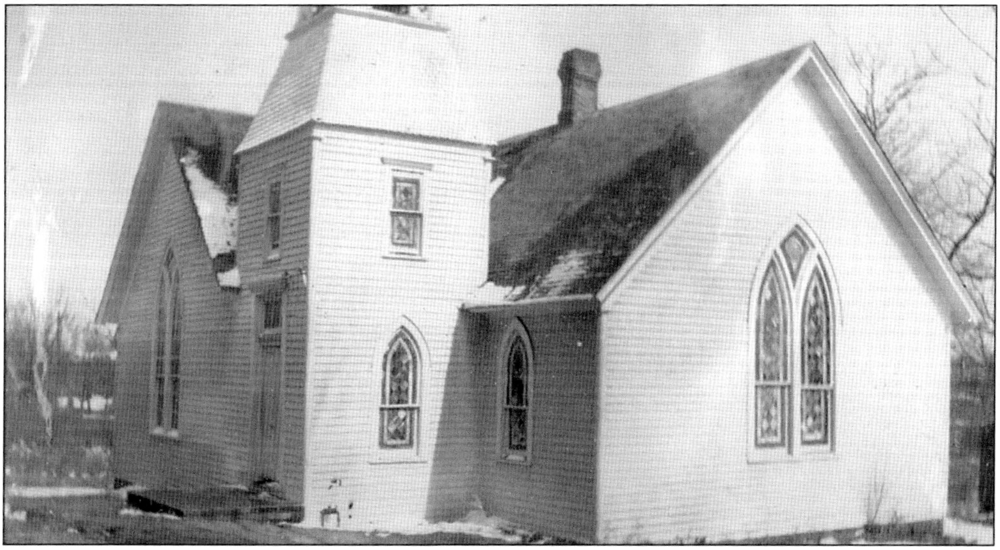

**ORONOGO METHODIST CHURCH, 1937.** Church records do not show when the church was started, only that it was organized sometime before 1872. The congregation's first building was destroyed in a tornado, and the church was reconstructed in 1883. Unfortunately, this photograph does not show the building's unique bell tower.

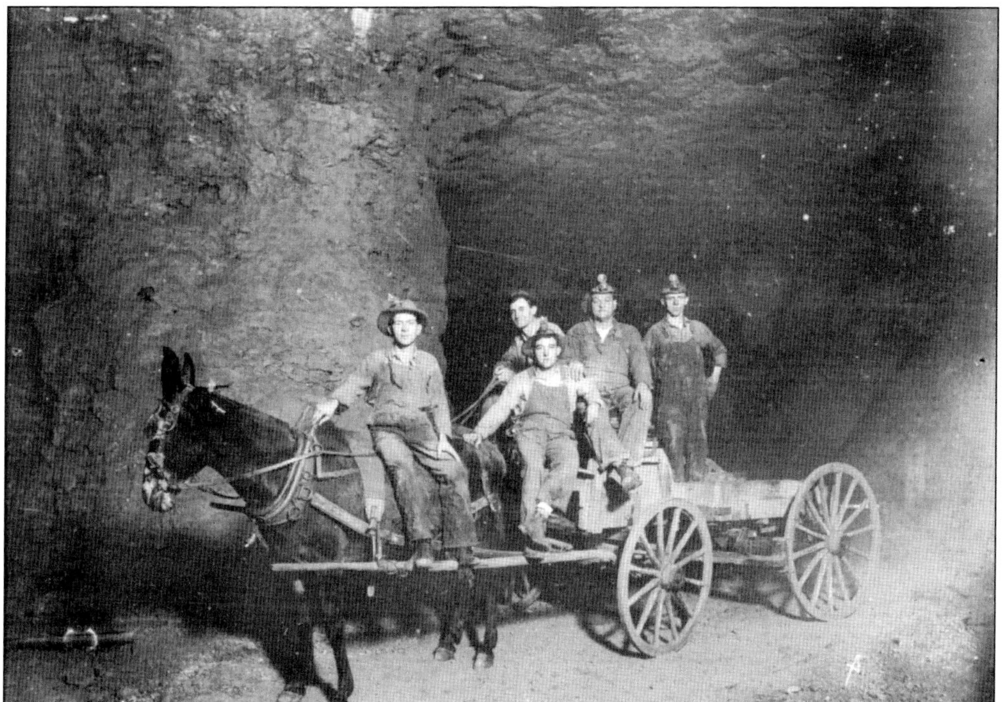

**DAVEY MINE, CARTERVILLE, 1915.** Mules were used to pull ore carts throughout the mine. Flatbeds like this one were called "jack wagons," a nickname left over from the days when zinc was considered waste and had no value. (Courtesy of the Missouri digital Archive)

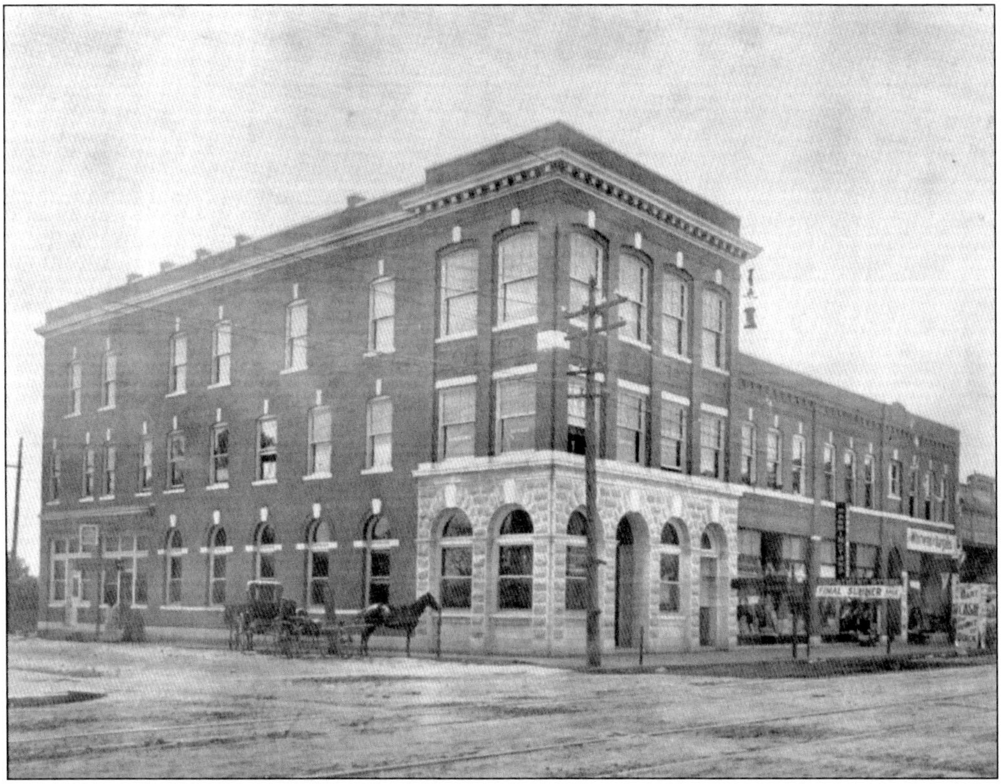

**Bank of Carterville, 1907.** W.B. Kane, Henry Weyman, and W.A. Daugherty established the bank in 1890. The name was changed to First National Bank of Carterville five years later.

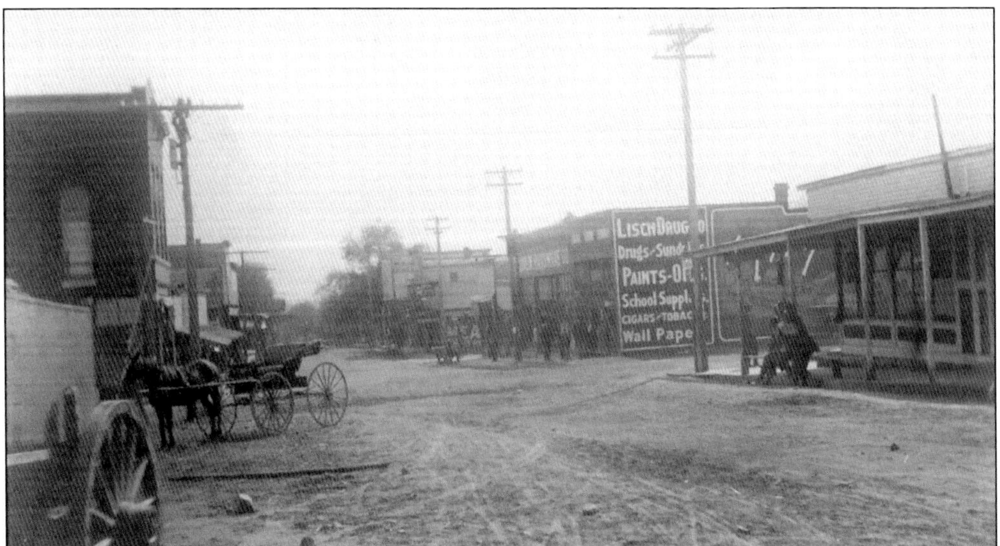

**Second Street, Oronogo.** Before 1840, Thomas Livingston had a trading post in Oronogo. He traded tobacco, whiskey, and supplies for furs. Like most boomtowns, the city has a rowdy past. Among other incidents, the town's bank was robbed by Bonnie Parker and Clyde Barrow.

**Cloyd Victor Boyer, c. 1955.** The Boyer family lived in Alba, Missouri, just outside of Webb City. Cloyd was the oldest of the 14 children and seven sons of Chester Boyer and Mabel Means. He was a pitcher for the St. Louis Cardinals from 1949 to 1952 and for the Kansas City Athletics in 1955. Later, he became a scout and a major-league pitching coach. All seven boys played professional ball at some time, with three making it to the major leagues.

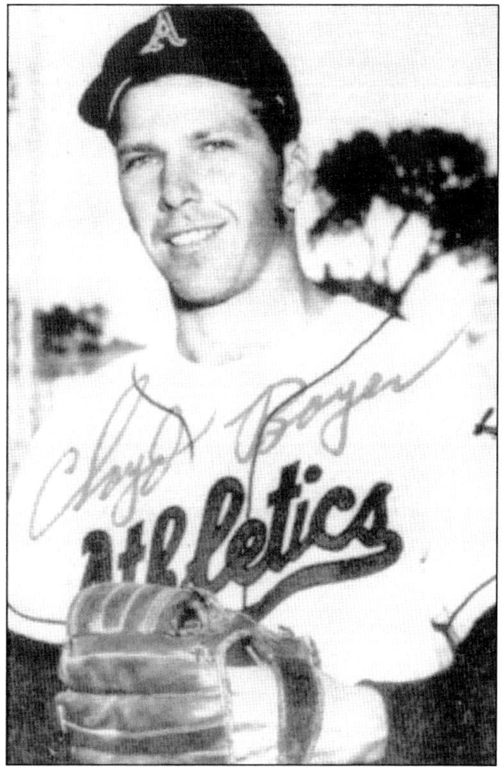


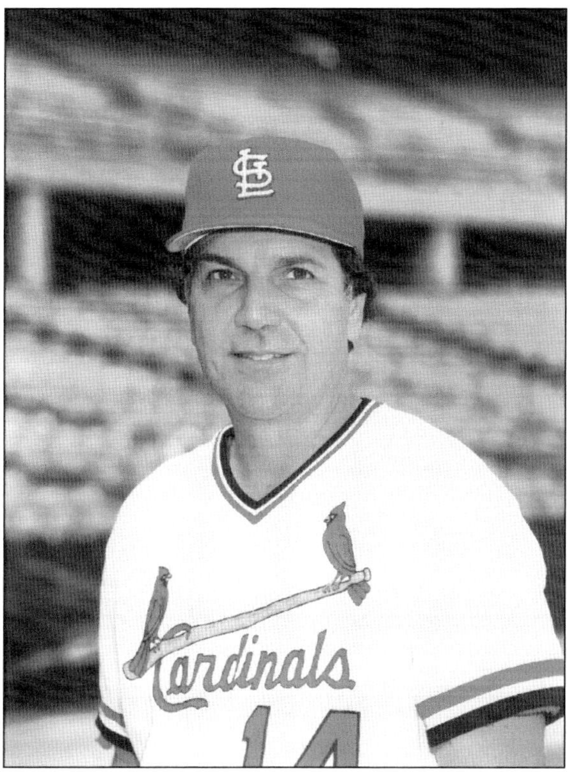


**Kenton Lloyd Boyer, c. 1960.** Ken Boyer was a third baseman for the St. Louis Cardinals, New York Mets, Chicago White Sox, and Los Angeles Dodgers. He was inducted into the St. Louis Cardinals Hall of Fame in 2014.

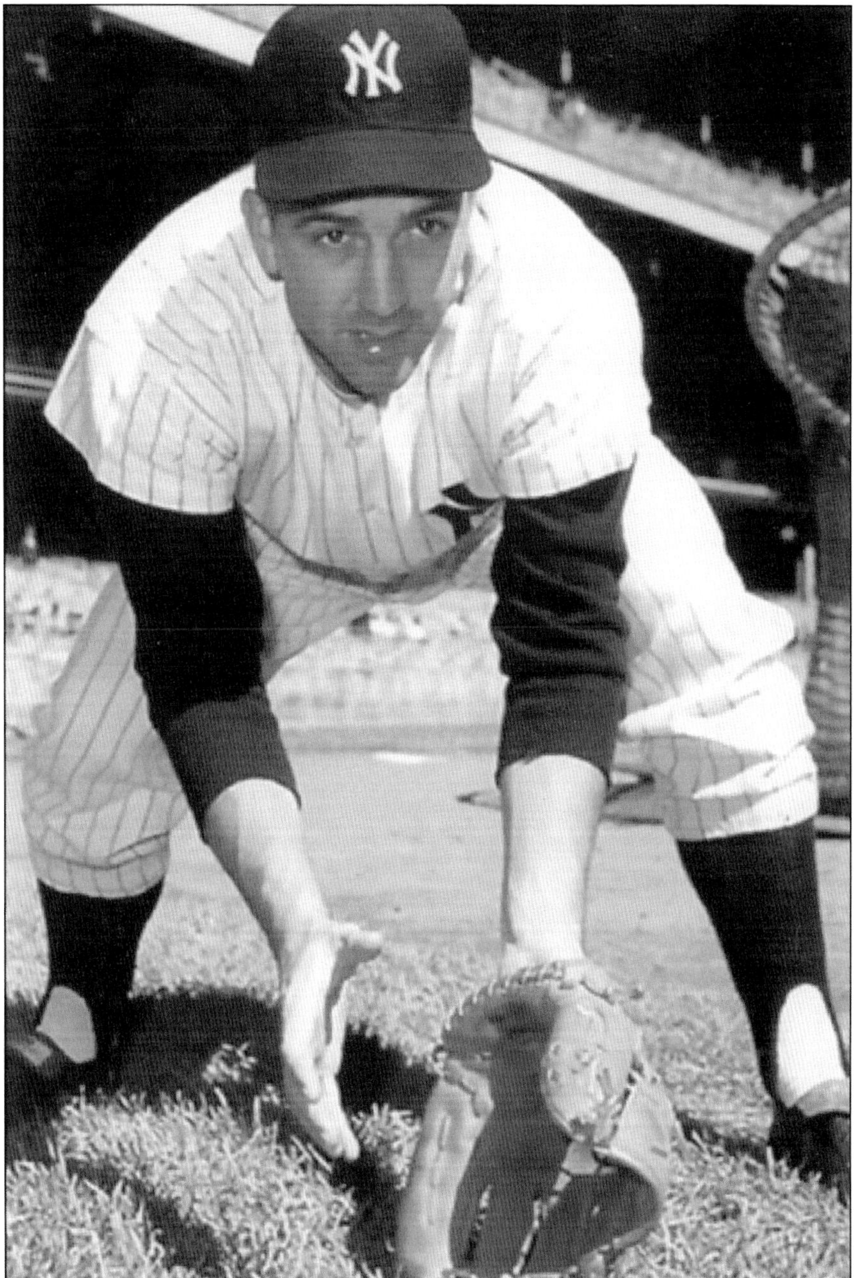


**Cletis Leroy "Clete" Boyer, c. 1960.** Clete was a third baseman who also played some shortstop and second base. His major-league teams included the Kansas City Athletics (1955–1957), New York Yankees (1959–1966), and Atlanta Braves (1967–1971). He also played for the Taiyo Whales, a Japanese Central League team, for four seasons. He was the fifth of seven Boyer sons and the third to play in the major leagues. He was a teammate of Yankee greats Roger Maris and Mickey Mantle as they chased the home run title.

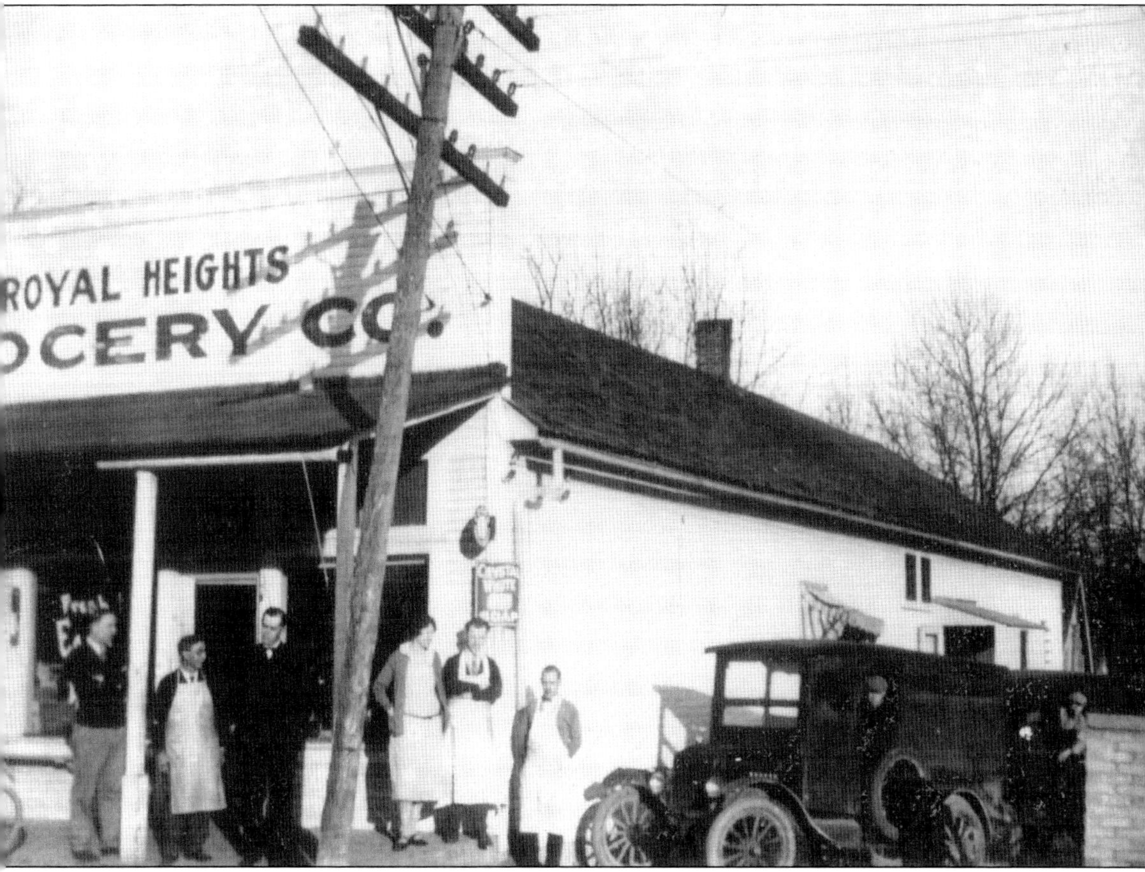


**GROCERY COMPANY, ROYAL HEIGHTS, 1925.** In 1926, the highway in front of this store became Route 66. Royal Heights was a small Missouri community that today has merged with Webb City and Joplin. (Courtesy of George Twigger.)

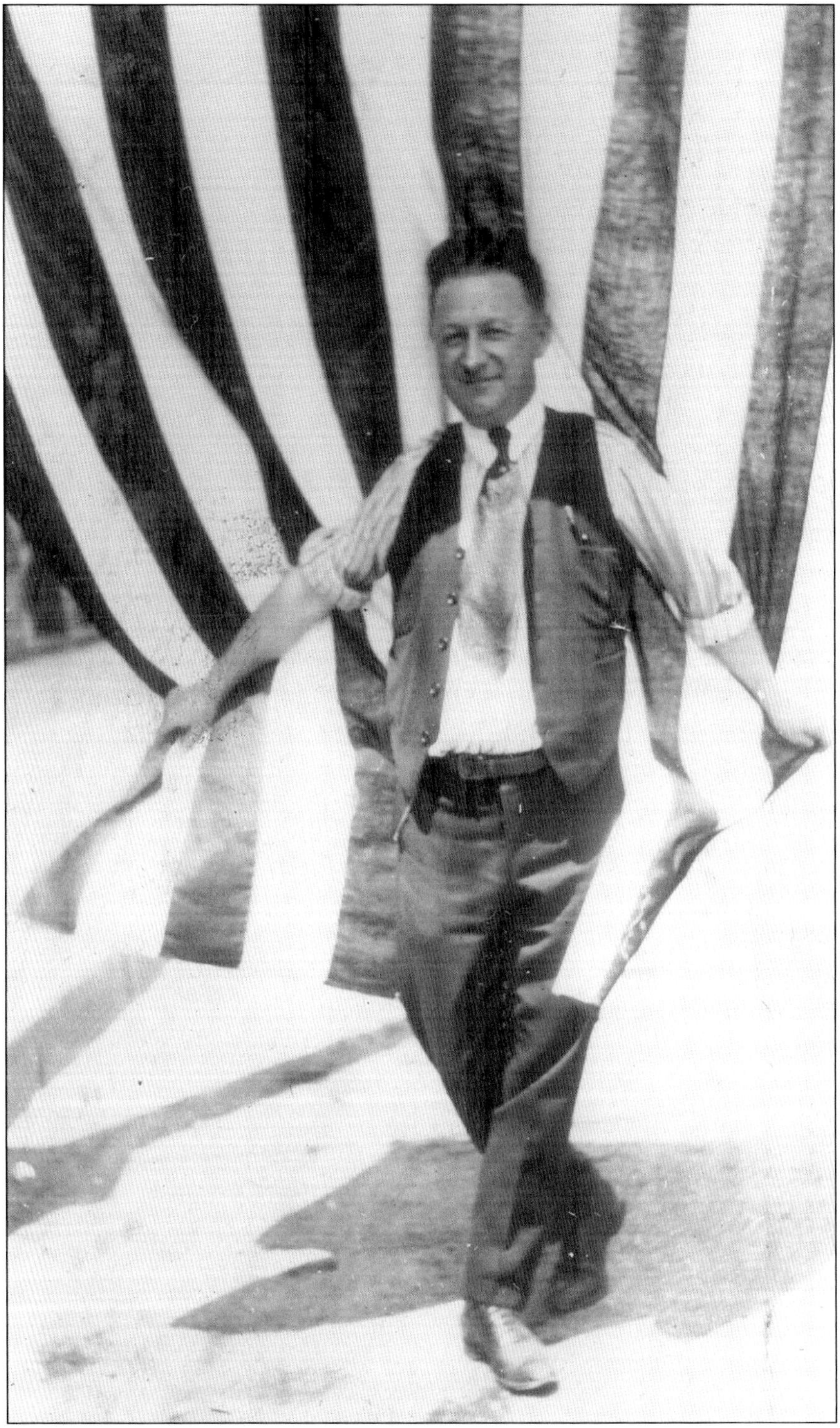

**J. Fred McDearmon, 1920.** Here, McDearmon participates in a parade of some kind. He is walking in the street with an American flag behind him. He was a Carterville druggist. (Courtesy of the Bob King Collection.)

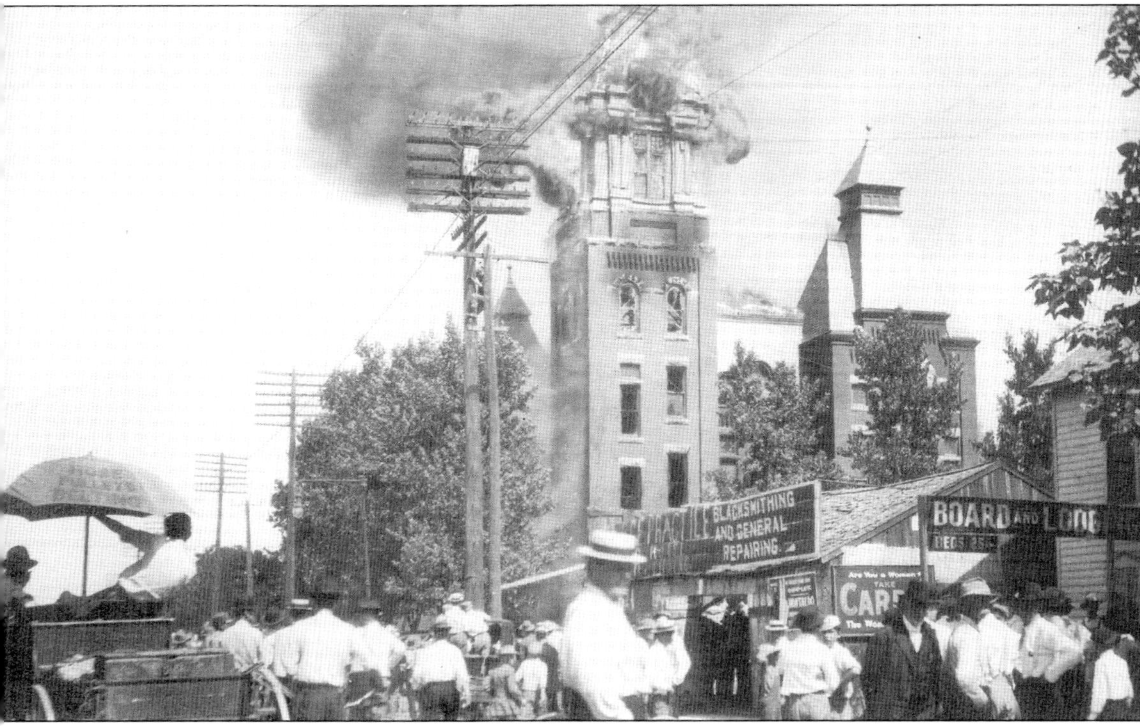


**Joplin Courthouse Fire, June 13, 1911.** It was speculated that a 10-gallon can of disinfectant exploded and caused the fire at Seventh and Virginia Streets. The three people inside the courthouse at the time of the blaze escaped unharmed. The building was a total loss. (Courtesy of the Bob King Collection.)

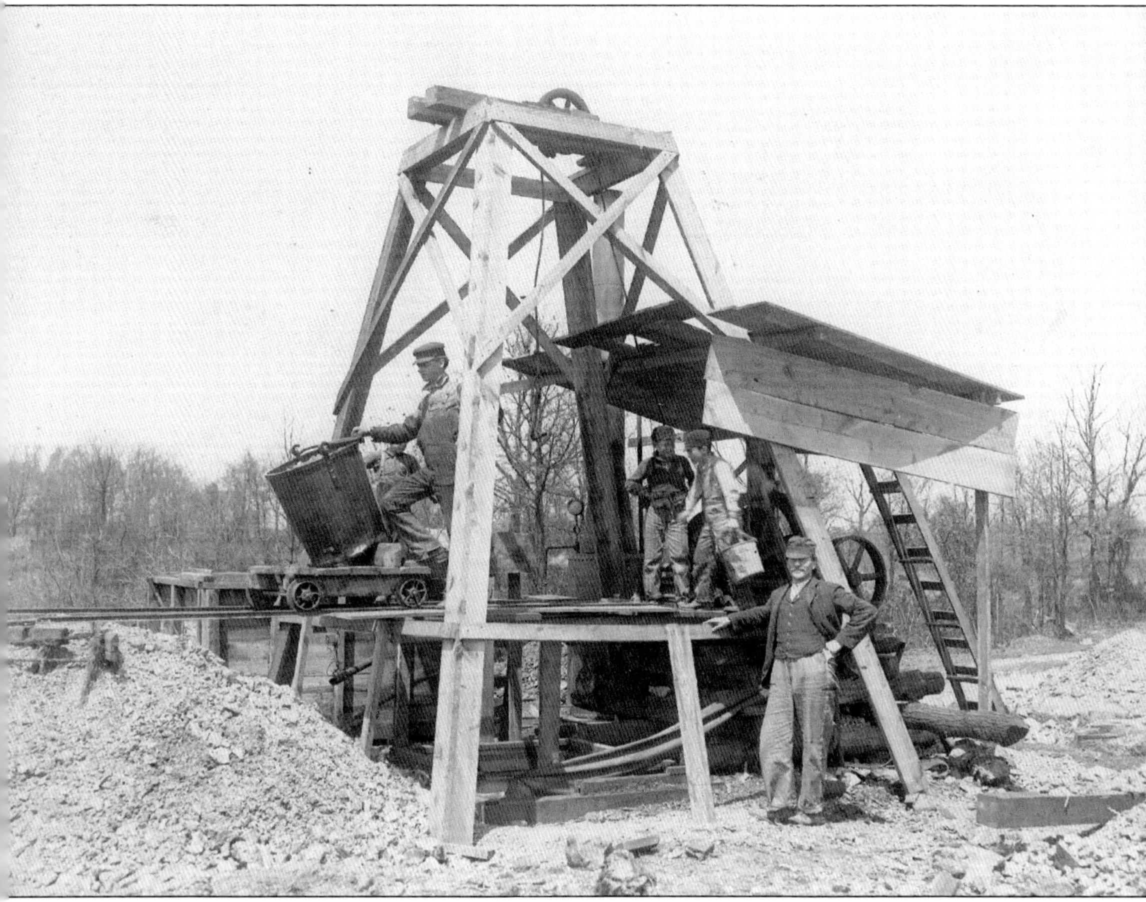

**Carrie Mine, Alba, Missouri, 1890.** Due to the hazard of carbon dioxide in the air inside mines, ventilation tubes like the one shown here were attached to steam-powered fans to keep fresh air circulating. It was a common practice for children to work for mining companies. In 1890, the two boys in this photograph would still be allowed to work. The Fair Labor Standard Act of 1938 changed child-labors laws. Children under 16 were no longer allowed to work in hazardous occupations. (Courtesy of the Missouri Digital Archive.)

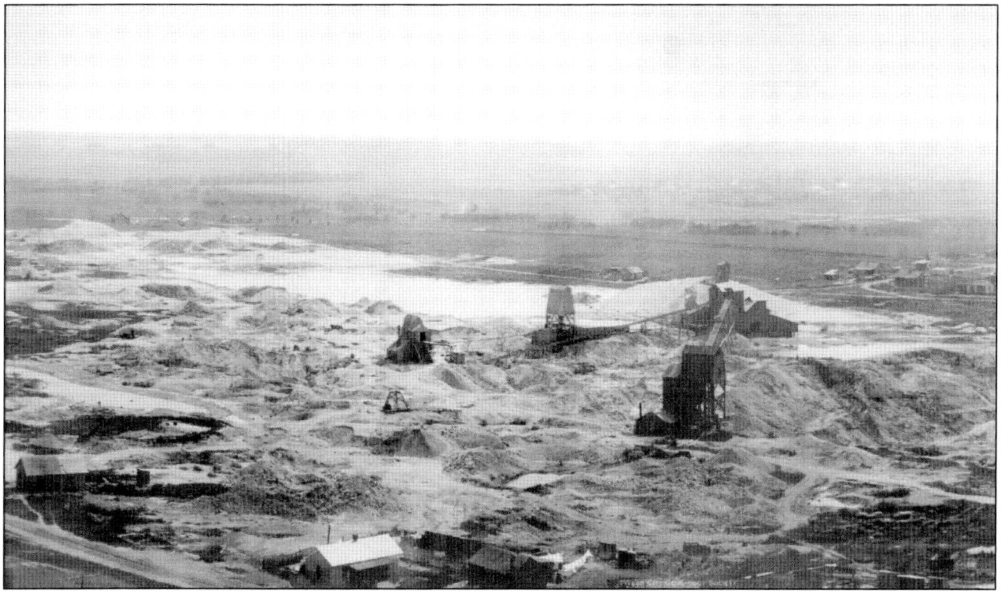

**Outskirts of Webb City, 1919.** Beyond the city limits of Webb City were miles of mining land. This aerial photograph shows how close the mines were to the homes of Webb City residents. Both large and small operations, along with shallow shifts nicknamed "gopher holes," can be seen. (Courtesy of the Bob King Collection.)

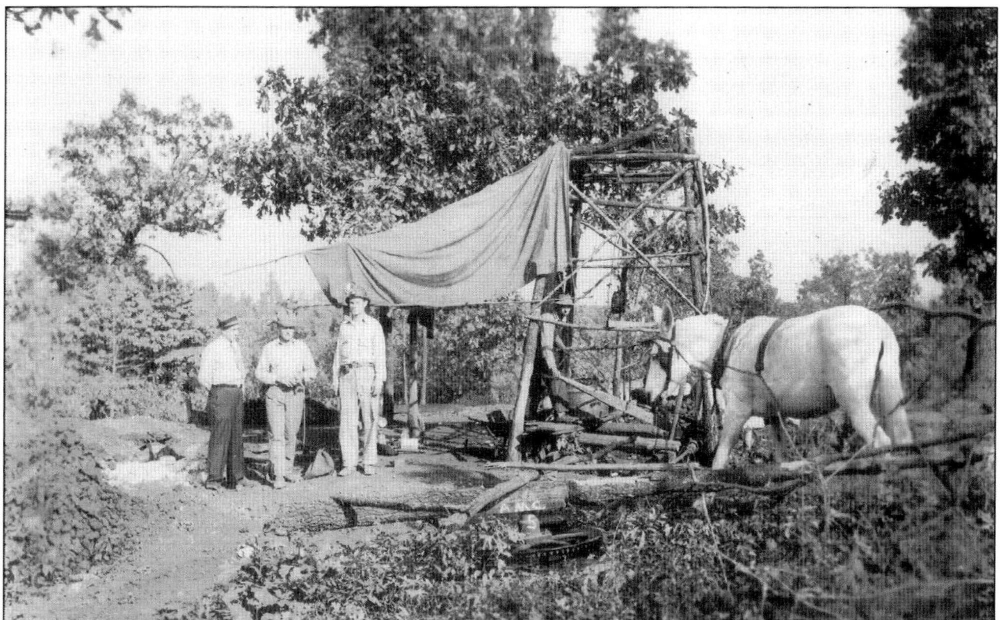

**Mine, Nick City, Missouri, 1930.** This mine is believed to be an individual operation on private property due to the primitive equipment. What looks like a brush pile on top of a gear is actually a log on a gear nick. The log is attached to the gear and is turned as the mule walks in a circle. The gear then turns the shift that powers the hoister. Under the derrick is a man holding a lever to control the hoist. By this manner, the men bring ore and waste up out of the mine. (Courtesy of the Missouri Digital Archive.)